Praise for *Engineering a Life*

"*Engineering a Life* is a story not only of determination and grit but also of hope. Bedi's indomitable spirit, positive attitude, and work ethic are a joy to read about."

—*Foreword Reviews*

"A remarkable memoir about a young immigrant who becomes a successful engineer in the US after years of hardship . . . Throughout his vivid account, Bedi shows amazing resolve and determination in achieving his dreams. Readers will likely applaud the author as he skillfully narrates his many trials on the road to forging a stable life in his new home. This engrossing and timely book should appeal to anyone wishing to learn more about the immigrant experience in America."

—*Kirkus Reviews*

"*Engineering a Life* is so many things: a touching and humorous coming-of-age story; a starkly honest and revealing chronicle of colliding cultures; a testament to faith, humanity, and The American Dream. But most of all, it's a compelling reminder that no matter who you are or what your provenance, life is not a straight path but a labyrinthine maze—and that it isn't the detours or even the final destination that define us, but how we meet the obstacles and challenges along the way."

—Grant Jarrett, award-winning author of *Ways of Leaving, The House That Made Me*, and *The Half-Life of Remorse*

"In *Engineering a Life*, Krishan Bedi describes what will be very familiar to many immigrant families in the United States today: a twisting and turning journey that was never predictable but always rewarding, sometimes in the most unexpected ways.

Navigating a course that has left him straddling two cultures, he manages to find his way home with humor, pride, and a deep appreciation for both cultures. Readers will leave this book with a better understanding of both the indignities and triumphs of a life bravely reimagined in another land."

—Rana Lee Adawi Awdish, MD, FCCP

"This is the story of a man from a village in India who didn't know how to drive a car and could barely speak or understand English but was determined to make a career in America as an industrial engineer. It's a brutally honest voice of the hardships he overcame to attain the American dream. A detailed account of the immigrant experience, this memoir is an inspiration for those who are searching for a chance at a better life and a lesson in perseverance to become American."

—Anoop Ahuja Judge, award-winning author,
blogger, and TV anchor

Engineering A Life

Engineering
A Life

A MEMOIR

KRISHAN K. BEDI

SPARKPRESS

Published by SparkPress, a BookSparks imprint,
A division of SparkPoint Studio, LLC
Tempe, Arizona, USA, 85281
www.gosparkpress.com

Published 2018
Printed in the United States of America
ISBN: 978-1-943006-43-4 (pbk)
ISBN: 978-1-943006-42-7 (e-bk)

Library of Congress Control Number: 2017953913

Interior design by Tabitha Lahr

This memoir is fondly dedicated to Raj,
my lifetime companion, and also to my wonderful sons,
their loving wives, and our beautiful grandchildren.

Preface

In 1961, at the age of twenty, I arrived in the United States, landing at the port of New York after three weeks at sea with only $300 in my pocket. Coming from a small village of only 200 people, I had never seen anything like New York City before. I had made it here on sheer faith, staying focused on my goal of an education in the United States. I'd overcome peer pressure to stay in India, lack of funds, the feeling that I was abandoning my family, and so much more just to get here. And now that I was here, I had to make it work. There was no other option but to succeed. I didn't know what would be waiting for me as I made my way to Tennessee, nor did I anticipate the culture shock of being not just in the United States, but in the South in the 1960s, which is where I spent my early years in the States.

This is a story of succeeding against the odds, and of my perseverance and determination to create the life I'd always dreamed for myself as a little boy in India, where my options seemed anything but limitless. I didn't know when I started out that my dream would take a much more convoluted path than I could ever imagine. My experience of being an Indian college student in the South at a time when many people did not know much about Indian culture brings a unique perspective to a story that also focuses on following one's dream and never giving up despite unfavorable circumstances.

Writing my memoir has been a wild experience, a long journey which started approximately eight years ago. After I regaled a colleague with tales from my student life in the 1960s in Tennessee, she exclaimed, "You should write a book!" She nearly died laughing at my stories, and her words planted a seed in the back of my mind that maybe one day I really would write a memoir. A couple of years later, my daughter-in-law listened in awe as I told her some of my stories from my younger days as an Indian going to college in the States and trying to get a date to blend in with the other Americans. "Your experience is very unique," she told me. "Everything you went through back in the sixties. You should definitely write a book."

As I began writing down my memories, it amazed me how much I remembered in clear detail about the early years of my life. Not even my closest family members knew some of my experiences or emotions, many of which I had kept to myself because it had been a hard time. It was my way to put on a cheerful face, especially later, for the sake of my wife and sons.

While I began writing my memoir, I knew I would encounter difficult memories as well as funny stories. At times, tears came to my eyes as I delved into my past to remember every detail, even if it was painful or embarrassing.

My memoir will entertain and inspire as it takes you through a life of hard work and perseverance, eliciting laughs at young and foolish days, and in the end, illustrating the power of hope in difficult circumstances.

—Krishan K. Bedi
March 17, 2017

Chapter 1

"The Muslims are coming! The Muslims are coming!" The cry of the watchmen rang through our small village of Malaudh in Punjab, India. Gunfire sounded in the distance as shop owners hurried to close up shop, fearing the dozens of men on horseback brandishing weapons and riding our way. My father, a shop owner himself, rushed home to help my mother herd me and my siblings to the outskirts of Malaudh, where a *maharaja*, a wealthy landowner, had built a fortress known as a *qila*. Shouts filled the air as dozens of families rushed for safety. Six years old at the time, I struggled to keep up with my parents. The chaos around me struck fear in my heart, and my feet trod the dirt path quickly.

It was the year 1947, and as Hindus, we found ourselves fearful of the anger and hatred set in motion by the partition of India. The partition drew new geographic lines, turning the northern part of India into a new nation, Pakistan, and forcing many Muslims to move north to the new country. The Hindus living in what is now called Pakistan were forced to migrate south. My family and I lived at the heart of the conflict because there were many Muslims in our state of Punjab, and they did not want to move. The partition bred violence—Muslims killing Hindus and Hindus killing Muslims.

The fortress, surrounded by fifteen-foot-high walls, covered ten acres, and contained three residential buildings, stables, a jeep, and an open area for the water buffalo to graze. My family and I felt safe with the guards pointing their guns through small holes in the wall, allowing them to shoot if the enemy came near.

Approximately two hundred families from Malaudh entered the qila and waited in an open area. My two older sisters and older brother formed a tight circle around me. My father, Mukandi Lal, paced back and forth, occasionally speaking in serious tones to other men standing nearby.

Seeing the fearful look in my eyes, my mother, Maya Wanti, spoke soft encouraging words. The early afternoon heat thickened, and dust rose in little clouds at any movement of wind or person. The heat and dust were a constant part of our lives, but this new thing, this violence and fear, made everything else fall to the background. As the noise outside the fortress grew closer, my father stood straight and still, like an immovable tree. Angry shouts and the thunder of hooves echoed outside the walls. A few gunshots blasted the air as the men passed us by on their way to the next town. My mother's soothing voice came like a powerful mantra to drown out the frightening sounds. She prayed to the gods of our Hindu faith, asking for safety and protection, for blessings to fall on us. Grandmother sat quietly. My father's uncle, whom we called Grandfather, also spoke strong, hopeful words to us.

The leaders of India thought it would be a peaceful migration, but after the hasty withdrawal of the British, centuries of peaceful coexistence was laid waste as Hindus, Muslims, and Sikhs engaged in a bloodbath that killed two million people. Rumors reached our village describing the ghost trains carrying nothing but corpses with their heads removed from their bodies, an act executed by both sides. With the angry Muslims crossing deeper into India every passing day, no one was safe, either on the roads or in the villages.

My family fled to the qila four times during the next few months. The Muslims could not reach us behind our high walls, and each time, we emerged from our hiding places to resume our ordinary lives.

Ordinary life for me took place in a small house behind my father's cloth shop. Like most homes in Malaudh, ours had a front yard where we kept our water buffalo. Every morning, I led her to a common place, and from there, a village boy steered the herd of buffalos and cows to a field to graze. Despite its small size, the village of Malaudh was the *kasba*, the center of commerce, for the surrounding thirty-six villages to buy their goods. Neither Malaudh nor the other villages had running water or electricity. Those too poor to afford a hand pump drew water for cooking and bathing from a central well, located in each residential street. My family owned a hand pump, but occasionally, we still used the well near our house.

School became a regular part of my life as I progressed through primary school, middle school, and finally, high school. Every day, I walked a mile outside the village to the high school, a compound of two buildings behind an iron gate, where we learned math, science, history, geography, English, and Hindi. One hundred and fifteen boys from Malaudh and the surrounding villages attended the school. Our Hindi teacher held class beneath a large *neem* (Azadirachta indica) tree. Its cooling shade refreshed us from the overbearing midday sun as we drank water out of clay jars, which kept the water from the hand pump cold.

Teachers did not hesitate to discipline with physical punishment, hitting us with sticks or slapping our faces if we misbehaved, answered incorrectly in class, or failed to complete the homework. They fabricated ways to embarrass students as well. One day I was sitting in class, pretending to listen to the physics teacher. The teacher asked a student a question. The student made a show of thinking hard. "I-I don't remember," he finally said.

"This is the third time you have come unprepared to class," the teacher said sternly. "Come to the front."

The student slowly stood and trudged to the front of the room.

"Bend forward," the teacher said.

Frowning, the student leaned over, his arms dangling near his toes.

"Now put your arms through your legs and touch your ears." We all watched anxiously, yet curiously, thankful we were not in his position.

The boy bent his knees so that he crouched awkwardly, his rear end sticking in the air. He grimaced as he stretched his arms as far as he could through his legs, finally latching on to the tips of his ear lobes. Several students snickered. The *murgha* (chicken) pose is one of the more humiliating punishments the teachers used. If the student lowered from the position even for an instant, the teacher would strike him with a long stick on his rear end.

After school, I helped my father in his shop, which adjoined the back of our house. The wooden shelves held stacks of beautifully woven, vibrantly colored fabrics. My father would greet the customers and ask what they would like to drink. Then I'd bring them either lemonade or hot tea. The drinks made the customers feel close to my father, and they would not bargain too much.

A thin woven rug covered the floor, and on top of the rug, we placed a sheet. My father sat on a round white pillow, signifying he was the owner, and the customers sat cross-legged before him. After an initial greeting, the customers would tell him what sort of cloth they were looking for (blue shirt material, perhaps), and then my father would order me to bring several bolts of cloth for the customers to examine. Once they made their choice, my father measured and cut the cloth before passing it to me to fold and wrap in paper. On weekends, I sprinkled water on the dirt road in front of the shop to keep the air free of dust. When the shop closed, I helped my father count money until 7:30 p.m.

My father was strict, well-built, and hard-working. He managed his income wisely, spent frugally, and never wasted a rupee (Indian Currency). At times, he exhibited a demanding character. For instance, if my mother did not prepare the food to his taste, he would dump the meal on the floor and chide her. With the help of my paternal grandmother, she would prepare the meal again. I couldn't bear to see my mother upset as she bent to pick up the food, mumbling under her breath and crying to herself.

My mother was kind and hard-working. Every day, she rose at dawn while everyone was still sleeping so she could make our hot tea and pump water for our baths. Afterwards, she prepared food for the water buffalo. While we washed ourselves in the tepid water from the pump and drank sweetened black tea, mother cooked a breakfast of *prantha*, whole wheat bread layered with ghee, yogurt, and potatoes cooked in spices.

My mother held a special place in my heart. She personified love by placing grain on the ant hills after it rained so they could eat too. Most days, she fed three of six young sisters who lived nearby. Their parents did not feed them much because they could not carry the family name as a son could. The girls came to our home, and my mother snuck them *chapatis* and *sabzi* behind a door where no one could see them. My father and brother guessed what was going on and were not happy about it, but my mother continued to help the girls anyway.

My mother also fed a crippled man who would come to our house around 2:00 p.m. every day. He sat, squatting on the balls of his feet, and used two wooden pads to drag himself across the ground. The man said kind words to my mother and my siblings. "One day, you will be a big man," he told me. "Cars will be all around you."

At that time, cars were prestigious, not common luxury at all. If someone owned a car, he was respected and considered rich. I couldn't imagine how his prediction would come true. Later, I learned that a man gave my brother's classmate a similar blessing. Soon after, my brother's friend moved to New Delhi, where he became a traffic policeman. Cars were all around him, but he did not own any. I hoped his prediction would not turn out the same way for me.

During my last year of high school, the National Board of Examination became my primary focus. There were only two years of schooling at my village high school, and the teachers spent the entire time preparing us for the exams we would take in March of our second year. These exams were our passage to better education, and if we did well, we qualified for college pre-med and pre-engineering programs. If the exam scores fell within the middle range, students qualified for degrees in liberal arts. However, if a student failed even one subject, that student had to take the exam again as many times as he needed.

The National Board Exams began on March 1 and ended on March 23, 1956. My father arranged for me to stay in Mandi Ahmed-Garh, the testing center, with a family I did not know. Mandi Ahmed-Garh was considered a small city, thirteen miles away from Malaudh. At that time, I felt a mixture of excitement at being in a new place, as well as apprehension about taking the exams, hoping I'd do well and not disappoint my family by failing.

The exam results declared three months later in June 1956. I walked into the chemist's shop and asked to see *The Tribune*, an English newspaper the chemist purchased and brought to Malaudh. If we passed, our ID numbers appeared in the paper along with our total score on the exams. I skimmed the columns of numbers until I spotted mine. Thirty-five percent! Scoring below thirty-three percent meant I would need to retake the exams. Grateful to have not embarrassed my parents in such a way, I walked home with a bounce in my step, eager to share the news. My parents, ecstatic to know I'd passed, congratulated me and spread the word to their relatives and friends. They also passed out sweets to our neighbors and to the poor who lived in the surrounding area.

Over the next three years, I attended the Vishvakarma Institute of Engineering Technology, an engineering college in Ludhiana, working toward a diploma in civil engineering. My time at the institute gave me a taste of living in a place much bigger than Malaudh, and in some ways, it seemed more sophisticated. I made a good friend named Jasbir Singh Mann. We liked to study on the floor, and when we grew tired of reading and memorizing terms, we fell asleep on the floor surrounded by books and papers. We felt that studying and sleeping on the floor showed that we were serious, hard-working students.

In the summer of 1959, I received my Diploma in Civil Engineering, second division, not without some bribery and approach to the teachers. I treated the professors to dinner at a nice restaurant or took them to the movie theater in exchange for questions on the test. In addition, Jasbir helped me study for the final exams. At Vishvakarma, most students completed two to four years of college in physics, chemistry, or math programs. Students at this school usually didn't qualify for admission at a more prestigious engineering university.

My parents were happy I had completed three years of Diploma in Civil Engineering in one try, especially since my brother twice failed his final year of engineering college before passing the exam. My parents arranged a big celebration in our village when I came home. My father proudly distributed sweets among the poor and to his colleagues, and he sent sweets to our relatives. Once the celebration was over, I asked myself what I would do next. If I was lucky, I might be able to work as an overseer, supervising the construction of buildings, roads, and dams; or a surveyor, inspecting land to determine elevations or depths where a new road or building would be constructed. However, a diploma from a small, unknown college such as the Vishvakarma Institute was not impressive, and most employers looked for workers with experience or a bachelor's degree from a well-known university.

My brother worked as an overseer at the time and would tell me stories about his boss, the Sub-Divisional Officer (SDO) who was responsible for a large, geographic area called a sub-division and had much more authority over the overseers working for him. In a way, he was like a ruler or rajah, and his chauffeur drove him all over the territory he was responsible for. Did I want to work as an overseer with little authority over anyone or a surveyor who had even less responsibility and power?

The SDO position appealed to me more than the others, but I discovered that I could only qualify for the title after eight or ten years of service as an overseer. I wasn't sure if I could get a job as an overseer with my engineering diploma from a small unknown college. It wouldn't mean anything to anyone, and I didn't have any on-the-job experience to qualify right off the bat.

I decided to take an examination at a well-respected engineering college in Nilokheri, 150 miles from my hometown. If I passed the exam in all subjects, I could find a good job as an overseer and eventually become an SDO.

My brother arranged for me to stay in a room near the college, but several days into my stay, I developed a bad rash under my arms. It was painful and scary to look at, and even worse, it prevented me from preparing for the exams. The frightening appearance of the rash worried me. After several days of no improvement, I consulted a doctor. He administered eight shots into my arms, and slowly the rashes disappeared. Somehow, I still could not concentrate on studying for the exams, which were spread out over a three-week period. Before taking each exam, I knew I would not pass. It was no surprise when the newspaper declared the results, and my roll number was missing. My dream of becoming an SDO was ruined. Not knowing what to do or where to go, my only option was to stay at home and work with my father.

The sun shone brightly through the front door of my father's shop as I brought a cup of freshly brewed tea to a customer haggling over prices with my father. She took a sip. "Thank you, Krishan," she said. "Just how I like it." The middle-aged woman was one of the regulars, but she still persisted in bargaining over prices with my father. "I have children to feed," she'd always say. "I can't be taking whatever first offer of price you throw at me, Respected Mukandi Lal."

"I have a family to feed as well," my father would say. "I can't always sell my goods for almost free."

I began folding bolts of fabric and organizing them by their colors. A moment later, my father walked over to me. "We reached a good price this time," he said. "She is a good customer, but she is always trying to swindle me."

I reached for an unrolled bolt of red cloth and began folding it carefully. "It must have been the tea. She is always happier when she gets a drop of tea in her."

My father laughed. "Yes, Krishan. I don't know how I've done without you these few months. It's been a hard time with you gone. You are a big help to me."

I reached for another bolt of cloth without meeting his eyes. How could I tell him that I didn't want to work in his shop anymore? What would he say when he found out I wanted to go to America?

My desire to travel to America began several weeks earlier when my father told me about my two cousins who traveled to America, or "Amrika," as most Indians pronounced it.

"We just received news from your cousin Ved who went to Amrika two years ago," he said. "In 1959 I believe. He is getting his Master's in Business Administration at the University of Tennessee. Very successful boy! Did you also know that another one of your cousins traveled to Amrika in 1955? He earned a PhD in Chemistry at a university in Michigan."

"I didn't know."

"Yes, it seems that traveling to Amrika is becoming popular. It offers much more opportunity, and if someone has a degree from the US, they can get any job they want. Think of all the money they must be making over there!"

Making tons of money sounded good to me. It seemed the people with the most money were also the most respected in India.

A few days later, I ran into a friend from the Vishvakarma Institute in Ludhiana.

"Do you have a job yet?" he asked. He knew about my dream to work as an overseer so I could become an SDO.

I shook my head sadly. "No. I had to take an examination in Nilokheri, but I didn't pass.""That's too bad," my friend said.

"But did you know there's another way to become an SDO? It is much quicker too. There are engineering programs in the US. You can go there and earn your bachelor's degree in two years since you have completed your Diploma in Civil Engineering.

Then all you need to do is remain in the US for eighteen months of practical training, and when you return to India you can get the post of Sub-Divisional Officer right away!"

That night, I spoke to my father about going to the US for further studies. He seemed reluctant for me to go so far, and my mother also felt it was too far away.

"Krishan, find something here," my mother told me. "You are so helpful to me, and I will miss you so much."

Regardless of my parents' discouraging opinions, I wrote a letter to my cousin Ved Bedi in New York City, asking him to help me get admission at the University of Tennessee in Knoxville. He asked the Dean's Office of Admission to send me the admission forms, and my brother-in-law Vijay Kaura helped me complete them so I could send them back as soon as possible. My father was still not enthusiastic about the idea, but he did not try to stop me. Part of him felt having a son living in the US sounded prestigious and would impress his friends. He neither discouraged nor encouraged me.

Toward the end of April 1961, I received a letter of admission from the University of Tennessee. Soon after receiving the letter, I set out to procure my passport, currency exchange permit, and visa to come to the States. However, to qualify for an exchange permit, my father needed 14,000 rupees ($2,950) in his bank account to prove he would be able to support me and pay my university expenses while I lived overseas. My father did not have this kind of money. In the last eighteen months, he had paid the expenses of three weddings. My two sisters had married six months apart, and my brother had married six months afterwards. My sisters' dowries had drained my father's cash savings that he kept tucked away in a small tin box at our house. Now he had nothing left to offer me. Still wanting to help, he talked to his friends and our local relatives, but no one had that kind of money either. My dream of becoming an SDO skidded to a halt.

Chapter 2

"Krishan! Pay attention, Son!" my father called from the other side of the shop. "I need your help over here." I shook my head from a cloud of daydreams and trudged over to him. With no money, I felt trapped in the village while my mind longed to go on to bigger things. I wanted to reach out and grab what I wanted in life, but that was like plucking a star from the sky. Unfortunately, money did not grow on trees in India, not like it did in America.

I would live in Malaudh the rest of my life, working in my father's shop, folding cloth, and serving customers. I moped around the shop. Customers came and went. They haggled over prices. I served them tea or lemonade and watched my father negotiate. He sent each customer off with a smile and a blessing. I sprinkled water on the dirt in front of the shop, and sometimes when business was slow, I sat on the ground outside and watched the women and girls walk by in their bright-colored saris.

I did not smile, and I rarely talked if I did not need to.

My father ordered me around. "Krishan, sweep the floor. Fold this cloth. Bring the customers tea."

I slowly obeyed his orders with a grave expression on my face. Perhaps my father thought my dark mood would pass. He hoped I would get over it eventually and accept my role in Malaudh. But when a week passed and I still had not cheered up, he finally told me about a friend in Ludhiana, the owner of a large spinning mill. "Maybe he will lend us money," he said.

"Is this true, Bai Ji? Will you take me there?"

"Yes," my father said. My eyes cleared and a smile brightened my face.

I hugged him and ran out of the shop to tell my mother the good news.

The next day, we visited the mill owner, and my father's friend agreed to transfer fourteen thousand rupees to my father's account. Once again, I felt that my life was about to truly begin.

Over the next few months, I worked toward obtaining my passport and visa, and my father supported me with whatever money I needed along the way. There were nearly a dozen trips to and from New Delhi, and I had to complete many formalities. My father tried to be happy, but in truth, he did not want me to leave Punjab State. At times, he wept sorrowful tears as if this display of emotion would change my mind. Seeing my father cry was not pleasant, but I would not give up my plans. At other times, my father appeared neutral, neither encouraging nor discouraging about my venture to the US. He wanted me to be happy.

My brother-in-law helped me contact a travel agent in Ludhiana, and I arranged to travel by boat from Bombay to London and from there to New York. One week before my departure for Bombay, I visited my relatives in neighboring villages to tell them goodbye. One day, while traveling to see my uncle in Mandi Gobind-Garh, I started a conversation with a man sitting next to me on the bus. The man asked what I was doing and where I was going. I had brought my documents in a purse to show to my uncle. I took them out and showed them to the man, explaining my plans to study in the US. After he looked at them, I placed them next to me on the seat.

When I arrived in Mandi Gobind-Garh, I picked up my bags and walked the half mile to my uncle's house. After greeting my uncle and several other relatives, I reached for the purse holding all the documents and saw it was not there. Immediately, I went into a state of shock. All my hard work had disappeared before my eyes.

The bus had left a while earlier, so my uncle borrowed a friend's car, and we followed the bus forty miles to its next destination. When we arrived, the bus was empty, and my purse with the documents was not there. We returned to Mandi Gobind-Garh at 8:00 p.m., and I was devastated. The whole night I stayed awake, on the verge of tears, thinking, *God, why have you done this to me? What do I do now?*

The next morning, we hired a local drummer to announce throughout the town, "Krishan Bedi has lost his documents, passport, and visa to the US. Anyone who finds it will be rewarded." Yet the documents never turned up.

When I returned home, my father did not show much emotion about my predicament. He was relieved that I would be staying in Punjab. Both my father and mother felt that Paramatma, the Supreme Spirit in Hindu theology, had taken care of my fate. It was my destiny to remain with my parents. This was the accepted explanation, and there was no more discussion about my future plans.

I did not like my destiny.

For the next few weeks, I helped my father in the shop. I told my parents that I would stay in Malaudh and join the cloth retail business. However, this was not what I wanted to do. I did not want to sell cloth for the rest of my life. This time my depression was even worse than before. I withdrew from all extracurricular activities, avoiding anything pleasant or happy. I even asked the barber to shave my head, causing embarrassment to my parents because I looked like a monk. After a month of plodding sullenly around the village, my mother realized my sadness was not lessening with time.

"Krishan, it is very hard for me to see you unhappy," she said one day, while I sat in the courtyard watching two pigeons strut back and forth. "I know how much you want to go to Amrika. I think if you really want to go, you should try again. Go. Apply for admission. Prepare the documents again. It is important that you are happy."

"But it is so hard," I complained. "Do you know how long it took me the first time? Four months! I do not think I can go through it all again. All that work I did, and it was all for nothing." I picked up a stone and hurled it angrily at the wall enclosing the yard.

"Krishan, if you really want something, you should not give up simply because it is too hard. Please, you have my blessing to try again."

She walked away. I lay on the ground and stared at the darkening sky for nearly an hour. It was pitch black, and the stars had appeared in multitudes when I finally decided she was right. I could not back down from my dreams. It only made me miserable and hard to be around.

When my father learned my mother was talking to me about applying again, he tried to discourage me. "It is too hard, Krishan," he told me. "You cannot do it. You will not be able to get all the formalities completed again."

Hearing this challenge, I immediately decided I would. If I wanted to do something, then I could do it. I would show my father it was possible. As I started preparing the documents once again, someone recommended that I go to an astrologer to predict the future and remove any obstacles that might prevent me from traveling to the US. I thought this would be a good idea. Perhaps the astrologer would know whether I should continue my pursuit to travel abroad. The astrologer lived forty miles away from Malaudh. He prepared my *janampatri*, a prediction of the future in Sanskrit, including diagrams that show my prospects in terms of health, travel, education, and wealth. The diagram was based upon the day, time, and year of my birth. The astrologer told me, "Yes, overseas travel is in your stars, but there will be obstacles along the way. To overcome them, you must pray a mantra 1.1 lakh (110,000) times in thirty-seven days."

The Sanskrit mantra he gave me translates to:

Oh God, the Giver of life. Remover of pain and sorrows, Bestower of happiness, and Creator of the Universe, Thou art most luminous, pure, and adorable. We meditate on Thee. May Thou inspire and guide our intellect in the right direction.

In the Hindu religion, it is believed that your troubles can be resolved by reciting certain types of prayers. I believed this wholeheartedly and resolved to follow the astrologer's instruction.

"How will you complete this mantra on your own?" my father asked. "This is a very difficult undertaking. It takes an intense amount of focus and determination that is not simple for the average person."

We consulted a *pundit*, a priest, who would repeat the mantra for a fee. The pundit and several other priests would say the mantra for several days and finish within the specified time. In addition to paying money, we would need to feed them breakfast and lunch. My father hesitated to spend so much money. In the end, I declared that I would say the mantra myself.

I calculated that it would take five minutes to say the mantra one-hundred-and-one times. I kept a record of the mantra count in a notebook, and I repeated it for six to eight hours a day. Toward the end, my sister-in-law helped me, and we completed all the repetitions in the required time frame. Afterwards, a *pundit* performed a completion ceremony for me, involving a large feast served to several pundits. The ceremony was considered *Yag*, meaning to feed the Brahmins and please our god, Paramatma.

One day, three Americans came to our village to work on an agricultural project. One of my classmates from primary school knew a little bit of English and had been conversing with these Americans using sign language as well. He knew I had lost my documents and was having difficulty obtaining them all again, so he told me I should speak to these Americans. Perhaps they would help me.

The next day, I spoke to them in broken English, explaining my situation and asking if they could help me. They wrote down my name and address, saying they would try their best.

To my surprise, two weeks later I received a letter in the

mail, admitting me to the University of Tennessee for the following quarter in January 1962. With renewed vigor, I acquired the remaining documents in less time than it had taken before. I completed all the formalities by October and made arrangements through a Ludhiana travel agency to reach the US by sea. My journey would begin in Bombay on November 26, 1961. The ship would take me to Genoa on the coast of Italy, and then I would take a train to the French city of Calais. From there, a ferry would take me to the port, and then I would board a ferry to cross the English Channel to get to London. Finally, I would board one last ship, the *SS United States*.

My brother, Sat Pal, and my brother-in-law Krishan Chand accompanied me on the train ride all the way to Bombay. As we left the Ludhiana station, I sat with my face pressed to the window, watching my parents waving after me. My heart grew heavy at the distraught expression on my mother's face. I wore the fragrant garland of marigold flowers around my neck that my parents had draped over me, and their gift of money, called a *shagan*, sat securely in my pocket. "May Paramatma keep you healthy and wealthy," my mother had said as she placed it in my hands.

She also had prayed over me in Hindi, her words meaning, "May God keep you safe and happy." Holding back tears, I had touched her feet to receive her blessings. The moment I boarded the train, I could not stop crying, thinking that I did not know if I would see my parents again.

Fifty people had come to see me off at the Malaudh bus stop just a few hours prior. There were shouts and a clamor of excitement as everyone hugged me, wished me well, and ushered me onto the bus with my two suitcases, an extremely heavy trunk, and a bistra bandh, filled with bedding my mother had insisted I bring with me.

At noon on November 26, I arrived at the port in Bombay to check in with my luggage. Ships lined the dock, and people swarmed around me. I moved off to the side to say goodbye to Sat Pal and Krishan. Then I fell in with the jostling crowd. Once on the ship, I stood on the upper deck and waved to Sat Pal and Krishan for the last time. At that moment it truly hit me: I was leaving India. *This is it*, I told myself. *There is no turning back.* Tears filled my eyes as the ship pulled away from Bombay's port. An hour later, I could see nothing but water sparkling in the sun.

Chapter 3

The journey from Bombay to London took fourteen days. For another week, I stayed in a guest house in cold, foggy London before boarding the SS *United States* bound for New York. After six long days at sea, we approached land and sailed into the harbor. I joined the crowd flocking to claim their luggage. The man at customs asked me a question (perhaps about the contents of my luggage), but I couldn't understand a single word. His pronunciation was remarkably different from the British accent I was accustomed to. I kept saying, "No, no," and the man smiled understandingly. He motioned for me to open the large trunk and saw it was almost overflowing with lentils and pickles.

"Are you a student?" he asked, speaking slowly and clearly.

I understood him this time. "Yes," I said proudly.

"What school are you attending?"

"The University of Tennessee."

"Good school. Good luck."

He approved my luggage, and two porters helped carry it away from customs. I stood by my luggage and waited for my cousin in the icy December air. The frigid ocean breeze blew right through me. I pulled my oversized coat up to my chin and wondered where Ved was. Half an hour passed, and he still did not come. Had he not received my aerogram informing him of my arrival date? Finally, I signaled a taxi to take me to Ved's apartment. The driver helped carry my luggage, saying, "Heavy, heavy," as he loaded it into the car.

Around noon, I arrived at Ved's apartment building. The taxi driver unloaded my luggage and placed it on the sidewalk in front of the door. He showed me his hands. "The luggage. Too heavy!" he complained. I paid him the price on the meter, but he showed me his hands again. "More money."

"No, no," I told him. "I need to save money. Go!"

The driver stormed away, muttering to himself as he slammed the taxi door and drove off. I knocked on Ved's door, but no one came to let me in. Realizing my cousin must not have received my aerogram, I sat outside on the cold steps to wait until he came home in the evening. About twenty minutes later, an Indian man walked up to the apartment building.

"Who are you?" he asked.

"I am Krishan Bedi, cousin of Ved Bedi."

"Oh yes. He told me you were coming, but we did not know when your ship would arrive. I live with your cousin. I will open the door for you."

He helped carry my luggage into the apartment and asked if I wanted something to eat. I was starving so he made me a sandwich, and although I had not developed a taste for this type of food yet, I ate it anyway. After lunch, Ved's roommate returned to work, leaving me alone in the apartment until evening.

At six o' clock, my cousin came in carrying the mail from the mail box in the hallway.

"Krishan, you are here! I am so glad to see you. What a surprise!" He embraced me, and then showed me the mail.

"Look!" he said, laughing. "I got your letter today."

When Ved saw my luggage, he exclaimed, "What is this? So much luggage! How did you bring it all? And a *bistra bandh*. This you will not need. Your landlord or landlady will provide all your bedding in Tennessee."

"Yes, but it was my mother's wish," I explained. "I could not say no to her. I wanted her to be happy before I left."

Ved just laughed. "Shall we have a cup of tea? I want to hear all about your journey."

❀ ❀ ❀

The snow fell in large clumps, covering the sidewalks and streets. I had never seen snow before or imagined it could feel so cold. Car exhaust turned the snow from sparkling white to gray in the streets, but the layers and drifts on buildings, houses, and store awnings shimmered brilliantly.

I had one week to learn about American culture and customs before I left for Tennessee. Red and green Christmas ornaments decorated storefronts and streets everywhere, while Christmas songs played on almost every radio station. I heard "Jingle Bells" so often I became amused and tired of it at the same time, even though I had not heard the song before. My cousin worked most days and spent the evenings with me. One night, he prepared a special drink for the Christmas season. "You'll like it," he said. "It's just sweet milk, and it will make you feel good." The first time, I drank it quickly. "Wait, drink it slowly," he said. "There is whisky in it."

"Oh boy, this tastes good!" I said. "What else is in it?"

"Sugar, beaten eggs, and cinnamon. It is called eggnog. People drink it during the Christmas holidays."

One day, Ved asked Poornima, a good-looking Indian girl, to show me around New York City while he worked. At first I thought she was my cousin's girlfriend, but later I learned they were just friends. She took me to the shops and treated me to lunch at a diner. I ordered a ham and cheese on rye bread with fruit. It was only my fourth day in America, but Poornima thought I was becoming Americanized well because I would say, "Yeah, yeah," instead of "Yes" as teachers taught us in India. Actually, I couldn't understand her accent, so I pretended to know what she was saying.

After spending six days in New York with my cousin Ved Bedi, he arranged for me to ride with a friend traveling to a small town in Virginia. From there, I took a bus to Knoxville, Tennessee. At 10:00 a.m. on December 29th, I arrived in Knoxville, where it had snowed several inches the night before. Ved had given me the address of the place he had stayed when he lived in Knoxville, Tennessee, and I gave the piece of paper to the taxi driver. Once we arrived at the house, the driver helped unload my luggage. He became upset, groaning and muttering loudly as he hauled the heavy luggage up the steps. Finally, we unloaded everything by the front door, and I paid him the money shown on the meter.

When I knocked, an old man in his eighties, came to the door.

"Ved Bedi. My cousin. He say you let me stay here," I said in broken English. I showed him the address written on the piece of paper.

The old man looked at it blankly. "Eh? What do you want?" He tilted his ear toward me and spoke loudly. "If you're selling something I'm not interested." He started to shut the door.

"Stop," I pleaded. "I am Krishan Bedi. You know my cousin. Ved Bedi. I am new in Amrika, need place to stay. I pay rent. Money," I said loudly.

The man mumbled something I couldn't understand. Frustrated, I pushed my way inside and held up the paper with the address. "Ved Bedi, Ved Bedi," I repeated.

The man must have finally understood what I was trying to say, because he showed me to the bedroom and pointed out the kitchen and refrigerator. He opened the refrigerator. "Eggs," he said, in case I was hungry. He coughed weakly into his hand, wandered out of the kitchen, and ambled up the staircase. Starved from traveling all night, I found a pan in a dusty cupboard, cooked the eggs, and ate them with bread and butter.

Afterward, I went to my room for a nap. Only the bedrooms were heated, using coal heat from a small grate built into the wall. I crawled underneath the heavy quilt on the bed and fell asleep.

The next day, I contacted Mohinder Sood, a friend of Ved's. He invited me for dinner and introduced me to an Indian student who took me to see the university campus. After three days, I moved to a room in a house with three Indian students for twenty-five dollars a month. The old man had coughed constantly, and I feared I might become sick too. In India, coughing is a sign of tuberculosis.

On registration day, I went to the basketball stadium and wandered around for a few minutes before asking a student what I needed to do. He explained, but I stared at him blankly, not understanding his accent at all. Finally, he pointed at a row of desks pushed together with thick course booklets for the winter quarter piled on top. I watched students get in line, grab a booklet and a white index card, and sit on the floor to look through the booklets. I did the same.

An hour went by before I found my three courses and the sections I would like to be in based upon the timing of the other courses. Flipping through hundreds of pages and scanning thousands of lines took more than my limited knowledge of English would allow, but no one helped me, and I wouldn't have understood them anyway. I joined the long line stretching from the front of the room to the back. When I reached the front, a lady called out, "Next!" and I gave her my card. She looked at it and checked the numbers with the data in front of her.

"I'm sorry, hon. These course sections are all filled up."

"Excuse me?" I said, not sure if I'd understood her correctly.

"These. Course. Sections. Are. Full," she repeated loudly.

I stared at her in disbelief.

"Choose different course sections." She gestured to the space behind me. "Next!"

Wishing I had saved the page numbers, I sat down on the floor again to go through the long process of flipping through the Winter Courses booklet. Then I joined the long line once again, wishing I had eaten more for breakfast. At the front of the room, a different lady took my card.

"These sections are full," she said.

My heart sank as I trudged away to begin all over again.

It was late afternoon by the time I returned to my house, feeling exhausted, depressed, and hungry. My housemates were lounging around the house, relaxed and in a good mood. Slowly, I made tea for myself, wishing for my mother, father, and sisters. Here in America I had no one to make tea for me or listen to my troubles and encourage me. Even though I was exhausted, I made the hot tea and drank it as I shared my registration experience with my housemates.

Two of them laughed. "It took us only two hours to register," they said.

The other student felt bad. "I am sorry you had such difficulty. Tomorrow will be better."

Before collapsing into bed, I ate a meal of peas and potatoes with bread and butter, washing it down with milk.

Yes, tomorrow will be better, I told myself. *Hopefully.*

❋ ❋ ❋

For the first week of class, I wore a suit and tie, alternating between two hand-stitched suits I had brought from India. I wanted my professors to think I came from an educated family in a big city, but several Indian students told me I didn't need to dress up for class, so I began dressing casually like the Americans.

Friends in India told me not to worry about my studies. The teachers would take it easy on me because they understood I was far from home. Unfortunately, the teachers did not show me any sympathy. Hundreds of students attended their classes. I was lucky if they even remembered my name. Earning a passing grade was solely my responsibility.

Even though I could not understand the lectures, I still took notes, copying whatever the professor wrote on the chalkboard. As the weeks went by, these notes remained stuffed in books or strewn across my desk, forgotten and not in the least understood.

Between classes I returned to the apartment, cooked a meal, and chatted with the other students I lived with. This soon became a comfortable routine. My studies fell by the wayside as socializing became my favorite part of my new life. If nothing else, I excelled socially. However, certain activities I did not understand.

For instance, I had never heard the term "dating" before. I was clueless about how to approach a girl and start a conversation.

It seemed a necessary part of student life. My Indian friends advised me on how to approach girls.

"While you are in between classes," one guy said, "if you see a nice-looking girl walking alone, ask her the way to the campus post office. Pretend you don't understand the directions and ask if she will show the way. While walking to the post office, ask her name. If she is talkative, ask if she would like to go on a date."

I decided to give it a try. One day while between classes, I saw a girl with long hair walking by herself. Underneath one arm, she carried several books. "Excuse me, excuse me," I called out, jogging to catch up to her.

She stopped and turned around. "Yes?"

"Could you tell me the way to the post office?"

"Sure." She started to explain, but I interrupted.

"I'm sorry. Could you show me the way?"

She smiled. "Of course."

We started walking and talked briefly about our classes. She asked where I was from and if I liked living in the US so far. Before we reached the post office, I worked up my courage and asked, "Would you like to go on a date with me?" She looked surprised. "Uh, sure. What do you have in mind?"

"We could go to a restaurant. But I don't have a car so I can't pick you up. Do you have a car?"

"Yes. I can pick you up, I suppose," the girl answered. "Where do you live?"

I told her my address just as we reached the post office. Before parting ways, we set up a time to meet. Then head down, deep in thought about where I might take her to eat, I made my way home to prepare lunch.

The next night, the girl picked me up in her car, and we drove to a cafeteria. Although my English was still rusty, I could converse well enough as long as I stuck with things I knew about, such as school, my life in India, and my journey to the States. I asked questions about her life, and even though I was still not accustomed to the accent, I understood most of what she said.

On the car ride home, I decided I would kiss her. "American girls like to be kissed in the car," a friend once told me. At every stop sign, I tried to kiss her, but she only pushed me away, gave me a strange look, and continued talking. She didn't act embarrassed or step on the gas to get me home quicker. Instead, she treated me kindly and talked about certain aspects of the town she thought might be useful or interesting to me. I wondered why she didn't kiss me. Maybe not all American girls liked to be kissed in the car. She dropped me off at my apartment, and when I asked if we could get together again, she did not reply. She simply said, "Bye," and drove away.

I hoped this would not be my last date, so with that in mind, I made preparations in case I brought a girl home in the future. Although I didn't smoke, I kept a pack of Menthol Cools, a popular brand among girls at our school, in my section of the refrigerator. Even though I did not drink beer regularly, I kept Budweiser and Schlitz, popular brands, I'd heard, among American girls. If my date came to my place, I could offer her a beer and a cigarette.

My housemates told me, "It is customary to bring a girl to your place after two or three dates." However, living with three other students made it difficult for this to happen. I couldn't just bring home a date with three guys wandering around the house, listening to everything we said, and watching to see if the girls were cute. If I did invite a girl over, I would need to bribe my housemates to go to the library or see a movie. Then, if the girl agreed, I could bring her to my room and offer her a beer and a smoke. I rarely brought a girl home, but when I did, the guys were anxious to come back to their rooms and take a look at her.

Early in the quarter, I learned that a minister of a Baptist church had asked American families to invite foreign students to their homes for lunch on Sundays. One Sunday, the Regis family invited Hathi, one of my housemates, to come for lunch. My housemates and I suspected they asked him because he was good looking with blue eyes. Elizabeth Regis, the young, pretty wife, seemed eager for Hathi to join them, but Hathi was hesitant about going and told me he did not want to go at all. At the same time, he did not want to stand them up, since they were trying to do a nice thing.

"Hathi, I will go for you," I said. In addition to wanting to help Hathi out, I was also curious about meeting this American family. I liked the idea of a free lunch. My housemates thought I was joking. Hathi stared at me as if I had just told him I wanted to quit school and fly to the moon.

"Are you serious?" he asked.

"I am serious."

Everyone felt it would be strange, but it didn't seem like a big deal to me, so I didn't care what they thought.

"What will she think?" one of my housemates asked.

"What if she says no when she sees Bedi and asks for Hathi anyway?" said one of the others.

"I don't think it's a good idea. She'll never invite anyone to lunch again."

They all turned to me. "Are you sure you want to do this?"

"I am sure."

At about eleven o'clock, I got ready and waited for Mrs. Regis to arrive in her car and take me to her house. Hathi hid in his room. Shortly after eleven, Elizabeth knocked on the door. Instead of Hathi, I came down the stairs. She looked at me for a second, and then introduced herself, shaking my hand. Politely, I said, "Hello. My name is Krishan Kumar Bedi." She didn't ask a thing about Hathi.

Elizabeth took me to her home, introduced me to her husband and two children, and served lunch. Afterward, Elizabeth and her husband gave me a tour of the Kingston Pike residential area before dropping me off at my house. Her husband, the owner of Regis Steakhouse in downtown Knoxville, gave me his card. "It's been a pleasure having you, Krishan," he said as I got out of the car.

When I entered the house, all the guys were anxiously waiting for me. "What happened?" they asked. "What did she say and do? Where did she take you?"

"Calm down. Nothing happened," I said.

❀ ❀ ❀

In the meantime, while I met new people and made many friends, my grades suffered. I rarely studied and was never prepared. One day, my professor announced a pop quiz.

I leaned over to the student sitting next to me. "What is a pop quiz?" I asked.

"Mr. Bedi, do not talk while you're taking this pop quiz," the professor scolded. "If I see it again, I will throw you out of the classroom and give you an F on the quiz."

I'd come to Tennessee thinking I would study for final exams only, and that is what I did. It's what I'd done in India, and I did well there. So the night before my calculus exam, I studied Indian style, the way my friend Jasbir Singh Mann and I studied at Vishvakarma Institute. I laid my bedding, the bistra bandh, on the floor and studied my notes. I stayed awake the entire night and went to class the next day for the exam. Studying did not help me. Instead of learning the math formulas, I tried to memorize the practice problems in the book. I studied those problems so hard and was sure I would pass the exams. When the teachers posted grades on their classroom doors, I had received an F in Differential Integer Calculus, an incomplete in English for Foreigners because I was sick and missed the exam, and an X in Electricity and Magnetism for skipping the final. UT was tougher than I'd imagined.

Each week I mailed my parents a letter on aerogram paper for eleven cents. When an aerogram did not provide enough space for all I wanted to say, I used onion sheets, extremely thin sheets of paper that allowed me to write as much as I wanted for a cheap price. Several sheets of onion paper weighed the same amount as one aerogram, allowing me to write several extra pages for the same cost. I told my parents that school was tough and I had made many friends, but I did not tell them I was failing my classes or that I was dating American girls. I knew they would only worry about me, and there was nothing they could do, thousands of miles away in a tiny village.

Early in the spring quarter of 1962, the president of UT invited the foreign students to his home for snacks and soft drinks. He lived in a large brick mansion a few miles from campus. We all ate in a spacious dining room around a large polished table set with fancy china plates and shiny silverware. The president's daughter, an attractive high school girl, ate with us. My Indian friends and I spent the afternoon flirting with her, hoping it would be our lucky day and at least one of us would score a date. I was determined, but the daughter politely ignored my overtures and those of the other students. After the evening snacks, we all stood outside on the front lawn, wearing our best suits. People gawked at us as they drove by, and we smiled and waved. Being an Indian in Tennessee was much like being a celebrity. No one had seen the likes of us before, and they'd slow down to get a good look at the brown-skinned foreigners smiling at them in their nice clothes.

Weeks earlier, I had taken part in a downtown fair with a friend I had met in Punjab shortly before traveling to the US. His name was Jagtar Singh Dhesi, and he arrived in Knoxville a few months after me. Meeting him in Punjab seemed like a good omen because he was planning to attend UT as well, and once he arrived, we rented a house together. At the fair, Dhesi and I, along with other foreign students, were asked to wear traditional Indian clothing and stand outside a booth so people could look at us, take pictures, and ask questions. We wore turbans and kurta pajamas, enjoying all the attention we received. The foreign student advisor, Nelson Nee, liked putting us on display because we made the university look even more prestigious.

❀ ❀ ❀

As the year passed, my grades continued to suffer, especially in math. One day, Mohinder Sood's brother, Ravinder, took me to a restaurant to help me study. He was in his late twenties and had received his bachelor's in mechanical engineering from UT in 1959. Currently, he worked for the Tennessee Valley Authority and was completing his master's in mechanical engineering at UT. We sat down at a table with my book and pages of notes, which might as well have been chicken scratches for all I understood. Ravi picked up the top page of notes and began explaining the formulas. When he looked up at me and saw the blank look on my face, he stopped talking.

"Do you know calculus, Bedi?" he asked.

"What is that?" I asked.

Ravi's mouth dropped open. "You are taking junior-level courses and you don't know what calculus is? Bedi, you need to drop this class as soon as possible."

I dropped the math course with no penalty and tried to focus on the remaining three courses. However, my grades did not improve, and my social life slowed down as well. I wrote to my cousin Ved for help and began applying to different schools. Unfortunately, I wouldn't be going anywhere else. UT was an easy school compared to the universities in the East, such as NYU, Columbia, and Yale, or the engineering schools, such as MIT and Virginia Tech. By the end of second quarter, I had received an Incomplete in Material of Engineering, a C in Highway Design, and an F in Fluid Mechanics.

Instead of registering for summer classes, I began looking for a job. Thinking it would be a good idea to find a civil engineering-related job, I responded to many ads on the bulletin board. To my surprise, a man in Atlanta called, asking if I could fly there for the interview.

"Come as quickly as possible," he said. "I will reimburse you for all the expenses incurred for the interview."

I purchased a round-trip air ticket for $120 and left the next day. The flight went through with no problems, and the man met me at the airport. While riding to his office, he asked me if I had brought sufficient clothes to stay in Atlanta. His question gave me the impression that I would get the job. When we arrived at the construction site, he ordered food, and we ate while he explained the job responsibilities. The position involved making interpretations from the blueprints and communicating them to the construction manager.

The man spoke quickly, running through a number of details and pulling blueprints out of his desk drawer to show me examples and ask questions to determine my experience level. I kept saying, "Yeah, yeah," through the whole interview, having no clue what he was talking about. As I ate my meal, I began to panic, hoping he wouldn't notice my lack of knowledge. By the end, he realized I had not understood anything he said, nor did I know how to read blueprints. He immediately drove me back to the airport and gave me airfare money to fly back to Knoxville—$130, including $10 for dinner.

With $130 in my pocket, an idea hit me. A few months earlier, some friends had told me about hitchhiking. Since I did not get the job, I decided to hitchhike back to Knoxville to save money on the return ticket. I spent four dollars on food and passed the night in a bus station near the airport. At around 6:30 a.m., I drank a cup of hot tea and washed up in the washroom. Still wearing my dark gray, baggy suit, I stood near the main road with my thumb out, hoping someone would give me a ride if I looked educated.

I spent hours on the side of the road trying to hitchhike from Atlanta to Knoxville, Tennessee. Most of the time, no one even bothered to slow down. If someone did stop, they were able to take me only twenty or thirty miles at a time. At 7:00 p.m., I reached Maryville, Tennessee, and after another hour and a half wait, a man driving a small truck agreed to take me the remaining twenty three miles to Knoxville. The entire ride, I struggled to stay awake. I was exhausted from standing for hours, my clothes were sweaty, and I was famished. I couldn't wait to reach my house, take a shower, and change into clean clothes. Then I would sit with a cold beer and ask Dhesi to fix some good food for me.

The truck pulled into Knoxville and dropped me off on my street at around 9:00 p.m. I walked to where my house should have been, but in the dark, I could not find it. *That's strange*, I thought. *Maybe I'm on the wrong street.* I walked a little farther. Even though I was tired and could not think as clearly as usual, I recognized the other houses, so I could not be on the wrong street. Then I came to where my house should have been. At first I thought it was an illusion. In the dark beneath the moon and scattered streetlights, all that remained were blackened foundation and ash. My house had burned nearly to the ground.

Slumping to the curb with tears in my eyes, the awful reality crashed down on me. I had nowhere to go, and I could not take a hot bath, drink a cold beer, or eat good Indian food. The fire had consumed my belongings, and most importantly, I did not know what happened to my housemate, Jagtar Singh Dhesi.

Half an hour passed while I sat on the curb in despair. After a while, three Indian students approached me coming from the library.

"Are you the guy who lived in that house?" one student asked.

I nodded miserably.

"That fire was a big one. The fire department put it out sometime between ten and eleven last night, but at three o'clock this morning, the fire started again."

"Do you know where my housemate, Jagtar Singh Dhesi, is?" I asked. "Is he okay?"

"I am sorry. We have not seen him," they said. "Do you have a place to stay? If not, you can come to our house for tonight. In the morning, you can find your friend and figure out what to do."

They took me to their house and prepared a meal for me while I cleaned up. Once I ate, they showed me to a bed. Despite my exhaustion, I tossed and turned sleeplessly the entire night, thinking about my belongings and legal documents lost in the fire. Everything was gone. My bistra bandh, the quilt my mother made me, the trunk filled with dal and mango pickles, my hand-stitched suits, the slide rule, and my books. I was particularly concerned about my passport and the certificate of my diploma in civil engineering.

The next morning, I walked past the ruins of my house and up the hill toward campus. In the distance, I saw Dhesi walking toward me. We saw each other at the same time and walked faster. He looked just as bad as I felt. He was still wearing his turban, but it was dirty, and his clothes were wrinkled. We embraced and sat on the sidewalk, unable to keep from crying. Crying felt good. We were still in shock, and although I did not know what would happen, I felt better with Dhesi next to me. After several minutes, Dhesi dried his tears with his shirtsleeve and explained what happened.

"It was awful, Bedi. Two days ago, while I was at the library, the house caught fire. After the firemen put out the fire, they allowed me to enter the house and bring out our important documents. When the owners arrived, they said it was not advisable to sleep in the house, but it would be okay to leave our belongings there. That night, I slept at a friend's house. At around three o'clock in the morning, the fire started again. Everyone was sleeping, so when someone finally noticed the smoke pouring out of the house and flames blowing out the windows, it was too late."

We decided to consult Nelson Nee, our foreign students advisor. Nelson told us to prepare a list of all the belongings lost in the fire, so we could get reimbursed. However, the owners of the house could not be found. They had left the city, and later on, we were told an investigation was going on. Police suspected that the owner of the house might have started the fire, because he didn't make enough money from renting it out to students. As a result, Dhesi and I did not recover any money for our lost belongings.

In the meantime, Ravi Sood arranged for us to stay in a house he owned six blocks from campus. It needed renovation work, but he said we could stay in one room on the ground floor for thirty dollars a month.

I was still wearing the same grimy suit from the interview two days before. Dhesi and I desperately needed clean clothes. Once Nelson Nee contacted several churches and told them about our situation, a Baptist church near campus organized a collection and gave us clothes.

The clothes were huge on us. Dhesi and I, of small stature, knew nothing about sizes because all our clothes were hand-stitched in India. We held up our pants so they wouldn't fall off our hips. The shirts were like small tents, and we looked ridiculous. All summer, we wore sleeveless undershirts instead, the coolest option and the best-fitting of all the donations. Still, the undershirts were so long they came to our knees, nearly covering the long underwear we wore in place of pants. It looked like we were wearing some kind of dress or nightgown, and people laughed when they saw us walking around the house or on the street.

The meager savings left from the money my father sent for spring quarter had burned in the pillow case. I needed money to pay for rent and tuition in the fall, but I could not tell my parents what happened. It would only worry them, and being so far away, they could not help me. My father was in no financial position to send me more money.

Desperate for a job, I contacted Mr. Regis, hoping he could hire me at his restaurant or knew of other opportunities. Mr. Regis lined up an interview for me with the owner of McDonald's. He told me that if I wanted to work there I could start Monday, and my hours would be 7:00 a.m. to 3:30 p.m. with a pay rate of eighty-five cents per hour.

"Go to the McDonald's on Chapman Highway," he said. "Talk to Bill. He's the manager. He'll get you started."

The next day, I walked a mile across the river and met Bill. After asking me several basic questions, he said, "Well, let's get ya started. Basically, your main job is to keep the place clean. You'll sweep and mop the floor, pick up trash, those sorts of things." He handed me a broom. "You can start right over there. Customer made a mess just now."

On the fourth day of the job, Bill told me to pick up the lot.

I looked at him, confused, and he pointed to the parking lot. "Cigarette butts, cups, wrappers, whatever customers throw out of their car windows. Throw it in the dumpster in the corner," he said.

The McDonald's contained only one small room for making hamburgers, french fries, milkshakes, and soft drinks, with a basement below for storing raw food. The building did not have seating, so people ate in their cars parked in the lot, and then threw their trash into bins placed around the lot. The smaller pieces of garbage did not always make it into the bins, so I spent a majority of my time picking up trash and emptying bins into the dumpster.

I felt ashamed. I came to the US to earn a civil engineering degree and become an SDO, yet here I was, performing menial work only an untouchable would do in India. In India there are four primary castes: *Brahmin*, the priests; *Kshatriya*, warriors and nobility; *Vaisya*, farmers, traders and artisans; and *Shudra*, tenant farmers and servants. My family and I were in the Kshatriya caste. Not even included in the system were the *Harijans*, in other words "outcasts." We referred to them as untouchables, because they were only allowed to perform jobs such as sweeping streets, cleaning up cow dung, collecting garbage, and cleaning the open sewer drains. Not allowed to touch anyone from the four castes, they could not even drink at the same well lest their shadow fall on us.

Bending over to pick up a dirty napkin and trudging over

to the garbage can to throw it away, I thought about my Harijan friend from India, Neela, who attended primary school with me. Too little to hold prejudices, we became close friends. Another untouchable, Nachattar Singh, became a close friend in high school, and I always shared my lunch with him. Sometimes after school, I went to his hut, built of straw and mud, surrounded by other huts of the same material and children running around half naked. My mother did not mind that I was friends with an untouchable, although my father and brother looked down on the friendship. My mother's heart softened toward Nachattar Singh's mother, and she too visited the hut of straw and mud to bring food and kindness.

Even though two of my friends were untouchables, it didn't mean I wanted to be one too. I was trying to make my way upward in society. As I picked up garbage, I felt so low I would sit behind the dumpster and cry. After a few minutes, I would dry my eyes. There was no one to encourage me but myself. Many Americans worked lowly jobs so they could attend college.

McDonald's employees took a half hour lunch break and ate a free meal, consisting of a cheeseburger, french fries, and a milkshake. Eating cow's meat is against the Hindu religion, so I picked off the hamburger and ate only the cheese and bun. Although several thousand cows wander freely on country roads and city streets, no one eats beef in India. If a cow lies down at a busy intersection, the cars don't stop and honk. They back up and drive around her.

The buns and cheese did not fill me up. I still felt hungry and tired, but it was ingrained in me that I should not eat beef, so I persisted. On the fourth day, I prayed to God and asked for forgiveness. *I am sorry, God, but I am in this environment, and it is not in my hand. There is no other alternative, and I don't want to feel tired and hungry at work anymore.*

Then I picked up the cheeseburger and took a big bite. It was my first time eating cow meat, but I hardly paid attention to the taste, because I was only trying to satisfy my hunger.

Later on, I became accustomed to American food and regularly enjoyed cheeseburgers and Coke.

Two and a half weeks later, I received my first paycheck for thirty-four dollars, which amounted to thirty-one dollars after taxes and social security were taken out. Deciding to buy gifts, I went straight to a store and bought fifteen dollars' worth of gifts for my brother and sisters' children and my parents. I shipped the package by sea, including a note saying, "These gifts are from my first earnings. Please enjoy them." Later that week, I donated five dollars of my check to a charity recommended by Ravi Sood. I also gave ten dollars to Mrs. Pruett, a kind-hearted woman who ran a guest house called "Little UN" where she bought groceries and cooked meals for Indian students living there. In some cases, the Indians either did not make payments or they procrastinated, saying they would pay later. I learned she couldn't afford to run the guest house anymore and planned to move to Washington, DC. In a conversation, she mentioned she did not have enough money to cover the bus ride. I was more than happy to give her the remainder of my check.

To this day, I teach a similar philosophy regarding money to my sons, nieces, and nephews. They should donate a portion of their first earnings to their favorite charity. With another portion, they should buy a gift for their parents. Last of all, they should reward themselves. If any money remains from their first paycheck, they should use it to celebrate with family members.

"Just enjoy it, and God will give you more," I tell them.

In July 1962, I began washing dishes at a new drive-in restaurant called Shoney's Big Boy. I didn't want to waste any time when I could be making money for school. After three days of working at McDonald's, walking to and from my apartment in the afternoon, catching the bus to Shoney's and working until 1:00 a.m., I was exhausted. Then I slept only a few hours before getting up at 6:00 a.m. to start the routine all over again. My feet were sore from standing and walking almost eighteen hours a day. The fourth night at Shoney's, my feet hurt so much I decided I would feel more comfortable if I took my shoes off toward the end of my shift. While another employee and I were cleaning the floors, the manager walked by and saw me.

"Kris! What do you think you're doing in your bare feet?!" he yelled.

"My feet hurt, so I took my shoes off." I didn't understand why he was so angry.

"Put your damn shoes on!" he yelled. "I don't want you working in bare feet."

I didn't understand how serious he was. After indicating that my shoes hurt my feet, I simply continued cleaning the floor, thinking he would accept my plea and let it go.

"That's it! You're fired!" he shouted. "I do not want to see you!"

I did not understand the word "fired," but I understood not wanting to see me, so I said, "That is simple, just close your eyes and you will not see me." I was trying to be funny, but I didn't think the manager was being serious, nor did I think that my remark was disrespectful. The manager looked astounded. Then he yelled at me. "You are fired! You leave now!"

I looked at the other guy for clarification, and he explained, "Kris, he does not want you to work here anymore. It means that you punch out your card and leave this place." When I finally realized what "fired" meant, I actually felt relieved, and when I got home, I slept for twelve hours straight.

Right away, I found another job, this time a position with a transportation company for a traffic surveyor. The survey involved determining the expansion of a road near my house that merged onto the bridge crossing the railroad tracks. The company hired me to work from 3:30 p.m. to 11:00 p.m., giving me just enough time to change out of my McDonald's uniform and walk to the traffic site, where I relieved the other worker.

The job lasted six weeks and paid $2.50 an hour. Every day, I sat on the bridge, counted vehicles, and marked the number of cars and trucks driving by.

✳ ✳ ✳

One morning, while working at McDonald's, I met Melissa, a high school girl who showed an interest in me. We exchanged phone numbers, and on my lunch break, we ate cheeseburgers, French fries, and milk shakes for our first date. Wishing I could take her to a nice restaurant, I told Ravi Sood about Melissa, and he offered to help. From then on, Ravi and I picked her up in his car and brought her back to my apartment where we drank tea, ate Indian food, and listened to American music on the radio.

Ravi and Peggy enjoyed giving me advice about how to treat Melissa, and Peggy thought she was a nice girl. During the nights at my apartment, Melissa taught me how to dance the cha-cha and other dances. At times, she talked seriously about getting married. I didn't know what to say. My main purpose for coming to the States was to earn a degree. Besides, I was failing my classes, and it seemed it would be a while before I graduated. I asked Ravi Sood what I should say to Melissa.

"Tell her that you want to finish school first," Ravi said. "Then you can discuss marriage."

The next time Melissa came to my place, I told her this, nervous to hear her response.

"Okay," Melissa said. "That's fine. I understand."

I was relieved that Melissa did not seem upset. "Can we at least go steady, Kris?" she asked.

"What is this 'go steady?'" I asked.

"I won't date anyone else, and neither will you."

"Oh. Yeah. We can go steady."

Later, I asked Ravi Sood what I should have said. He was married to an American girl, so I figured he would encourage the relationship.

"It is okay to say yes," he said. "But you should see how it works out first."

Feeling that I needed to focus on school, I decided not to pursue a relationship with Melissa anymore.

❀ ❀ ❀

One weekend, two coworkers from McDonald's, Ken and Lee, asked me to go cave exploring with them. Naturally, I said yes, although I didn't know what a cave was or what we would explore there. They went every weekend and collected rare stones. Sometimes they used a map, but other times, they took random paths and walked wherever they wanted.

I eagerly anticipated the adventure and invited Dhesi to join us. We navigated underground tunnels, and when the pathways became too narrow, we squeezed through single file. At other times, the passageways widened to allow us enough space to walk freely without stooping or bumping our heads on cold, drippy stalactites and various rock formations. As we walked deeper into the caves, waterfalls and streams flowed over rocks and gathered in pools. Ken and Lee marked each stream and waterfall on their homemade maps.

One time, bats flew at us from the darkness. Ken and Lee cursed, and we all bumped into each other, trying to run away from the flapping wings, high-pitched screeches, and beady eyes. We all yelled as we wildly swung our flashlights to scare the bats away, and we ran from the rest that weren't afraid of a few flashlight-wielding explorers.

On our way back, the passage caved in, leaving a small opening. Panicked, we dug through the dirt and rocks with our hands so we could crawl out. With no way to communicate with relatives or friends on the outside, it took more than two hours to dig ourselves out. Our hands and legs were scratched and bleeding as we emerged. Dhesi and I never went back to the caves. *I came to get a degree*, I thought to myself. *Not end up dead in a cave.*

Chapter 4

The summer of 1962, Dhesi and I were still living in Ravi Sood's rental house. Ravi came by almost every day to make repairs, and soon we became close friends. Ravi paid me fifty cents an hour to help him convert several houses near campus into apartments for UT students. I worked in the evenings, although I knew nothing about tools or repairs.

"I will show you as long as you are willing to learn," he said. "Other students who helped me in the past were lazy and unwilling to learn construction." He raised an eyebrow and held out a hammer. "Are you ready to learn?"

The work involved changing the interior of the house so we could separate it into two or three apartments, each with a kitchen, bathroom, and separate entrance. In one house, we spread insulation in the ceiling to conserve heat. Afterward, my throat itched and my spit and nasal discharge turned black. "Ravi, help me. Everything is coming out black, and my throat won't stop itching!" I said.

"You'll be fine after you wash up and clear your throat," Ravi assured me.

In the back of my mind, I wondered if the dark material in the insulation would cause me to become severely ill, but after washing my throat thoroughly, the itching stopped.

Because I followed instructions and paid attention to detail, Ravi considered me a good worker. He noticed that I worked hard with my McDonald's and traffic surveying jobs, and that I tried hard to adapt to the American lifestyle, especially important to him since his wife was American. Most Indians did not approve of Indo-American marriages, but it did not matter to me.

Years later, I would come back to Knoxville every two or three years to visit Ravi, and he always told me he would not forget one thing I taught him during our time working on the houses together. *What could he possibly learn from me?* I thought. I felt it was Ravi who taught me so much during that time.

Ravi said, "Remember when you were standing on the top of a ladder one Saturday morning, waiting for further instruction? I told you, 'Wait, I'm thinking.' You said, 'Nights are to think and plan. Days are to work and to execute the plans.'"

As the end of summer neared, I talked to Ravi about working part time at McDonald's and going to school during the fall quarter at UT. He said it would work, but perhaps I should buy a car because, with all my classes, I wouldn't have time to walk a mile to and from work. One day we saw an ad in the newspaper for a cheap DeSoto. Ravi arranged for the owners, a father and son, to bring the car to a common place near campus so we could examine it.

"It's a good car," Ravi said after examining it thoroughly. "You should buy it."

The father was asking $120 for the car. We offered $90 and then negotiated to finish the deal at $105. I paid the father in cash and asked if they wouldn't mind driving it to my apartment.

Puzzled, he asked, "Don't you know how to drive?"

I answered no, and the two men looked at me strangely.

"Is it a crime to buy a car and not know how to drive it?" I asked.

"Oh no, no," they said. "We are sorry. We will be happy to drive it to your place."

I couldn't believe I actually owned a car. It was a 1951 DeSoto, a gray, two-door stick-shift with two and a half gears. Feeling good about my purchase, I couldn't wait to share my excitement with someone who would support me and be happy about it. I called my former housemate Ravi Aggarwal, a native of Calcutta, who was working on his MBA at UT. The other Indian students I lived with advised me to not get too close to him. "He is a city-slicker," they said. Ravi was fluent in English, came from an affluent family, and received his bachelor's in commerce from Xavier University. Students knew him as a talkative and cunning person who easily took advantage of people. "Stay away from him," they warned. "He is up to no good."

"He may be the type of person you are describing," I replied, "but I would like to know this person and have experience with him before I accept your impression of him."

As time passed, Ravi Aggarwal and I became close friends. Even though he was from Calcutta, his parents were from Punjab, and he knew Punjabi culture, one of the reasons we became such close friends. When I told Ravi Aggarwal about the car, he said, "Oh no, Bedi. You did not."

"Yes, I did," I answered. "Come and see it."

Ravi was glad to know I had bought a car, but he told me it was not considered good for foreign students to own cars. Americans figured that if foreign students owned cars, they could go on dates easily and have a good time instead of studying.

"Our advisor, Mr. Nelson Nee, is from China and is married to an American woman, and even he doesn't own a car," Ravi informed me. "He does not advise foreign students to own cars either."

"Well, I didn't ask Mr. Nee, did I?"

"It is great that you have a car. Just don't publicize it."

I finally persuaded him to come to my house and look at the car. "Get in and I'll show you how it runs," I said.

Ravi got in the car, and I pulled onto the street. I had driven half a block when Ravi asked if I had a driver's license.

"No," I answered, nonchalantly. "This is my first time driving."

"You don't know how to drive!" Ravi exclaimed. "You have to go back right now!"

Slowly, I drove back to my house and parked the car. Ravi sat stiffly in the front seat, praying I wouldn't run over the curb or veer into oncoming traffic.

"Bedi," Ravi said, once we were safe in the driveway. "You cannot drive this car until you take driving lessons and get a driver's license."

The next day, Ravi and I went to the DMV and brought home the driver's education book so I could learn how to operate a car and memorize the rules of the road. Two weeks later, I passed the written test for a learner's permit. As soon as Ravi gave me driving lessons, I could get my license.

When the fall quarter started, McDonald's did not offer me a job for the rest of the year. I could only afford to take three courses, the minimum requirement. Ravi Sood suggested I offer parking spots to earn extra money. I could fit three extra cars in the driveway at Ravi's rental house. On football game days, I made a sign that said, "Park–$3," and stood by the side of the road for all the passing cars to see. Friends and classmates laughed at me standing there, holding my sign. But I made nine dollars almost every home game, and I didn't care, even when the gossip was about Bedi standing on the street with a sign.

In the beginning of the fall quarter, I became friends with Sarbjeet Sandhu, a PhD student who had just moved from Punjab. Sandhu came to my apartment for lunch or hot tea several times a week. Four years older than I was, he had completed his Master's in Agriculture in India and worked for several years. He had married an Indian woman a year earlier and missed her terribly since leaving her in Punjab. Sandhu was not adjusting well to the environment in America, and he found studying in the US not as easy as he had been led to believe.

One day, while we sat in the kitchen drinking tea, Sandhu mentioned that he needed to open a bank account.

"I have a car. I can take you!" I responded immediately.

Sandhu hesitated. "I don't know, Bedi. You don't have a driver's license yet."

"Don't worry. Ravi Sood has given me lessons, and I can drive now."

Sandhu didn't look too convinced, but he agreed.

The next day, I drove to his apartment, but he was not outside yet. I honked the horn a couple of times, but he still did not come out. Deciding to park on the side street outside his house, I yanked the steering wheel too hard and could not straighten the car since it did not have power steering. My Desoto crashed into a parked car with a loud crunch. Panicking, I looked around to make sure no one had seen me before I drove away.

About twenty yards down the street, I came to a stop sign. In a hurry to get away from Sandhu's house and the car I'd hit, I ran the stop sign, slamming into another car in the middle of the intersection. I climbed out of my car and approached the two ladies sitting in their dented car—a mother and daughter, I presumed—the latter appearing to be in her twenties. The mother glared at me as I walked around the front of my car, stepping over the water gushing from it. The women did not appear injured, but the daughter began to cry.

"I am so sorry about this," I told them. "I will pay for your car to be repaired. But please, do not call the police. I don't have any insurance." I also did not have a license, causing this accident to be an even more serious offense. My stomach was in knots, and with the sun bearing down on me, I could feel beads of sweat forming on my forehead and sticking to my shirt. The moment I said I didn't have insurance, the daughter cried louder. "I'm hurt," she whimpered. "I'm hurt."

I tried to calm her down, but she only ignored me and continued crying uncontrollably. A moment later, a policeman arrived at the scene. When he asked for my driver's license and insurance card, a lump formed in my throat, and I could barely speak. I managed to say that I didn't have either. Then I showed him my learner's permit. The disapproving look on his face caused me to sweat nearly as much as the sun did. He pulled a pad of paper from his chest pocket just as a colored man charged toward us, holding a paintbrush.

"Officer, I saw everything. I was painting on the second floor of that house over there, and I saw this man hit a parked car."

Confused, the policeman looked at where the man pointed, and then he looked at me. After walking over to the parked car and observing the dent, he thanked the man, who looked quite proud of himself. Feeling his work was done, he looked me up and down smugly and strode away, paint brush swinging jauntily.

The situation could not have gotten any worse. Pen poised, the officer shook his head in disbelief, and added another offense to the growing list.

As he wrote out the ticket, I glanced over at the two women. The mother was glaring at me, arms crossed over her chest. The police officer began reading me the charges.

"These charges are for a hit-and-run, missing a stop sign, hitting another car, injuring two ladies, and having no driver's license or insurance," he said. "What do you have for identification?"

I showed him my student ID. Since I was a foreign student at UT, the policeman did not know what to do. He called his captain and explained the situation. The captain did not know either, but told the officer to keep me there, and he would come shortly. When the captain arrived, he asked where I lived and the same questions the first officer asked. Then he contacted my foreign student advisor, Nelson Nee, and told him to come to the scene. While waiting for Nelson, I spoke to the ladies and told them I would take care of any medical expenses and the repair of the car. I did not have any cash on me, but I said I would work part time and pay them later. They did not look too reassured.

Ten minutes later, Mr. Nelson Nee came huffing and puffing up the hill. "When did you buy this car?" he snapped at me.

"A month ago."

"Why?" he yelled. "You do not have driver's license!"

"I have a learner's permit," I murmured. I was beginning to feel scared. Before, the entire situation seemed surreal, but now, after the ordeal with the police, the unknown outcome, and my advisor fuming at me, I thought, *What if they put me in jail?*

The captain, the officer, and Nelson Nee held a conference right on the spot. My case was unusual. The officers rarely dealt with foreign students, but they decided I must appear in court. They gave me a ticket requiring that I appear before the judge. Nelson Nee said, "I assure you, Mr. Bedi will be at court on that day."

The police officers helped push my damaged car to Ravi Sood's house, a little way down the street. After the officers departed, Nelson Nee scolded me again, and then he left too. I walked back to my apartment feeling sad about the whole situation and disappointed that I couldn't show off by driving Sandhu to the bank in my car.

Within several hours, the news had spread among the Indian students that Bedi had been involved in an accident, two ladies were injured badly, and the cops took Bedi to jail.

Ravi Aggarwal called me and sounded surprised when I answered the phone. "I thought you were in jail for a hit-and-run," he said, "but I called to make sure. Tell me what happened. Everyone is saying you are in big trouble!"

"Everything is okay," I assured him. "Please calm down."

Ravi immediately came to the apartment to see if I was okay. By the time he arrived, I was fixing the evening tea and asked if he would like some.

"Bedi, are you all right? Are you hurt? Are you in pain?" Ravi asked.

"Let us have tea first, and I will explain what happened," I said.

He was more anxious to know about my well-being and the accident than to drink tea.

"Are you sure you're okay?"

"Yes, I am!" I said.

He shook his finger at me. "What did I tell you? Never drive a car without a driver's license! Very bad, Bedi. Very bad. At least you are not hurt. Now we will see about this court date."

While waiting for my court date, Ravi Sood took me to the UT parking lot for driving lessons. A few weeks later, I got my license. Now I could go anywhere I wanted, and I felt more self-assured when asking girls out since I could pick them up in my banged up car.

On my court date, Ravi Aggarwal accompanied me to the courthouse. We entered a large room with no windows. At the front of the room, an austere man in black robes was conferring with an officer and another man wearing a suit. I waited anxiously, sitting on the hard bench while other cases were taken care of. I could hardly tell my parents in a letter that I had been sent to jail. I would never get my degree, and I would be the laughingstock of Malaudh. When my case came up, the judge announced the hearing, and the police officer described the hit-and-run and the accident, adding that I did not have a driver's license.

"What does Mr. Bedi have then?" asked the judge.

"He has a learner's permit, your Honor," said the officer.

The judge looked at me. "Can you speak English?" he asked.

"Yeah, yeah," I said nervously. I met his eyes and then glanced over at Ravi, who gave me a reassuring nod.

"What do you have?" he asked.

I stood up and said, "I have my driver's license." I pulled it out of my wallet and showed it to him.

The judge looked at the officer. "Mr. Bedi has a driver's license," he said.

Clearing his throat, the judge looked around the room where a few other people were sitting. "Are the ladies involved in this accident present?"

There was no response. The two women were not there. Neither was the owner of the other car I'd hit before driving away.

"Judge, I am so sorry all this has happened," I said, showing him my driver's license again.

He exchanged a look with the officer and said to me, "Do not do this again. Case dismissed."

Ravi Aggarwal and I returned to my apartment, laughing in relief at the quick trial and my good fortune that they had not made me pay a fine or thrown me in jail.

❀ ❀ ❀

One day, Ravi Sood told me about Dr. Cheema, a professor at Knoxville College who had grown up in Pakistan and knew about Punjabi culture. I contacted Dr. Cheema, and he invited me to his house for dinner. I was surprised when I met his wife and discovered that we were distant cousins. Bilques, or Billo as everyone called her, was happy to meet me. She fixed a variety of foods, including several Indian dishes, and afterward we drank tea and reminisced about our families and the past.

After dinner, I explained my circumstances to Dr. Cheema and Billo. Starting January 1963, I would have no source of income, and to make matters worse, I was failing all of my courses at UT. If I did not maintain a 2.0 GPA, I would be thrown out of the university. At that point, my GPA was 1.0.

"Would you like to attend Knoxville College?" Dr. Cheema asked. "I can see if the president would grant you free room and board along with some pocket money."

"I can help you apply for admission and financial assistance," Billo offered.

I couldn't say no, and a few weeks later, I received admission. The college granted me financial assistance to cover tuition and room and board, but they denied the pocket money on the grounds that the college had exhausted its cash fund. Knoxville College, a school attended mostly by black students, was glad to have one more student to add to its small community of foreigners. The other students could learn more about Indian culture, and it was considered prestigious for a smaller school to have foreign students on campus.

At first, I worried about what my friends and family would think if I went there. Knoxville College was not as prestigious as UT. After some serious thought, I knew it was the best choice for me at the time. Since the college did not offer civil engineering, I chose to pursue a bachelor's in math instead. While part of me felt embarrassed at this change in my circumstances, it was the only door open for me.

❋ ❋ ❋

The third week of January 1963, I moved into a dormitory at Knoxville College. In addition to Saran Bhagta and me, the only Indians, there were three students from Cuba and three from Africa. I did my best to fit in, observing how the black students dressed, how they walked, what beer they drank (Colt 45), where they took girls on dates, but most of all, the way they talked, perhaps because that was the easiest thing to catch on to.

"Hey man," they said to each other in the hallways.

"Hey, you black ass," they hollered while crossing campus.

"What's up, my niggah?"

"Hey Mo Fo. Come here."

Usually, I would see the same people ten to fifteen times a day, and in these instances, the students would point their thumb and index finger at me, a simple way to acknowledge the other person without saying anything. At other times, they'd say, "My main man."

In an attempt to blend in, I tried talking like them.

"Hey, you blackie," I'd say, or, "Hey, you niggah."

They roared with laughter at this. "Did you hear what the foreigner just said? Did you hear?"

A tall black guy, a basketball player from my dorm, slapped me on the back, his teeth flashing white as he laughed. "Kris, you ain't nothin' but a yellow niggah!"

So far, taking showers at the dorm was the most difficult adjustment I faced. In India, we bathed from a bucket filled with water from the hand pump, always keeping our underwear on. The guys in the dorm shower room undressed completely in front of each other. It was embarrassing and uncomfortable for me to even *think* about stripping down in front of a bunch of strangers, so for the first week, I kept my underwear on. The guys looked at me strangely, but they didn't ask questions.

One day, my roommate asked me why I took showers with my underwear on. I shrugged and tried to explain that's how we bathed in India. He raised an eyebrow and laughed, unable to fathom such a practice. The next day, I decided to do as "the Romans do," and I began undressing completely for showers, still feeling self-conscious. However, I would not walk naked down the hallway back to my room with the towel slung over my shoulder like most of the guys did. The first few times I saw them walk that way, I was taken aback and thought, *What is this?* I didn't care how normal it was to them—I always wrapped the towel around my waist. They also brushed their teeth and shaved naked. It felt strange to stand there in my clothes while shaving or brushing my teeth with the others naked on both sides of me.

In the meantime, I enjoyed getting to know the students at their house parties, and I learned to like their music. The students mimicked James Brown's quick feet as they danced to "I Feel Good." We listened to the silky voices of the big-haired Supremes in "Baby Love" and "Where Did Our Love Go." We swayed to Aretha Franklin's soulful, hair-raising voice. Their parties relaxed me and lifted the pressure I felt from my classes and lack of money.

In the meantime, even though I did not need the class for my degree, Dr. Cheema persuaded me to take his freshman chemistry course which took place every Saturday at 8:00 a.m. Functioning on only three and a half hours of sleep, since I came home from my new job at Andy's restaurant at 3:30 a.m., I figured I could sit back and relax. On the first day of class, I thought to myself, *This will be simple. Dr. Cheema knows me well and will give me a good grade to help improve my grade point average.* Dr. Cheema had assigned pages for us to read, but my chemistry book sat untouched on my desk all week. *That is fine,* I thought. *Dr. Cheema and I are close, so he will take it easy on me.*

As soon as class started, Dr. Cheema asked a question about the reading assignment. Without skipping a beat, he turned to me and said, "Mr. Bedi, please explain this to us." He gave me an encouraging smile. Why was he asking me? Out of the whole class, he chose me to answer the question. My mouth dropped open as I stared at him in shock. What did I ever do to him? I invited him and his wife to my apartment for Christmas. I cooked a nice meal and showed them respect. What about the times I massaged his headaches away? And on top of all that, his wife was my cousin. Did that mean nothing to him?

Dr. Cheema's question flew right over my head. Feeling betrayed, I could only say, "I don't know."

As the weeks passed, I learned Dr. Cheema's idea of helping me was different than I expected. I thought he would breeze me through the course. Instead, he always asked *me* the questions, showing he did not expect any less from me than he expected from everyone else. At the time, I did not see it that way. I just thought he had it in for me.

With work and my other classes, I felt I did not have time to read the assignments. Chemistry was supposed to be an easy A. Billo was the director of Public Relations at Knoxville College, so one day I went to her office and told her that her husband was giving me a hard time in his class. I became so emotional that I cried, while she listened intently and tried to console me. "I will talk to him," she promised. "Continue going to your classes."

To my dismay, Dr. Cheema only persisted. Knowing I worked Friday nights and was not prepared, he still asked me questions I could not answer. Enough was enough. I dropped the class, later learning from other chemistry students that Dr. Cheema was astonished to discover I had dropped it.

Chapter 5

At the end of spring semester, the Dean of Student Affairs told me about Wildwood, a summer resort town on the coast of New Jersey. "There's a group of students going there on a bus," he said. "It should be easy to find a job at a hotel or restaurant."

In need of a job, I packed a suitcase, and wearing my baggy suit, I boarded the bus. We switched buses in Philadelphia and arrived in Wildwood late in the evening at a house that served as an employment agency office as arranged by the college employment office. The owner of the employment agency, a black woman in her sixties, welcomed us into her home, showed us to our rooms, and told us she would explain the job situation in the morning.

The next day, we sat on the floor, while the woman informed us there was only one job opening, a short-order breakfast cook position.

"Does anybody know how to cook?" she asked.

After she asked twice, and still no one said anything, I hesitantly raised my hand. I had never cooked for a restaurant, but how hard could it be? I'd worked at McDonald's, where they served breakfast, and Andy's restaurant served scrambled eggs, fried eggs, and omelets. I felt confident that I could make the food on my own.

"Do you know how to cook?" the woman asked. She looked doubtful.

"Yes," I said in a firm voice.

"Okay. Where have you cooked?"

"McDonald's," I answered. Several students chuckled.

"Okay, you've got an interview at the Dorsey Hotel at eleven o'clock. I'll call the owner, Mrs. Whitesell, and tell her I'm sending you over." She scrawled the address on a slip of paper. "It is already 10:30, so you need to head there right away."

The day was warm with clouds overhead and a cool breeze carried the scent of ocean waves. As I walked, drops of rain fell, turning into a thick downpour and soaking my suit and hair in no time. A few minutes later, I approached the Dorsey Hotel, a four-story white house. After climbing the steps and knocking on the door, a tall, casually-dressed man let me inside.

"My name is Kris Bedi, and the agency has sent me for the short-order cooking job," I said.

The man just looked at me, a foreigner dripping puddles of water on the lobby's wooden floor. Later, I learned he was Mr. Whitesell, and apparently, the Whitesells weren't prepared to consider a foreigner for the job. In the past, the employment agency had sent only black people for the cooking position.

Mr. Whitesell went to get his wife, who handled the hotel staff and took care of management. She led me into a small room as her husband went away shaking his head.

Despite my soggy and disheveled appearance, Mrs. White-sell spoke courteously, asking my name, where I was from, and what foods I could cook. Suddenly I couldn't think of any names of food from McDonald's or Andy's. I was cold, wet, and nervous, but I had to answer something.

"You name it, I know it," I said.

"Can you make scrambled eggs?"

"Yes," I answered.

"Fried eggs?"

"Yes."

"How about meatloaf?"

I had never seen anyone cook meatloaf before, so I replied, "I can learn your way of cooking meatloaf, since each person has a little bit of a different recipe. If you show me, I will be able to do it."

She nodded pleasantly. "Do you know succotash?"

I never heard of this word. To sound truthful, I said, "No,

ma'am. I don't know how to cook that. But if you show me once, then I will cook it.

"Oh, no problem," she said. "I'll show you."

At the end of the interview, Mrs. Whitesell still wasn't sure if she should hire me. "Wait here while I discuss it with my husband," she said.

A few minutes later, she came back with a smile on her face. "Kris," she said, looking at me standing there in my wrinkly, wet suit. "You have the job."

The Dorsey Hotel was open from mid-June through Labor Day weekend. Two weeks prior to the opening date, the hotel staff cleaned and repaired the hotel, preparing for guests. Before Mrs. Whitesell hired me, she had cooked most of the meals for the hotel staff, but now it was my job to cook breakfast for them every morning. When the chef arrived a few days before the opening date, I would help him cook for the guests.

The Whitesells paid me $250 a month, including room and board. I slept in the basement quarters with the black employees, in my own small room, with one bed, no more than a thin mattress on top of a wooden frame. The white employees worked in the dining room as servers and slept upstairs in the comfortable beds.

The next three mornings, I fixed eggs for the hotel staff, while Mrs. Whitesell made sandwiches for lunch and prepared full meals in the evenings. I assisted her and watched how she prepared the meats and vegetables in case I would have to make the same foods.

On the fourth day, an employee came up to me while I was cooking scrambled eggs in the kitchen. "Do you know how to make pancakes?" he asked.

"Sure," I said, even though I had no idea.

"Good, we are tired of eating eggs," he said. "Tomorrow could you make pancakes?"

"Of course," I said.

Each afternoon for two to three hours, I strolled down to

the boardwalk with the dining room help to play games and look at the sea. That afternoon, I said I didn't feel well, and after everyone left, I hurried to the phone booth to make a collect call to Billo Cheema in Knoxville.

Thinking there was an emergency, Billo immediately accepted the charges. "Kris, what's wrong?" she asked. "Are you okay?"

I only had three minutes to talk. At the end of three minutes, the operator would ask if Billo wanted to accept a further three minutes. Unsure if Billo would accept more time at two dollars for each additional minute, I spoke quickly.

"Never mind about that," I said. "I have a job now."

"Oh, Kris, I am very glad," Billo said. "What kind of job did you get?"

"A cooking job."

"Oh my God, Kris. You don't know how to cook!" Billo exclaimed.

"Don't tell me whether I do or not. Now I have this job, so I'm calling you to find out how to make pancakes."

Billo just about died laughing. "Kris! How could you do that? How did you get this job?"

"Never mind that," I said. "Tomorrow morning I'm supposed to make pancakes. So quickly, tell me how!"

"The pancake mix usually comes in a box as some type of powder. You need to mix it with milk or water to make a paste. Read the directions on the box," she said. "It will tell you how to do it. Once the batter is prepared you just pour it in the hot pan. When one side is done you must turn it over to the other side. It should look brown on both sides." Billo laughed again. "Kris, I can't believe you are a cook!"

The next morning, I woke up earlier than usual and hurried to the kitchen. Mrs. Whitesell was already unlocking the pantry and making sure we had everything for breakfast. While she started the bacon, I found the pancake mix. Turning my back to her to hide the fact this was my first attempt at making pancakes, I poured the powder into a big bowl and mixed it with water to form a thick paste. The hotel staff began lining up while I heated the grill and transferred the batter into a container with a long spout resembling a watering can. Once I poured the batter onto the hot grill, the white mixture spread quickly, forming a giant thin pancake. Hovering nervously over the grill, I tried to figure out how to flip the pancake with my small spatula. Finally, after looking around to make sure no one was watching, I scraped the pancake off the grill.

This time I stirred more pancake mix into the batter until it was thick. The pancakes formed small, thick circles, and in no time at all, the outsides of the pancakes turned dark brown. Flipping the pancakes onto plates, I proudly served them to the staff. A moment later, an employee returned with his plate. "Kris, this pancake needs more cooking," he said. "It's done on the outside but gooey on the inside." Realizing I made the batter too thick, I added more water and reduced the grill's temperature. Finally, the pancakes were as they should be. Mrs. Whitesell smiled and nodded at me while I served everyone the properly cooked pancakes.

The chef arrived three days before the hotel's official opening. I should have felt nervous for, as the story went, the Whitesells could never keep a short-order cook for a whole summer. No one could stand the chef's hostile behavior and the long hours in a hot kitchen, so my job usually had two to three turnovers during the three-month period.

With the chef in charge, the kitchen environment changed drastically. Now the staff ran around trying to please him and avoid getting yelled at. Two of the guys had worked with the chef before. "He will try to keep his recipes and cooking methods a secret," they warned. "You will never learn anything from him."

True to their word, the chef did not talk to me. He did not show me how he prepared the food, and he refused to answer any of my questions. A day before guests started arriving, the chef ordered me to fill a tall pot with water and set it at low heat on the stove.

"Chef, what are we going to do with this?" I asked.

He ignored me and proceeded to chop an onion, two carrots, and a stalk of celery, which he threw into the pot. Throughout the day, he continued throwing leftover scraps of vegetables and meat fat into the pot of simmering water. Unable to contain my curiosity, I asked again. "Chef, what are we going to cook with this?"

He still would not answer.

After I asked several more times throughout the day, the chef grew exasperated and snapped, "It is a stock pot to cook soup and gravy. The pot will sit on the stove over low heat all day." He pointed his finger at me. "You will fill the pot with water every day and adjust the heat. No more questions!"

The next day, the chef announced we would be cooking lobster meat and freezing it for lobster Newberg and lobster bisque. The shipment of live lobsters arrived in a big truck, and as the chef's assistant dumped the live lobsters into a tub of water, I stared at the green-shelled creatures with snapping claws. To my dismay, the chef's assistant dropped the lobsters one by one into a large pot of boiling water.

"Kris, you help too," the chef demanded.

Hesitantly, I picked up a large lobster and dropped it into the churning hot water. Taking a deep breath, I dropped another and watched it move its claws helplessly as it slowly became lifeless. Something inside me cringed. *Oh God,* I prayed silently, *this is my job, and they are asking me to kill lobsters, but I just can't. It's against my religion. My conscience is not allowing it.*

When I told the chef I could not put lobsters into the boiling water anymore, he looked at me like I was crazy and stormed off to tell Mrs. Whitesell that I was not following his orders. She came to the kitchen and spoke to me.

"I'm willing to do anything you or the chef wants me to

do," I explained. "But I cannot put a live lobster into the boiling water to kill it. It is against my religion."

Mrs. Whitesell spoke to her husband, and then said, "Kris, you don't have to do it. I'll talk to the chef."

The chef was angry, but there was nothing he could do. I thanked God the situation ended in my favor.

On the opening date, 130 guests arrived, filling 80 of the rooms of the Dorsey Hotel. At this time, more staff came—a coffee boy, a hostess, several waitresses, a busboy, and extra kitchen help. The chef took a liking to Charlene, a black girl who helped in the kitchen pantry. He flirted with her when she cleaned and brought raw food items to the kitchen. She flirted back, but only because she wanted to keep her job. Another guy in the kitchen liked Charlene too. They went on dates, and they always smiled at each other and laughed while they did chores. The chef watched them with jealous eyes and grew more irritated at the rest of us in the kitchen, snapping his orders and picking on the smallest details that weren't to his liking.

Every day, I listened carefully and asked many questions, so I could help prepare the meals exactly to the chef's preferences. Maybe my constant questioning wore him down. Or maybe he detected sincerity in my efforts to follow his instructions. After a couple of weeks, when it became apparent I had no intention of quitting my job, he became friendlier and would explain his cooking methods in more detail.

After the first month at the Dorsey Hotel, the Whitesells raised my pay from $250 to $275. They were happy with my work and glad I did not plan to leave the hotel before the end of the summer. For the first time since they started the business, a cook had stayed the entire three months. At the end of the season, they gave me a $100 bonus and invited me to their home in Broomall, Pennsylvania to relax before school started. I thoroughly enjoyed the reward for working long hours in the hot kitchen seven days a week.

Once I returned to Knoxville, I walked from the bus stop straight to the Cheemas' house to pick up my Oldsmobile (purchased a few months earlier after selling my DeSoto), and my belongings, which they said they would keep for the summer. When I neared their house, my car was nowhere in sight, and their car was not in the driveway. After knocking on the door, I peered through the dark window, shocked to see an empty living room. More than a little confused and worried, I went to the registration office in Knoxville College's main building. The Cheemas had left a note with the dean, saying I could find my belongings at the residence of Mrs. McGennis, the business and typing instructor.

After getting directions, I walked quickly to her house.

"The University of Delaware offered Dr. Cheema a job," Mrs. McGennis explained as she set my belongings on the kitchen table. "He and his wife moved there in July."

I thanked Mrs. McGennis and loaded my boxes into the trunk of my car, which was parked in the driveway. The news of the Cheemas' abrupt departure upset me greatly. I had counted on them for advice and comfort. Part of me asked, *Now what will I do? Who will help me through my difficulties?* To console myself, I said, *God helps those who help themselves. Whatever happens, I must continue.*

As fall semester 1963 began, I realized Bs and Cs were not good enough. If I wanted to do well and take my education seriously, I needed to make As and Bs. I started associating with the students who made those grades, telling myself, *If they can do it, I can do it too.*

I spent extra time with the teachers, asking them questions after class to make sure I understood the subject matter. To stay organized, I created a weekly schedule for classes, homework, extra studying, and social activities. The schedule helped me keep track of assignments so I could finish them in a timely manner and have time to spend with my friends at UT. The changes in my routine affected my grades in a positive way, encouraging me to continue pursuing my bachelor's degree. Over and over I told myself I had not come to America to cook and clean. I'd come to get a civil engineering degree so I could become an SDO in India.

❀ ❀ ❀

Before the end of spring semester in 1964, I wrote to the White-sells to see if they would offer me the cooking job again. They responded that they would not only offer me the job but would raise my salary to $350 per month with room and board included. When summer came, I packed my suitcase and boarded the bus to Wildwood, New Jersey.

A friend I had known in Punjab, Jasbir Singh Mann, was in Knoxville at the time. We had studied together at the Vish-vakarma Institute of Technology and stayed in touch after I left India. He also decided to attend the University of Tennessee two years after I did. He surprised me one day, showing up at my dorm room at Knoxville College. It was a wonderful, yet awk-ward, reunion because I'd never told him that I was not going to UT anymore, and I was slightly embarrassed about it. Jasbir had looked all over for me until one of my friends from UT told him where I was.

Jasbir was having a hard time at UT as well, and he con-fided in me that he didn't want to spend the summer in Knox-ville. He came to Wildwood a few weeks after I did. I asked the Whitesells if they could give him a job, and they offered him a busboy position as well as a room to sleep in upstairs with the dining room staff.

Right from the start, I prepared breakfast easily and learned new methods to cook eggs to go with bacon, sausage, or ham. Confident in my cooking skills, I needed Mrs. Whitesell in the kitchen very little. In fact, I was so confident that my salary seemed low, especially considering I worked seven days a week and long hours each day. I learned that cooks in other restaurants made $640 a month working only five days a week with two days off to enjoy themselves or work another job. I wouldn't be getting free room and board the way I did at the hotel, but the money was still significantly more. I began looking around Wildwood for available cooking positions.

In a short time, a restaurant offered me a job, and while I wanted to take it, my loyalty to the Whitesells made me hesitate. They treated me like a family member and gave me all the comforts at their home in Pennsylvania. When they heard I might be leaving, the Whitesells offered another fifty dollars per month, saying they would love for me to stay.

Looking at my calculations again, I figured I would still be working seven days a week with no days off, and I really wanted the extra two days, so I could work another job. Sadly, I told the Whitesells I would be leaving the Dorsey Hotel.

The next day, I rented a room near the restaurant and began working forty to forty-eight hours a week at a diner, covering the breakfast and lunch hours from 6:00 a.m. until 2:30 p.m. It was a fast-paced environment, and I learned how to break an egg in each hand at the same time. For parties of eight to ten, all orders needed to be finished and served at the same time.

During the weekdays, I was the only cook, but sometimes Lee, the manager, helped out if I was in a jam. Lee's wife, Linda, helped manage the place. At one time, she had worked as a waitress in the restaurant until they fell in love and got married. Sometimes, she still waitressed if the place was really busy and we needed help.

Jimmy, a guy who went to college in Philadelphia, helped during the weekend breakfast hours, since it was always extra crowded. He was considered a fast short-order cook, and he liked to brag about himself. Jimmy also liked to tease me while we worked. He gave me a hard time about being from India, and he always talked about how much the US was doing for foreign countries, giving them aid, and how the US was giving more aid to India than any country. For a few weekends, I tolerated the way Jimmy taunted me and treated me like a lesser person, but one day, while I chopped onions and Jimmy stirred the coleslaw, I couldn't take it anymore.

I slammed the knife on the counter and said, "Jimmy, nobody does anything for nothing. The US may have some vested interest or something to gain in the future, otherwise, the US would not be giving financial aid to India. If they are, they are not giving it to me! I'm in the US, and I am working equally as hard as you are, so don't tell me about this financial aid anymore!"

For a moment, Jimmy stopped stirring the coleslaw and just looked at me in amusement. "Okay, Kris," he said. "Okay." He resumed his work, but from that point on, his taunting only grew worse.

"Do not say this thing anymore," I cautioned him one day.

Jimmy laughed. "What are you going to do about it?"

Without thinking, I picked up the stainless steel dish rack and threw it at him as hard as I could. Jimmy was about eight feet away and quickly dodged the flying dish rack. It bounced with a loud clang and hit Linda, who was standing nearby.

Immediately, a great commotion filled the kitchen. Linda screamed, "Kris, how dare you?"

Lee ran in, grabbed both my wrists, and shook me hard. "What are you doing?" he yelled.

I tried to control my anger. The waitresses stopped to watch the scene, Linda stared at me, and Lee released my wrists, looking at me with a hard, serious expression.

"Lee, I'm sorry the rack hit Linda," I said, "but I cautioned Jimmy not to tease me in a condescending manner anymore, and he did not stop, so I had to do what I did. I am very sorry."

Lee did not know what to do. I was a hard worker and a good short-order cook. Jimmy was an especially fast worker and had worked at the restaurant for a long time with no problems. Lee finally told me to wait in his office while he talked to his dad, the owner of the restaurant.

When Lee came back, he said, "Kris, in the future, don't

do something like this. If Jimmy is still teasing you in any regard, come tell us, and we will take care of it." Lee talked to Jimmy separately as well. That weekend, the atmosphere was tense, but the work kept us busy, and Jimmy and I did not speak to each other at all.

In the meantime, I began working at a commercial laundry in the evenings and on my two days off. For eight hours, I folded towels and sometimes helped another employee feed sheets through the flatwork ironer. When the Dorsey Hotel closed a few weeks before the end of summer, my friend Jasbir Singh Mann joined me at the commercial laundry. It seemed his time as a busboy had gone well, although several times he expressed discontent with that type of work. One day, while I was folding towels, Jasbir got into an argument with two black guys who worked in a different area. I heard shouts, and looked over to see the black guys towering over Jasbir, their muscles flexing beneath their shirts. *Oh no,* I thought. *This can't be good. Jasbir has never been in a fight in his life, and those guys are twice his size.* Jasbir didn't seem to notice the disadvantage. He continued talking loudly in an angry voice. Suddenly, one of the guys grabbed him, threw him on the floor, and began punching him.

Just then, the manager rushed out of his office, a furious expression on his face. He separated them and yelled, "You're all fired! Get out!" The black guys cursed and spit at Jasbir, yelling offensive remarks at him. He looked ready to yell back, but this time he held his tongue. A moment later, he left the building and sat on the sidewalk, waiting for me to finish work. When I went outside, he began to weep bitter tears, a result of feelings he had been holding onto for months. I did not know what to say, but I knew how he felt.

I sat next to him on the sidewalk and listened while he angrily poured out how insignificant he felt and how he tried to understand life in the States, but he just couldn't. Jasbir came from a well-to-do family in India, much wealthier than mine. He and his brothers possessed plenty of farm land, and they even owned farming machinery, which was rare on most Indian farms during those days. Now he was in the US, working menial jobs and feeling completely out of place.

The black guys were not used to foreigners. They tried to put Jasbir down, perhaps taking out their own frustrations on Jasbir, who was not familiar with all the swearing and slang the blacks used. He misunderstood something they said and took offense at it. While I usually went with the flow, even when I didn't know what was going on or what people meant by their words, Jasbir was easily insulted. In India, he had spent money lavishly on his friends, and he was at the top of the social ladder. Everywhere he went, people looked up to him and respected him. Here in America, he was nearly broke, and no one cared who he was. When the black guys put him down and made fun of him, he couldn't take it anymore and defended himself vigorously.

Jasbir returned to Knoxville a week early. I offered to come with him, but he shook his head. "No, you should stay and make as much money as you can," he said. "You have two more weeks before classes start."

I felt sad. I wanted to help Jasbir, but I didn't know how. Just like me, he would need to figure out the American culture and try to fit in the best way he could.

Chapter 6

At the end of the fall semester of 1964, the president of Knoxville College invited me to a reception for honor roll students. The previous semester, I received As, Bs, and one C due to the extra time I spent studying. At the reception, I ate snacks along with the other honorees and listened to a message from the president. Afterward, my professors shook my hand and congratulated me. "Keep it up, Mr. Bedi," they said. Their words encouraged me to stay focused on earning good grades so my instructors would perceive me as a good academic. With my next set of classes, I didn't realize how difficult that would be.

In Music Appreciation, I didn't have the ear to hear the differences in keys. We listened to Bach, Mozart, and Beethoven, but no matter how hard I strained my ears, they all sounded the same to me. Square dancing, a requirement for physical education, was nearly as difficult. Introduction to the English Bible was challenging because there were so many stories, and it was difficult to keep them all straight as well as remember all of the names. In all three courses, I barely managed to earn a C.

In the spring semester of 1965, as I studied alone in my room, I felt sad that the other students were out having a good time. I struggled through my classes, studying harder than ever, and it seemed the others received good grades without even trying. *I am going to get a one hundred percent,* I told myself before each exam. However, I was so nervous before each test that I would cry out to God, *Look where I am. I'm stuck here for now. I don't know what I'm doing. Please help me. I don't want to fail my classes like I did at UT.* My prayer finished, I would dry my tears, put on a cheerful face, and go to class for the exam.

One day, while I sat in my dorm room, I remembered the

mantra the astrologer in India told me to recite 1.1 lakh (110,000) times if I wanted to travel to the US with no more problems. I started repeating the mantra 101 times a day while I sat at my desk with my books and papers piled around me. The words lifted my thoughts from my troubles and focused my mind on God.

Also, to cheer myself up and remind myself to stay positive, I wrote a few sayings at the bottom of my study-work schedule above my desk:

> *Life is full of happiness, enjoy it.*
> *Life is full of adventure, discover it.*
> *Life is full of challenges, face it.*

One evening, I came back to my room and saw another phrase scribbled at the bottom: *Life is full of shit, eat it.* To this day, I do not know who put it there.

❀ ❀ ❀

As winter turned to spring, I began receiving 94s and 95s on math exams, and at the end of the semester, my final grade in my math class was a B. At the time, an A started at 95 percent and a B was 85 to 94 percent. Now that I could understand the formulas in math and do well on the exams, I enjoyed solving the problems and spent extra time working on additional exercises.

Despite how stressed my classes made me, as was my nature, I still made time for friends and social activities. However, my hard work paid off. At the end of the school year, the president invited me to attend the reception for honor roll students once again. It was a great honor to shake hands with the president of Knoxville College and the dean of admissions. It felt great to show my professors I was a good student. I learned that once the instructors have this perception, the honored student consistently receives better grades in the following semesters. It could mean the difference between a B+ and an A- or a C+ and a B-.

❀ ❀ ❀

In the summer of 1965, I took a bus to Chicago to land a highly sought-after job as a waiter on an Amtrak train traveling from Chicago to cities such as Los Angeles, San Francisco, and Seattle. The job required standing on your feet eight to twelve hours a day while carrying trays or pushing carts, but $2.25 an hour plus tips was good money compared to the minimum wage of $1.25.

A new friend, Rajeshwar Chopra, accompanied me to Chicago, hoping to find a job working in a factory. We'd met while I was visiting friends at UT and had been good friends ever since. Pursuing his bachelor's in electrical engineering, he was struggling with his studies as well.

Chopra and I moved into the Michigan Hotel on 22nd Street, on the south side of Chicago and close to the Amtrak station, planning to stay only a week or two while we looked for a cheaper place. The next day, I completed the physical exam and passed the blood test required in order to qualify for the job.

Three days passed with no call from my supervisor with news of a train assignment. In the meantime, Chopra had already found a factory job paying close to $3.50 an hour. Tired of waiting, I walked several blocks to downtown Chicago to look for something else. A seven-story building with a huge sign for "Stouffer's" looked promising. I went inside to speak to the supervisor and told him about my experience as a short-order cook. Stouffer's turned out to be a hotel, and the manager said there were no cooking positions open, but I could start right away as a janitor from 3:00 p.m. to 11:00 p.m.

The first few days, the supervisor trained me to use the vacuum cleaner and a large machine used to scrub and wax floors. The vacuum cleaner was simple enough, and I figured the other machine would be easy too. I turned on the switch and pulled a lever on the handle, which controlled the machine's speed. The next thing I knew, the machine had bolted out of my hands, zoomed to the left, and zigzagged down the hallway, bouncing off the walls. Hearing the loud commotion, my supervisor ran into the hall. I was sure he would fire me, but instead, he assured me it was fine. I just needed to get used to it.

One night, I got off the L train after working until 11:30 p.m. As I walked under the railroad pass on my way back to the Michigan Hotel, I hoped that I wouldn't get mugged. My friends in Knoxville told me robberies were common in Chicago. "If you are stopped and are going to be robbed," they advised, "pretend you do not know any English. Take out your wallet and say, 'Take money. No harm. Please leave.'"

Just as I walked under the railroad pass, three or four black guys appeared out of the darkness and walked toward me. They were laughing, and one of them said, "Hey man, whatchya got? Hey, you Mo Fo."

Without hesitating, I took out my wallet and held it out to them. "Money. You take. Me no English. New, Chicago."

One of the guys took my wallet and laughed, saying, "This guy, no English." They continued making jokes, mimicking my speech, and saying other things I didn't understand. Then they gave back the wallet and told me to go. Relieved they hadn't taken my money or harmed me, I hurried to the hotel, where I tossed and turned the whole night. I could not stop thinking about what could have happened, and I did not want to find myself in that situation again.

The next day, I told Chopra about the incident. He agreed that we needed to find a new place to live. At the suggestion of an Indian student I'd met from The Illinois Institute of Technology, Chopra and I found a fraternity house that was more than half empty for the summer. The students living there let us stay for a dollar a night per person. Thirty dollars a month in Chicago with kitchen facilities and furnished rooms was a good deal. The students showed us to our sleeping quarters, a large room where everyone in the house slept on cots lined in rows on either side. They gave us bedding and towels, and we settled in right away.

One late night, two weeks into my job at Stouffer's, the supervisor approached me as I cleaned the hallway and asked me to clean the area near the locker room. I steered the scrubber toward the locker room and began cleaning the floor. The supervisor followed me and said, "Perhaps you should clean this room too." He pointed to a bedroom on the other side of the hallway. "Okay," I said, pushing the scrubber into the room, wondering why he was following me.

"You have been working very hard. You must be tired," he said. "Why don't you just lie down on this bed?"

Why was he saying this? I wondered. In all my time working in the US, no one told me to lie down on the job. I felt strange, and I didn't know what to do because he was my supervisor. Was he serious?

Seeing the questioning look on my face, he said, "I am your manager, and I can fire you."

It seemed I had no choice but to lie down. To my surprise, he lay next to me and put his arm on my chest. Immediately, I realized this was not right. Pushing him away, I rolled off the bed and walked away as fast as I could.

"Kris, what is the matter?" he said, following me out of the room. "I was just telling you to rest a few minutes. I am your manager, and I can fire you!"

I continued walking and did not look back. I never went back to Stouffer's to complain or do anything about what happened. Instead, I kept it to myself, not even sharing the story with Chopra, because I didn't know what he or anyone else would make of it.

To replace the Stouffer's job, I started working as a cook on the weekends at the Germania Club. Without any German cooking experience, I tried my best. The first day, I received a compliment from a customer, saying the lamb chops were delicious and done just right. But the second day, when the head chef asked me to get the Weiner Schnitzel from the walk-in refrigerator, I had no idea what it was. I couldn't find it and asked him to show me. He explained, and then, when I asked him to help me cook the dish, it became apparent that I knew nothing about German cooking. He had no choice but to let me go.

Fortunately, Chopra and I found jobs at the MaJournier Brothers factory on Pulaski Avenue in order to make money during the day. The manager put us on a thirty-day probation period, after which they would decide to keep us or not. We learned to read product blueprints, and we assembled the parts, using dye and raw materials they provided us. The supervisors liked us because we were punctual, and after finishing up one job, we would always ask the foreman what to do next.

At the end of thirty days, we received a good review from the immediate supervisor and our coworkers. As official employees, we were required to join the union for a seventy-five dollar fee, even though we could work for only two more months before going back to Knoxville. At the monthly meeting, the union members celebrated our initiation with beer, and they cheered for the two new members at their factory. Seventy-five dollars was a lot of money, but the job paid around four dollars an hour, so in the end, the initial fee was worth the much larger amount on our paychecks.

While I was working tiring physical jobs, I remembered my friend Jasbir, and I knew I could easily become just as discouraged if I allowed it. When I questioned my ability to continue working so hard, I would sing a song to myself in Hindi that I'd learned growing up in India:

> *I have an old lifetime companion / who knows to cooperate very well and stays with me day and night / and that is my right hand.*

I felt as long as I was healthy and able to work, I would be able to make money. These lyrics kept me going during the hard physical work.

Toward the end of July, I landed another cooking job. The husband and wife who owned the restaurant were impressed with my experience in Wildwood.

They hired me for the weekends, from 3:00 p.m. to 11:00 p.m. After showing me around, he demonstrated how to prepare the food, separating the lettuce leaves and slicing the tomatoes, onions, and ham before the customers arrived.

"You should always be prepared before the enemy attacks," he said. "The lunch rush hour gets hectic, and the last thing you want is to run out of food."

In the beginning, Gus helped during rush hour, but he saw I learned quickly and let me work on my own.

Every night after the supper rush hour when his wife left, Gus and his friends drank whiskey and played Blackjack in a small room at the back of the restaurant—his "office." Once in a while, he called me back and gave me a shot of whiskey. "Just enjoy it," he'd say, flashing a grin.

I became quite comfortable with my job and my boss, so comfortable that one evening I prepared curried chicken with spices found in the kitchen. When Gus came behind the counter, he saw the pot of chicken simmering with curry, garlic, and onions on the stove.

"What's going on, Kris?" he asked.

"I'm cooking Indian curried chicken," I answered. "I'd like you to taste it."

Gus seemed stunned. He was quiet for a few minutes, watching me stir the sauce and add a few more spices to the chicken. Finally, he said, "Sure, I'd like a taste. But from now on, try not to cook it here." He grabbed a fork and took a bite. "This is great, Kris," he said. "So much flavor."

Jokingly, I said, "Hey, we could put this on the menu."

Gus laughed and answered, "I don't think so. My wife would throw us both out."

One late night, I decided my Ford Galaxy, which I had bought earlier that summer, needed a good washing. Gus looked for me everywhere and found me out back, scrubbing down my car and hosing it off.

"Kris, there are orders stacking up in here," he exclaimed.

"It was slack time, so I thought I would have a moment to wash my car," I explained.

"All right, Kris. Just don't do it again, or the other employees might get mad."

I went inside and returned to work. With summer almost over, I worked as much as I could before school started. However, I eagerly anticipated going back to school, so I could eventually get a job in the field I came to America for. Unfortunately, a degree in civil engineering looked as far away as my home country, India.

Chapter 7

The previous spring, a classmate at Knoxville College mentioned he was taking industrial engineering courses at the University of Tennessee to prepare for his second bachelor's degree. I hoped I could do the same. Much had changed since I first came to America in 1961, and civil engineering no longer seemed relevant to my life. I decided to work toward an industrial engineering degree instead.

As soon as I returned to Knoxville for fall semester of 1965, I met with Professor Emerson, head of the Industrial Engineering Department at UT, to see if I could sign up for co-op classes. Professor Emerson reviewed the courses I had completed so far at Knoxville College as I sat anxiously in his office. I hoped he would accept me into the program, but I was not sure if my grades were good enough.

After a few moments, Professor Emerson cleared his throat and looked up at me.

"I see a marked improvement in your mathematics courses," he said, "as well as your other courses. It seems you are adjusting very well to life in the US, and from your transcripts, I can see you take your education seriously."

I held my breath, waiting for the final decision.

Professor Emerson smiled encouragingly. "I have had a consistently good experience with Indian students who have completed master's degrees in my department," he said. "I would be happy to take you on as a co-op student until you are able to attend UT full time."

My heart leaped with excitement.

"Thank you, thank you so much, Professor Emerson," I said, standing up and shaking his hand vigorously. "This means a lot to me. I will not disappoint you."

My focus was unwavering as I juggled several co-op classes at UT while completing the remainder of the requirements at Knoxville College for a mathematics degree. At the beginning, fifteen students had signed up for the math program, but now only five were graduating with a degree in the subject, as many students switched majors due to the rigorous coursework.

The excitement at Knoxville College was contagious as the students prepared for graduation in May of 1966. When the day of the ceremony finally arrived, it felt surreal. I had worked toward this moment for so long, and now I was preparing to walk on stage to receive my degree. Despite the general cheerfulness of the students, I felt a sadness I couldn't quite place. As cars arrived from all over the state and country, and parents and relatives stood on the lawns and walkways, smiling, taking pictures, and hugging the graduates, I realized I was missing my own parents. Weaving my way through the groups of families laughing and talking, I felt lonely. No one from my family would be there to hug me, drape marigold garlands around my neck, and throw me a big feast afterwards. At the same time, I was glad my family was not there. After all, what was so great about a mathematics degree from a community college? My eyes were still fixed on my true goal—to earn an engineering degree at UT. That would be the happiest moment of my life.

In June of 1966, Chopra and I spent another summer in Chicago. Once again, I worked at Gus's restaurant, and Chopra also got a job there as a cashier. We also found jobs across the Illinois border working in a steel factory in Gary, Indiana. The job involved carrying heavy steel blocks. It took two people to carry the beam, one at each end. The factory required us to buy expensive steel-toed boots to protect our feet. The pay was worth it, but after a couple of weeks, being of smaller stature, Chopra and I were struggling to carry the steel all day and grew tired easily. We quit the steel factory and found technical jobs in the

second week of July with A. B. Dick & Company, a manufac-
turer of copy machines and office supplies.

Whenever Chopra and I weren't working, we walked
around downtown Chicago or drove to the beach on Lakeshore
Drive. One day in mid-August, we were standing in line at an
ice cream shop. Two girls stood behind us and began laughing
and giggling when Chopra and I spoke in Hindi. Chopra and
I glanced at each other in amusement. Both girls were attractive. One was shorter and stocky with an innocent face and a
big, brilliant smile. The other girl was thinner and wore glasses.
After paying for our ice cream, we went outside and tried to
decide which way to walk. A few moments later, the girls came
outside. The shorter one smiled at me but was too shy to say anything. As they walked away, she smiled at me over her shoulder.

"Hey Chopra, let's try to talk to them," I said.

We walked after them, and the girls giggled and walked
faster. Just as we came close enough, I said, "Hi, we would like
to talk to you."

"About what?" the shorter girl with the big smile asked.

"Would you like to go out on a date with us?"

"Yes, but we don't know you," the girl said.

"Well, I'm Kris, and he's Raj," I said, shortening Chopra's
first name.

"I'm Larisa, and she's Zelia," the girl said.

"We are students at the University of Tennessee."

The girls laughed to no end. I didn't know what was so
funny, but Larisa gave me her number on a piece of paper and
said I could call her. Still laughing, they walked away.

For our first date, Larisa and I met downtown at the ice
cream shop. We walked around for a while, and then I drove
my car to Lakeshore Drive, where we walked along the lake.
Afterward, we sat in the car and talked. We went on a second
date after that, and on our third date, as we were walking along
Lakeshore Drive, Larisa said, "Zelia would like to go out with
Raj, too, if that is okay with him."

That night I told Chopra what Larisa had said.

"She wants to go out with me? That's great!" Chopra said.

Soon after, we started going on double dates. At first, Zelia seemed excited to go on dates with Chopra. After each date, I took Zelia home first, dropping her off a block from her house, and then dropping Larisa two blocks away from her home. She did not want her mother or her neighbors to see she was dating a foreigner. On Fridays, she had to return home before sunset, and from that point up until sunset on Saturday, I could not talk to her on the phone or see her at all.

"Why can't I see you?" I asked.

"It's the Sabbath," she told me.

"What is that?" It sounded strange to me.

"I am Jewish," she said. "And my father is a rabbi."

"What is a rabbi?"

"It's like a priest," she said. "And we go to synagogue."

"What's synagogue?"

"It's like a church. We go to synagogue on Friday instead of Sunday, and we must keep the Sabbath on weekends. We can't watch television or pick up the phone. We also must eat before sunset on those days."

On one of our dates, she further explained the Jewish faith and what they believed in. "There are three types of Jews. One group is Orthodox. They believe in the old way described in the Holy books of the Torah. The second group is Conservative, believing in a modified version of the Torah. The third is Reform, believing in the Torah, but they do not follow traditions such as not picking up the phone after sunset."

"Which group are you?" I asked.

"I am from an Orthodox Jewish family. Zelia is also Jewish. Her parents would also be angry if they knew she is dating a Hindu."

Lucky for Zelia's parents, her relationship with Chopra would not become an issue. One day, Larisa told me, "Zelia is not happy with Raj. He is too aggressive with her."

That night at the frat house, I brought up the subject. "Chopra, you need to slow down with Zelia. Larisa says she doesn't feel comfortable with you."

Chopra nodded. "Okay, I'll try."

But Zelia still didn't like how much older he was. Larisa and Zelia had just finished high school, and Chopra was nearly thirty, about five years older than I was, and he also looked a lot older and more mature than I did. Zelia decided to stop seeing Chopra, but Larisa and I continued spending time together.

Since Chopra and I lived at the frat house, I could not see Larisa in the evening during weekdays, nor could I bring her to my place so I could fix her curried chicken. This was a problem. Chopra and I looked for a two-bedroom apartment with a kitchen, and we found a nice place on the second floor of a building near the bus depot. It had a good kitchen and an entrance lobby with a couch, but there was only one bedroom. We decided one person would sleep in the bedroom, the other would sleep on the couch, and we would switch places every week.

It was a good arrangement because Larisa and I could see each other more often. She started showing a lot of love and affection and would say that she loved me very much. When she came by in the evenings, we would drink tea and cook dinner. I didn't have a TV, so we spent most of our evenings listening to the radio and talking.

In the later part of August 1966, I received a letter from UT offering me a teaching assistantship. This meant UT would cover my tuition fees and pay me close to $1000 for the academic year. I was overjoyed, thinking I had come to the US to learn, and now I would be teaching a course here. Larisa was happy for me, but at the same time, she felt sad. What would we do about our relationship?

In a way, we felt like the couple in *Fiddler on the Roof*, a play Larisa and I watched together. Larisa and I broke many traditions with our relationship. I knew my parents would want to arrange my marriage, and Larisa's parents would be angry if they found out she was not dating a Jew, but instead was going steady with a Hindu. In *Fiddler on the Roof,* Perchik breaks tradition by crossing the barrier between the men and women to dance with Tevye's daughter, Hodel. Later on, he breaks another tradition by asking Hodel to marry him. The father is appalled that they would ignore tradition and make their own match.

Hoping these problems would resolve themselves in the future, Larisa and I decided to continue our relationship. We would stay together and write to each other during the school year.

Larisa gave me a necklace with a centerpiece made of silver and her words engraved on one side, cleverly using the math symbols for *more than* and *less than.* "I love you > yesterday, < tomorrow." On the other side, she had her name engraved. Before leaving for Knoxville in September, I spent as much time with Larisa as I could. She spoke often of her plans to attend the University of Chicago to major in art that year. "I will write to you every day," she promised. "And here is my class ring to wear as a promise that we will not see anybody else."

When it came time to leave, I felt a physical pain I never experienced before. I missed Larisa so much, but I needed to focus on school. I arrived in Knoxville two days before the quarter started.

While looking for an apartment, I met Sewa Singh, a student who had just come from Punjab to work toward a PhD in UT's Agriculture Department. He lived in a house on the street farthest from campus with two other guys. He said I could stay in the room on the second floor. Sewa Singh lived on the first floor next to an Iranian student working on his bachelor's in civil engineering.

With four students sharing the kitchen, someone was always waiting to use the stove in the evening, and once there was a commotion in the kitchen over missing sugar. "Someone used my sugar!" the Iranian guy yelled. "Who used my sugar?" This went on for a few minutes, and Sewa and I only laughed. Why would someone use his sugar? The Iranian was upset, but we all kept our groceries separate, so we didn't see how someone could have gotten into his sugar.

That fall, I registered for three grad courses: Materials Handling in the Industrial Engineering Department and two math courses. On top of that, I would be teaching a course in math. I posted my school schedule and office hours so students would know when they could see me for help.

At the beginning of the fall quarter of 1966, I wrote to my father, saying, "Baiji, you would be very happy to know I am teaching at UT. Your son who came to US as a student to earn a degree is now teaching at the university."

My father wrote back to say how happy he was for me. He shared the news with everybody, and my maternal uncle, a qualified teacher who was running a business at the time, wrote to me in Urdu. "I am proud of you," he wrote. "A few people go out diving into an ocean. Some come back empty-handed and some come back with seaweed and shells. But some come up with diamonds in their hands. You, Krishan, have dived into the ocean and come up with diamonds." My uncle's words inspired me to continue trying my hardest at school.

As the semester passed, Sewa Singh and I became good friends. More than six feet tall and weighing close to two hundred pounds with a big chest and small waist, he was quite a ladies' man. He always wore a turban, a stylishly trimmed beard and mustache, and a big smile. All the girls were attracted to him, but since he didn't have a car, he needed me to pick up the girls and drop them off for him. Since I had lived in the US for five years, Sewa looked up to me as a mentor, someone to teach him about the American way of life. Not only that, our cultures were similar—both of us were from small Punjabi villages, and we both liked to party. When there was no party to be found, we started our own. Many nights, one could find us sitting on the street corner outside our house, drinking beer.

Every day at the house, Sewa lifted dumbbells for half an hour. He taught me how to lift weights too, but I would never be as strong as he was. On one of his first days in Knoxville, Sewa Singh was walking down the street carrying a leather briefcase when a group of guys started making fun of him. He looked different with his turban and beard, and most of them, from small Tennessee towns, had never seen anyone like him before.

"Hey, Santa Claus," the guys taunted. "Why you look like Santa Claus?"

Sewa kept walking, but the guys continued following him down the street.

"Didn't know there was an Indian Santa Claus," someone said.

Sewa asked them to leave him alone several times, but they wouldn't. Instead, they walked in front of him, blocking his way and teasing him about his appearance. Fed up with them, Sewa took his briefcase in both hands and swung it, knocking one of the guys down.

"Whoa, this guy is strong," the others said, backing away.

Sewa continued on his way undisturbed.

A year went by before Sewa finally shaved his beard, cut his long hair, and stopped wearing his turban. I was living with a group of American guys by then, and when Sewa came over for the first time after changing his appearance, all my housemates complimented him, saying, "Oh, you look so handsome." My friend certainly looked younger and more boyish. After that, Sewa became even more popular with the girls.

Somehow I did not think graduate course work would be more difficult than undergraduate studies, but it was. The math courses were abstract and required a deep understanding of theory and subject matter. I hoped, due to my status as a teaching assistant, my professors would not give me a grade below a C. Although I tried to stick to my study schedule as much as I could, sometimes Sewa Singh wanted to talk or go out. Of course, I would chat with him or we'd go to a friend's place.

Also, while I tried to adjust to the new routine, one thing stayed on my mind: Larisa. I constantly thought about her and the time we spent together. She wrote daily, and I read and reread her letters at every spare moment. Although I had learned to study hard at Knoxville College, I could not concentrate on my studies at UT. My mind was not in Knoxville. It was in Chicago with Larisa.

That fall I received a C in Materials Handling, and in my two math courses I received Ds. I felt the professors expected me to earn higher grades, but at that point, there was not much I could do. As soon as the semester ended, I drove to Chicago to see Larisa. By the time I left Knoxville at nine p.m., I forgot about my grades. I drove the entire four hundred miles in one night, arriving in Chicago at 5:00 a.m. and stayed with my old friend Jasbir Singh Mann in his hotel room. When Jasbir traveled to Chicago in the summer of 1965 to find a job, he decided to stay there. His experience of the US was not pleasant, and his undergraduate studies at UT were tough. No matter how hard I tried to persuade him to go back to his studies in Knoxville, there was nothing I could say to change his mind.

The next day, I met up with Larisa, and we walked around Chicago. Larisa loved art, and we often went to the Art Institute of Chicago and The Field museum in a different part of the city. We studied the paintings in the different rooms while we talked about life, our plans and hopes, and our experiences in college. Larisa, possessing an eye for beauty, enjoyed creating with a paintbrush and canvas. She wished she could show me some of her work, but if we wanted our relationship to continue, it was not possible for me to go to her house.

Not long into my stay at Jasbir's hotel room, I convinced him to get away from the hotel life. First, the room was too small, and I could not bring Larisa back so I could cook for her. Second, it simply was not a good environment for Jasbir. He worked during the day, and in the evening, he spent most of his time drinking at the bar before going back to the room to sleep.

It was the same routine day in and day out. With Larisa's help, I found him a one-bedroom apartment a few blocks away from downtown Chicago. It would be cheaper and hopefully save him money so he could continue his studies. As we bought groceries and a set of pots and pans, Jasbir kept saying, "Bedi, it's costing us so much money to buy all these pots and pans. How are we saving money?"

"The initial cost of fifty to seventy dollars will save you money in the long run," I replied. "Instead of eating out at restaurants every day, you can cook your own food."

Jasbir just laughed. "You're always thinking about how to save money," he said.

One day, Larisa met Jasbir. She found him interesting, and they discussed their different views of lifestyle and culture in the US.

"I hate it when someone replies 'I don't care' to a question," Jasbir explained. "What do they mean? I say, 'Would you like to have a beer?' And they say, 'I don't care.' Well, do you or don't you? It is so frustrating!"

Overall, Jasbir thought life here moved too fast. "People have no time to chit-chat," he said, frustrated that he could not make any new, sincere friends. On a lighter note, he knew poetry and enjoyed singing classical Punjabi songs. He spoke fondly of Punjab.

Two weeks went by fast. Knowing I would have to leave soon, Larisa and I became closer. "I love you," she said one afternoon as we walked along Lakeshore Drive. She had started saying this to me often. I didn't know what to think. I liked her a lot, but with school to focus on, our relationship couldn't get more serious until I finished my engineering degree. Besides, her parents would not approve of our relationship. If it went on any longer, they would surely find out. They might even disown Larisa if she didn't break ties with me. While Larisa enjoyed spending time with me, she was worried about the future as well. Neither of us saw a happy ending for our relationship. However, neither of us was ready to completely stop seeing each other. All these things weighed on my mind as I drove back to Knoxville at the end of the holiday break. I wasn't sure what to do.

❀ ❀ ❀

"Here's your room." My new friend Jim ushered me into the large bedroom where one of Jim's housemates stood up from his desk in the corner and shook my hand, flashing me a friendly smile.

"Nice to meet you Kris," he said. "Sorry we don't have an extra room, but I don't mind sharing."

I had met Jim while standing in line for registration for the winter quarter of 1967, and in addition to noticing his unique New Jersey accent, I learned he was an undergrad majoring in math. He lived with three other guys from New Jersey, and I got the sense that he was a studious person, someone I would be wise to associate with if I wanted to do well in my classes at UT. Sewa Singh, although a great friend and roommate, liked to socialize often, and I could never say no to a good party either. I knew that moving in with Jim and his friends would be a good decision.

While I was excited to stay with American students and observe their study habits, Jim was excited for a math teaching assistant to live in his rented house. He was sure I'd be able to help him. I didn't mention I'd received Ds in my math courses and was repeating them for better grades.

Jim was a serious student. With his parents divorced, he lived with his mother when he came home from school. He wanted to finish his degree so he could find a good job and provide for himself and his mother. Paul Kehir, an anthropology major, was a friendly guy with a girlfriend named Arlene, who worked as a nurse back in New Jersey.

Ray Eisenberg and Dan Bryant lived upstairs. Ray reminded me of Larisa, because he was Jewish. Dan was the son of songwriters Felice and Boudleaux Bryant. His parents worked as a team to write popular songs for famous singers such as the Everly Brothers, Roy Orbison, and Buddy Holly. They wrote "Wake up

Little Suzie" and "Bye Bye Love" for the Everly Brothers. Later on in the 70s, they even wrote hits for Simon and Garfunkel, The Grateful Dead, and Bob Dylan.

Living with the New Jersey guys, I learned more slang to add to my vocabulary. For instance, if Dan came home with exciting news about a girl, Jim would say, "Hey, do you have a dime?"

Dan would answer, "Yeah, why?"

Jim would say, "Go call someone who cares."

At first I didn't know what they meant about the dime until they explained it cost a dime to make a call from the phone booth. Now, whenever I came home with exciting news about getting a good grade or talking to a cute girl or anything else, they would flatten me with, "Do you have a dime?" No need to say more.

Whenever we sat around drinking beer, the conversation usually turned to girls. I thought it was funny that when a relationship didn't continue with one of the guys, he would say, "Eh, she bit the dust." I used the phrase every chance I could.

"Kris is learning," my roommates said with a laugh.

On the last day before spring break, as soon as I finished taking my exams and posted the grades for my assistant teaching class, I hopped into my Ford Galaxy and drove to Chicago to be with Larisa. At 4:00 a.m., I arrived at Jasbir Mann's apartment, where I slept restlessly, hardly able to wait until 9:00 a.m., when I would see her.

Larisa and I spent our days together, and occasional evenings when she didn't have to go to synagogue or when her family didn't expect her at home. Most of the time, we drove to Lakeshore Drive and walked along the sandy beach. A few times we visited Old Town, a center for hippy counterculture on Clark and North Avenue. During the day and on weekends, many street vendors sold peace signs, psychedelic print tee-shirts, and bead necklaces. Artists filled the sidewalks with their paintings for sale. Larisa, an artsy, eclectic type, enjoyed the color and creativity that surrounded us at Old Town.

During our walks through Old Town, we discussed our relationship. Should we continue seeing each other? If we did and we got married, what would be the religion of our children? I was a Hindu and did not believe in conversion. Larisa, an Orthodox Jewish girl and the daughter of a rabbi, wondered how we would raise our children because conversion was not an option for her either.

We also discussed other cultural differences. Mine was a strict lifestyle with tremendous social and societal pressure and no divorce, whereas in the US, it was easy to get a divorce, and there was much more emphasis on independence. We had each been brought up very differently. My parents expected to arrange my wedding. They would choose a girl for me based on her educational background, her parents' social status, and whether she was from the same caste as I was.

After thinking through the practicalities of getting married, we decided it would be too difficult. There would be problems with her parents from the beginning, and on top of that, I had not yet received my master's degree, nor did I have a professional job to afford a decent lifestyle. Also, how would my parents feel when Larisa and I visited them in India? In the end, we decided to go our separate ways. Although I wanted to keep it more than anything, I returned her ring which I always wore around my neck. If we were really going to end our relationship, it was best to let it go.

Larisa cried nonstop the morning I left. It was difficult to see her crying so hard, and the whole way home I felt like crying too. My sadness only grew stronger the closer I came to UT's campus. *Did I do the right thing?*

❧ ❧ ❧

Once back at school, I thought about what I should do to complete an industrial engineering degree. My grades had improved in math, but I was still getting Cs in the engineering courses. Was it possible the Engineering Department would not let me into the graduate program?

I discussed my concerns with the department head, Emeritus Professor Emerson, who was also my industrial engineering advisor. The "Emeritus" in front of his name was a title of respect for a hardworking professor with many accomplishments for the university and tenure of more than twenty years at UT. He had expanded the Industrial Engineering Department, and everyone knew him to be an extremely kind and understanding gentleman. He somehow understood a person's needs in all situations. Emeritus Professor Emerson saw my difficult struggle to maintain good grades, as well as my dedication to my dream. Eager to help, he offered me the chance to work toward my master's in industrial engineering.

One day, the phone rang at the house. "It's for you," Paul Kehir said, handing me the phone.

"This is Larisa's mother," a woman's voice said angrily. "You should stay away from my daughter if you know what's good for you. I know all about you. You are playing with fire. I am going to have you deported for dating my daughter. Stay away from her!"

My mouth dropped open in shock. *How did Larisa's mother get my phone number?*

"The day Larisa marries you, she will be pronounced dead, and we will have her funeral," Larisa's mother snapped. "If you don't stay away from her, I will call UT and have them suspend you. Then I will have you deported. Stay away from my daughter!"

After she hung up, I stared at the phone, not sure what to think or do. I knew she didn't have the power to deport me or suspend me from school, so I was not concerned about that statement. Paul Kehir raised an eyebrow at me. He could hear Larisa's mom yelling over the phone and the gist of the conversation.

"Kris, you better start packing your stuff to be shipped back to India," he joked. Then, more seriously, he said, "Kris, dating a rabbi's daughter, you *are* playing with fire."

Larisa had been writing to me on a daily basis, but after her mother's phone call, she wrote one more letter before stopping altogether. "My mother is watching me very closely," she wrote. "She found some of your old letters, and she called UT to get your phone number. She kept asking me if we were getting married, and she kept saying they would have my funeral on the day of our wedding. Kris, if we ever married, they would disown me and would not allow me to see them again for any reason."

Several weeks later, Paul handed me the phone again. "Someone from Chicago is calling for you," he said. *What now?* I thought, assuming it was Larisa's mother again. Instead, it was a man's voice. "Mr. Bedi, I am calling from the Chicago morgue," he said. "I am sorry to inform you that Mr. Jasbir Mann is dead."

I wasn't sure I heard right. "What? Could you say that again?"

"Mr. Mann is dead," the man repeated. "His body is at the morgue. We need to know what to do with the body."

In a state of shock, I could not speak.

"Sir? Mr. Bedi?" the man said. "I need to know if you want the body flown back to India."

"I'm not sure," I answered.

"Well, I can keep the body at the morgue until you get here," the man said. "Or you could opt for a pauper's funeral, a choice for a person with no money and no relatives in the area. The body would be cremated, and the minimum charges would be covered by the social security administration. You only need to send $275 so we can proceed with cremation."

I didn't know what to do. A strong sadness overcame me as I thought about Jasbir's difficult struggle in the US. I had been worried about him ever since I'd left his place in Chicago during spring break, but this was a complete surprise.

"Do you know what happened to him?" I asked.

"The cause of death is not certain," the man said. "I wish I could tell you more."

"Can you hold for a moment? I am going to talk to my roommates about the situation."

"Of course," the man said.

"What do I do?" I asked Paul and Ray after telling them what happened. "I do not have access to international calls so I can't call his family. Even if I could call them, I would have to book a call and wait several hours for the operator to get back to me. And then, I don't even know if his brothers have a phone because they live in a small village."

Jasbir was my best friend from college days in India, and now there was nothing I could do for him. I also did not feel comfortable making such a decision on his family's behalf, but as there was no way to reach them quickly, I had no choice.

"Perhaps, in this case, it would be best to cremate him," Paul suggested.

It did sound like the best option, so I told the man to proceed with the cremation and send the ashes to his brother since I wasn't sure if his mother was still alive, and I knew his father had passed away several years earlier.

That night, I tossed and turned in my bed. I could not rest knowing Jasbir had come to get an engineering degree and instead had died at the age of thirty. Paul did his best to console me, but my grief was too great. How could I sleep, knowing Jasbir had come to this country because of me?

To this day, I still do not know the cause of Jasbir's death. Receiving two phone calls within weeks of each other—each cutting off a connection with a person who had been important to me—was a blow harder than I knew how to deal with. Sadness overwhelmed me, and as I tried to drown it out with my daily prayers, I studied more than ever.

One afternoon near the end of spring quarter of 1967, my professor of Linear Algebra wrote a theorem on the board and asked if anyone knew how to prove or disprove it. This class involved a lot of in-depth theory and long algorithms to prove the theorems. Since the professor had recently returned from the military, he often needed to ask his students for the solution to a theorem. Of course, he acted like he was testing us, but soon we realized he simply did not know or was not completely sure.

When no one volunteered to solve the theorem, he asked again. I looked around, and still no one raised a hand. Slowly, I lifted mine into the air.

"Mr. Bedi, are you sure you know it?" the professor asked.

"I'm pretty sure," I responded.

"Are you positive?" he asked.

"Uh . . . I'm not that positive," I said hesitantly.

"Let's see who is more positive in the class," the professor said, looking around the room.

Another student raised his hand, and the professor asked him to write his solution on the blackboard. Annoyed that he hadn't let me try, I raised my hand again, remembering a saying my friend Hamrahi told me. I'd met Hamrahi at Knoxville College, and we had become very close friends.

"Yes, Mr. Bedi?" said the professor.

"There is a saying in my country that only fools are positive," I said.

The professor's face turned red as the whole class burst into laughter.

At the end of class, one of my classmates said, "That was pretty brave of you to say, but you are going to pay the price for it."

At the end of the quarter, I felt sure I performed well on the final exam for his class. But when I scanned the grades posted on the classroom door, there was a D next to my name. My jaw clenched in anger. My midterm grade was a B, and I knew I did well on the final exam. The professor had failed me on purpose.

Immediately, I went to the professor's office, but he was not there. Storming off to my room, I hatched a plan. My heart pounded and my hands shook. I had worked so hard to reach this point. I was so close to earning a degree at UT, and now it might not happen after all these years. Paul Kehir happened to be packing his suitcase when I arrived.

"What's the matter?" he asked.

"My math professor failed me!" I fumed, pacing the floor. I studied hard, and I know I deserved at least a B. I'm going to buy a gun, find him at home, and shoot him in the leg!"

"That's not a good idea, Kris," Paul said.

"I don't want to kill him, only hurt him enough so he will realize he has ruined my career," I said. "I might get thrown out of grad school now! I want him to walk with a limp or on crutches or be in a wheelchair so he will suffer for the rest of his life."

"You shouldn't do that," Paul said. "It will not be in your best interest. They could put you in jail."

"I don't care. My life is already ruined. If I am taken to jail, that's fine. At least this professor will learn he shouldn't try to ruin somebody's career and life."

Jim happened to be walking by the room and overheard me. He came in and tried to calm me down.

"That's not a wise thing to do," Jim said. "You need to stop and think."

I sat on the edge of my bed and crossed my arms stubbornly, still resolved to find out where the professor lived. The next day, the secretary of the Math Department told me the professor had only been employed at UT for one quarter and already left town. Disappointed, I returned to my room. The professor had been extremely lucky to leave town when he did because there was no telling what I would have done in such a state of anger. A week later, I received a letter accepting me into the industrial engineering graduate program. I was overjoyed and thanked God.

Chapter 8

"**K**ris, why do you want to drive a bus?"

I sat in an orange plastic chair and stared at the manager across from his desk. It was June 1967, and the Chicago Transit Authority (CTA) was hiring hundreds of temporary bus drivers for the summer, paying $3.50 an hour, about two dollars more than minimum wage. Chopra and I drove to Chicago soon after the school year ended, and we were contacted the next day to fill out applications.

"Sir, driving a bus is in my blood," I answered. "My father is in the transportation business, and my grandfather was in the same business. I want to do it too."

I really wanted this job, and the manager would never know if it was true or not. He would never attempt to track down my family background in India.

A day after our interviews, Chopra and I each received calls offering us a job. We were to report to the bus depot office the next day for training.

"You must accelerate gradually and apply the brakes gradually," the instructor urged. "Pretend an old lady is sitting in the very last seat, holding a bowl of hot soup in her lap. We don't want her to spill even one drop!"

As bus operators, most drivers wore two watches—one on their wrist and the second, a larger watch chained to their belt—to be punctual to the minute.

At the end of our week-long training, our instructor emphasized, "Keeping the schedule is of the utmost importance. People are going to their jobs and need to be on time. It is up to *you* to make sure they get there when they need to."

❀ ❀ ❀

The first day on my own, I arrived at the bus depot at 6:45 a.m., wearing my navy blue uniform, hat, black leather shoes, and a badge stating my assigned number. The man behind the ticket window supplied me with transfer tickets, a puncher, change dispenser, my route number, and the street name representing my route.

"There is a man in the parking lot who will help you find your bus," the ticket man said.

On my way, I asked another bus operator if he could explain my route to me because I didn't know which way to go. He explained the directions in a leisurely manner while I looked impatiently at my watch. It was 6:50. My route started at 7:00, and I still needed to find my bus. *How can I get rid of this guy?* I thought, unable to focus on the directions. *I can't be late on my first day!*

At 6:53 I interrupted him and hurried into the parking lot. For several minutes, I wandered up and down row after row of buses, searching for my bus. There must have been at least two hundred of them. Having no luck on my own, I found the man who could help me, and he showed me the bus right away.

Once in the driver's seat, I could not work the lever to change the route number on the sides of the bus and the street name on the front. I was running four minutes late in a city where the route must be followed by the second! Giving up on the lever, I turned the key in the ignition, shifted the bus into gear, and stepped heavily on the gas pedal. The bus lurched forward as I turned the wheel. *Screeeeech!* I slammed on the brakes at the metallic sound and stared in horror at the bus next to me—the side mirror, knocked clean off, lay smashed on the ground. I glanced around the parking lot anxiously, but no one was around to notice. Holding my breath, I maneuvered onto the street, the large bus bouncing over potholes and swaying slightly before I straightened it and accelerated toward my first stop.

Even though I was running six minutes late and did not know where I was going, I could not remember the last time I felt so important. Sitting behind the steering wheel of this large bus gave me a feeling of power. Moments later, I neared the first bus stop on my route where a line of passengers anxiously watched me approach. Needing to make up for lost time, I sped past them. Everyone stared after me in confusion and dismay. Stopping would only throw me off track. Now I was four minutes late, and the line of people at my next stop was even longer. Once again, I passed them without slowing down.

Passing one more bus stop in the same manner, I could go no farther. I remembered all I could of the man's directions before I stopped listening. At the next stop, I pulled the bus over to the curb and swung the doors open.

"Come on, people. Get on the bus!" I called out. The people just looked at me, looked at the front of the bus, and then looked at me again. No one moved. "What are you waiting for?" I asked. "Get on the bus!" I finally caught up with my schedule, and now these people were causing a delay.

"Sir, the street sign and route number…" a woman said.

"Don't worry about it," I said. "Get on the bus. I'll take you wherever you need to go."

"But the sign is not right," another person protested.

"Just get on the bus, and I'll take you wherever you need to go!" I commanded.

Hesitantly, the passengers climbed the steps, paid their bus fare, and took their seats. When everyone was seated, I called out, "Okay folks, which way do I go?"

No one said anything.

"Folks, tell me which way to go," I repeated.

Realizing that I truly did not know which way to go, the passengers began calling out directions. I smiled and pulled into traffic.

"Go straight!"

"Turn right!"

"Take a left up here!"

At one intersection, I missed a turn by several feet.

"No! Wrong, wrong! Stop!" they shouted. I halted the bus in the middle of the intersection.

"What are you doing?" the passengers demanded.

A car beeped its horn and swerved around the bus, the driver yelling at me as he went by.

"Don't worry. No harm done," I said. "We are going to back it up."

"You can't do that!" the passengers yelled at me.

I could not see behind the bus and so it was difficult to know if the traffic was clear behind me. Pointing at a young man near the front of the bus, I said, "You, get out and tell me when traffic is clear."

He stared at me speechlessly.

"Come on. Get off the bus!" I was determined to back up and make the proper turn. As everyone stared at the young man, he shook his head in disbelief, climbed down from the bus, and stood in the intersection, waving for the cars around us to stop. When all was clear, he motioned for me to back up. Just when I was in position to make the turn, a police car pulled up with its lights flashing. An officer got out and approached the bus.

"Driver, what's the matter?" he asked.

"I'm backing up the bus," I said.

The officer stared at me for a second. "You're not supposed to do that," he said.

"Gee, I didn't know," I said quickly. "But now I'm done, and I'm making the turn."

The officer looked at me strangely. "Okay, well don't do it again," he said, shaking his head as he walked away.

Miraculously, I did not lose my job that day. None of the stranded passengers complained to the Transit Authority, and most people understood that I was a temporary bus operator filling in for an employee on summer vacation. In a sense, I was lucky to be given such leeway, not even getting in trouble for the bus I damaged. It was my first day on the job by myself, and I knew that I could only improve from there.

❀ ❀ ❀

Every week, the CTA assigned me a new route. Some people were annoyed that the bus driver asked them for directions, but most of them understood I was a temporary summer driver covering for bus operators on vacation. I could always count on the older ladies to give me directions. I liked to drop them off near their houses, even if their street wasn't on my route. "I wish there were more bus operators like you," they would say.

The old ladies loved me, and always eager to show them respect, I rose from my seat to help carry their groceries onto the bus. Whenever grandparents took their grandchildren to see Chicago and go shopping, I was patient, where other drivers would have hurried them.

"Take your time. I am not in hurry," I'd say.

Within the first three weeks, some of the ladies mailed complimentary letters about me to the bus depot. When my boss shared their kind words with me, I felt encouraged and sure that I was doing the right thing. My mother had taught me kindness and respect through her own actions, and I felt proud I was carrying her values with me everywhere I went. Besides, why should I give these people a hard time when they may be tired of walking and carrying their shopping bags in the heat?

One morning, about a month into my job, a stocky middle-aged man with a cigar in his mouth boarded the bus. Pointing at the "No Smoking" sign, I looked at the man through the rearview mirror and said, "Sir, no smoking on the bus. Please put out your cigar."

"Just drive the bus. Don't worry about me." The man took another puff of the cigar and continued looking out the window.

"Please put out your cigar," I repeated.

"Just drive the bus," he said in a condescending tone, exhaling a mouthful of smoke in my direction.

I knew I must handle the situation to show the other passengers I was in command and he must follow the CTA rule.

Flipping a switch on the lever to indicate a mechanical problem, I coasted the bus to a stop on the side of the road.

"Everyone off the bus," I ordered. "There is something wrong, and I cannot drive any further."

Once we were all standing outside, I explained that we were waiting for my supervisor to come check the bus. The passengers were angry. They had jobs and appointments to go to, and most of them understood there was nothing wrong with the bus.

"Why didn't you put out the cigar?" the passengers scolded the man. "Now we're going to be late. Thanks a lot!"

"I will take you wherever you want to go," I informed the passengers, "but I will not take the guy with the cigar. You all are very nice people, and I am sorry you have to suffer because of him. But in a whole bushel of apples, one bad apple spoils the rest." Pointing at the man, I said, "There stands the bad apple."

The man glared at me. "I'm going to tell your supervisor about this," he growled.

"Please do so," I replied, pointing to my badge. "Here is my badge number."

Muttering under his breath, he stormed off to board another bus stopped ahead of us. Half of my passengers followed him, and the rest boarded on my bus. As the bus driver, I was in command and knew I had done the right thing. I wouldn't let anyone try to take advantage of me. Besides, the CTA wouldn't fire me after giving me two weeks of training and receiving complimentary letters from the older ladies.

At the end of the summer, I returned to Knoxville, intent on working towards my master's in industrial engineering. My favorite engineering class that fall was Advanced Work Measurement, where we learned to observe and analyze workers performing repetitive tasks. The professor dealt a deck of cards among four students, while the rest of us determined how quickly or slowly the professor passed the cards along. As future industrial engineers, we would need to recognize the normal pace of a certain task, so we could set a standard time for that task based on its pace and fatigue factor.

I applied the same focus to my other two classes as well. Instead of going out every night, I stayed home to study, and it paid off. At the end of the semester, I received one A, one B, and one C, a big improvement from the previous semester.

When Christmas break arrived, Paul Kehir invited me to his home in New Jersey. The first night at his house, we sat in the living room with his parents after dinner. Mr. Kehir drank whiskey, and Paul and I drank beer while Mr. Kehir told us jokes. I laughed at all of them, and as the night went on, Mr. Kehir seemed to enjoy having me there.

A day later, I met Paul's girlfriend, Arlene, when her parents invited us for dinner. Arlene was a pretty girl, and I could tell Paul really cared about her. However, Mr. Kehir was not too keen about Arlene's parents. Sometimes he made fun of them, but it was light, in the spirit of fun. Mr. Kehir was simply of the joking nature, so Arlene's parents never took it the wrong way.

Mrs. Kehir liked Arlene, and when we were back at their house, I overheard her telling Paul she wanted him to make a decision. Paul and Arlene's relationship was simple compared to my relationship with Larisa. Their parents approved of the match, they didn't have any religious differences, and the only trouble was deciding when to set the date after Paul popped the question to Arlene. I didn't know much about American weddings, but Paul told me that to propose to Arlene, he would buy her a ring, and then ask her if she would marry him. He was trying to decide how he would ask, but I was sure however he asked would be fine, and she would say yes.

That night, I told the Kehirs what marriage arrangements were like in India.

"The parents choose a partner based on certain characteristics and requirements," I explained. "Usually, the two people don't know each other at all."

"Wow!" Mrs. Kehir laughed. "I can't imagine getting married in such a way."

Somehow the discussion turned to other Indian customs.

"Aren't husbands in India strict with their wives?" Mr. Kehir asked.

I nodded. "In small villages, sometimes the husband takes his wife to a dark room and spanks her if she does not behave or treat her husband with respect and dignity."

They all got a big kick out of that, and whenever Mrs. Kehir disagreed with her husband in any way, immediately Paul or Mr. Kehir would say, "Take her to the dark room!"

Once Arlene complained about doing something Paul asked, and Mr. Kehir said, "Take her to the dark room!" Everyone laughed, and Arlene looked at them like they were crazy. Then we told her about the old Indian custom. It was fun for all of us, and we laughed about it at every opportunity.

After spending an enjoyable six days with the affectionate Kehir family, I visited the Cheemas, who lived twenty minutes away in Morristown, New Jersey. After I arrived, I filled the Cheemas in on everything.

"Wow, that is really something, Kris," Billo said. "You have a bachelor's in math, and now, you are starting a master's degree in industrial engineering. You really do not give up."

After I'd discovered that the Cheemas had moved to Delaware several years earlier, I'd called them and asked why they had left without telling me. I had also suggested that I could go to Delaware too and attend the university there. At the time, they both replied that I was not smart enough. Now, sitting in their living room over a cup of tea, I reminded them of their statement.

"Now look. I have made it back to the University of Tennessee," I said.

"See, our comment was a challenge to you," Dr. Cheema

joked. "And look at you now. You have finished your bachelor's and are working on your master's at UT. We are very proud of you."

❋ ❋ ❋

After a wonderful reunion with the Cheemas, I returned to school. While I struggled with Applied Digital Computer Engineering, my Operations Research professor, Russ Buchan, livened up his night class with jokes. Tired at the end of a long day, most students were not in the mood to sit in class for three hours. Sometimes Professor Buchan told me a joke in the hallway, and then, when everyone took their seats at 6:30, he would say, "Hey, Kris has a joke to tell." The students roared with laughter to hear American jokes coming from an Indian guy. Students in Nashville and Chattanooga, taking the course via satellite, went crazy hearing me over the speaker.

I liked Professor Buchan. He was passionate about industrial engineering and seemed to like me as well. In the spring, he became my major advisor, and I took Advanced Operations Research, choosing him to help me with my thesis.

As the deadline for payment of tuition approached for the spring quarter, I began to worry. Running short on money, barely able to buy food, I worried that I couldn't pay for three courses before UT tacked on a late penalty. One day, Professor Buchan asked me if I would like to work part time at the UT Hospital and Research Center.

Surprised, I said, "But I have no experience in hospitals."

"Don't worry about it," Professor Buchan said. "You'll learn."

He scrawled the name "Macks McFarland" on a piece of paper. "Go see him about working there. You'll be fine."

The next day, I took a bus to the UT Hospital and Research Center. Mr. McFarland interviewed me, and a few days later, he offered me the job. The hospital paid me three dollars an hour, letting me work as many hours as I wanted Monday through Friday. Grateful that Professor Buchan had come to my aid when I needed the job most, I thanked God for helping me at just the right time. The mantra I recited one hundred and one times a day strengthened my belief while I went through a tough financial time, struggling to pay for my coursework. I knew God was teaching me to trust him and assuring me he would provide for me when I needed help.

I discovered that industrial engineers were breaking new ground in the healthcare industry, and in hospitals, they were called management engineers. Using time analysis, the industrial engineer determined the number of people needed to perform certain functions throughout the hospital. As a management engineer at the UT Hospital, it was my job to save the hospital money.

Each day, the Housekeeping Department mopped and waxed the hallway floors while the Laundry Department washed, dried, and folded hundreds of pounds of laundry daily. After obtaining the square footage of floors they cleaned and the pounds of laundry they washed, management engineers would observe the amount of time it took to complete these tasks and determine the minimal amount of people needed.

"What do you know about hospitals?" Sewa asked when I told him about my job. "What are you going to do there?" It became a joke to my Indian friends who couldn't imagine what an industrial engineer would do in a hospital. Since I didn't have any more knowledge than they did, I simply went along with their jokes.

On my first day of work, Mr. McFarland gave me literature on industrial engineering studies in the healthcare field. The University of Michigan and Georgia Tech were pioneers in the field, and Mr. McFarland purchased their methodologies so I could review them.

After one week of hospital orientation, I began my first project—determining how many technicians were needed in each lab of the Pathology Department. Mr. McFarland made sure the supervisor, department manager, and pathologists knew what I was working on. "Provide Kris with full cooperation," he told them. "Give him whatever he needs and explain to him everything he asks so he can finish his project."

Throughout the week, the supervisor explained the Hematology Department to me while I took notes. Later, I elaborated on them at my desk, and if I came to parts I didn't understand, I spoke to the supervisor again. At times, I worked directly with the administrator, and since he was the top person, my recommendations carried weight. I was a part of the administrative team, and on a weekly basis, I met with the administrator, two assistant administrators, and the Pathology Department head to discuss major issues the hospital faced and possible solutions.

One challenge I faced as a management engineer was finding a non-threatening way to work with hospital personnel. They feared my recommendations would eliminate their jobs. "That will not be the case," I assured them. "I am here to help the hospital run more efficiently, not to jeopardize your livelihoods."

On top of the employees' suspicions, I felt pressure to succeed. Industrial engineers were expected to save the hospital three to four times more money than the salary paid to them each year.

Because I was not an American, everyone was extra nice to me and asked me about India and my family. They showed concern that I was so far from my family and asked how I was doing. I tried to be friendly as well, and did not act like I was any different from them. I asked about their educational backgrounds, their children, and where they were from. Soon I developed a good rapport with everyone in the Pathology Department.

For the most part, Mr. McFarland was an agreeable boss who treated me the way he did anyone else, but every once in a while, he would insult me in some way. Each morning, Mr. McFarland came to his office at 8:30, looked at the papers on his desk, reviewed his phone calls, and got a cup of coffee. Sometimes he gave Selma, his secretary, the money and asked her to get it for him. One day, Selma was not there, and since I also wanted to drink coffee, I offered to get it for him. He said okay, and I started to leave, thinking I would buy it for him. In the Indian culture, it was a common courtesy to pay for a cup of tea for your friend or your boss. Just then, Mr. McFarland took a dime out of his pocket and threw it on the floor. "Pick it up," he said in a demeaning tone. "Take this dime for the coffee." I looked at him for a moment, thinking about telling him off. But he was my boss, so I didn't say anything, just picked up the dime and left. I needed that job and wanted to turn it into a career.

Another instance that made me feel uncomfortable occurred in April 1968, while Selma and I were working at our desks. Mr. McFarland was sitting at his desk doing paperwork when he looked up and said, "Oh, a coon was shot yesterday." I didn't know until then, but Dr. Martin Luther King had been assassinated.

Selma said, "Mr. McFarland, you shouldn't be saying this."

But Mr. McFarland only said, "Oh, he was nothing but a coon."

I agreed with Selma. I didn't like him saying things like that, but it was not my place to correct him. He was my boss, and I was also a minority, so I kept quiet.

During the 1968 spring quarter, my professor-student relationship with Professor Buchan turned into a friendship. Whenever I invited him to my apartment, he would show up with a six pack of beer, and I would make curried food. He found me funny and felt comfortable with my straightforward manner. He was divorced and had a son, but he never talked much about his family. He often came to my parties with his girlfriend, and whenever the phone rang, he'd answer it and say, "Harry's Bar and Grill."

The person on the other line would be confused, and say, "I'm sorry. I have the wrong number."

Then when they called back a moment later, Professor Buchan would say, "Yes, who do you want to speak to?" Sometimes Professor Buchan also brought John Snyder, my professor of Special Industrial Engineering Problems, and he would always tell people, "Kris's place is the hottest spot in town."

As summer began, I started to work on my thesis, a requirement for graduation from the industrial engineering master's program. At Professor Buchan's suggestion, I decided to write my thesis about the hospital project in the pathology lab.

Early in the summer, I was the best man at Paul and Arlene's wedding. After the wedding, Arlene moved from New Jersey to an apartment in Knoxville with Paul. Every now and then, Paul and Arlene invited me to their place for dinner. The first time, Arlene cooked fish filets with rice and vegetables. As I chewed a piece of fish, I realized it was still cold and a little rubbery on the inside. Not wanting to embarrass Arlene, I moved onto the rice.

"Is the food okay?" Paul asked me after a few minutes. "Do you like it?" He had told me once that Arlene was not the best cook.

"It's pretty good," I said hesitantly. "But the fish is still a little cold on the inside."

Arlene's face turned red. "Kris, I'm so sorry," she said. "I'll put it back in the oven for a while."

She took our plates back to the kitchen while Paul teased her. "Arlene, you are feeding my friend frozen fish."

Sometimes Paul invited Bill and Cindy, their next door neighbors, to dinner also. When I found out Bill took flying lessons at the Knoxville airport, I started seeing visions of myself flying an airplane and someday owning one.

"It is really easy to get a pilot's license," Bill told me. "It is a great thing to have in life."

Bill gave me a coupon for one free lesson. After that, each lesson would cost sixteen dollars per hour. The first lesson involved completing paperwork and reading material about how to fly a small airplane. I thought it would be neat to have a pilot's license, as most people only have a driver's license. Then, once I found a good-paying job, I could buy a used plane and fly it all over the country. At the time, one could buy a used airplane for around $9000, and it seemed impressive to tell my friends and coworkers I owned a plane.

For my second lesson, the instructor took me up in a small two-seater plane. I sat in the control seat on the left side of the plane with the control wheel, or yoke, and all the gauges and buttons in front of me while the instructor told me exactly what to do. We leveled off at a thousand feet above the ground, over-looking the mountains and the Tennessee River.

"Make a left turn," he said at one point.

Pressing the rudder pedal, I turned the control wheel and watched the turn coordinator gauge at the same time. As soon as the plane turned, my door flung open, revealing the mountains all around and the ground miles beneath me.

"Oh shit!" I yelled. "Now what do I do?"

The instructor was trying to stay calm, but he was scared too. "Oh God, oh God," he kept saying. I took a deep breath, trying to calm myself down, thankful for the seat belt strapping me in.

"Pull the damn door and close it tight!" the instructor yelled over the rush of wind coming into the plane and the roar of the engine.

I tried several times, but the wind pressure kept knocking the door from my hand. At the same time, I accidentally pushed the control wheel forward, and the plane nosedived. Suddenly, all in one movement, the instructor took over the controls on his side, straightened the plane, and reached his arm across me to shut the door.

When we landed on the ground, we both let out a sigh of relief.

"I'm sorry, I should have made sure your door was shut properly," the instructor said.

My heart was pounding, as if threatening to fly out of my chest, and I could hardly speak. It was my first flying lesson, and it would be my last. With school and work to focus on, I did not want my time in America to end abruptly if something were to go wrong again.

Chapter 9

My study project report for the UT Research Hospital was due at the end of September 1968, and I devoted all my time and effort to completing the report, going to the office on weekends, cutting down on my social activities, and repeatedly telling myself, "You must sacrifice something to get something."

Professor Buchan and Mr. McFarland reviewed the report to make sure my staffing formulas and recommendations made sense. I was anxious, and my nerves were on edge. The chief pathologist, a member of the administrative team, carried a high status among the medical staff, and because my report uncovered the problems and weaknesses of the Lab Department, I worried that he might not agree with my findings and recommendations.

In October, Mr. McFarland presented my study to the chief pathologist and managerial staff. For clarification of any point, the questions were referred to me. There were no major surprises for the lab staff, and the chief pathologist seemed pleased with my recommendations. Before we left the room, he made a closing statement: "Kris Bedi did a good job of understanding the laboratory functions and activities, collecting the historical data, and making good observations. I will think through the staffing level recommendations and discuss it further with my supervisory staff."

I felt everything had gone well. The chief pathologist acknowledged me for the study, even though Mr. McFarland presented it. Mr. McFarland, on the other hand, did not hide his annoyance that the chief pathologist and managerial staff directed all their compliments to me. Without saying a word, he stormed out of the room.

❖ ❖ ❖

Shortly after Thanksgiving, I received a job offer for a position
I'd interviewed for two months earlier at Vanderbilt University
Hospital in Nashville, Tennessee. They were looking for a management engineer, and Professor Buchan immediately recommended me. The letter stated my title (management engineer),
start date (December 17), and salary ($9,000 a year). After grad-
uation, they would pay me $10,000 a year. Later, I learned it
took them so long to hire me because they were hoping to find
another candidate. However, there were not many industrial
engineers with experience in the healthcare field at the time.
I was thrilled to receive the letter, even though I was also disappointed it had taken them two months to decide about me.
Professor Buchan advised me to take the offer, so I sent an acceptance letter. While I was happy to have a job with a large, well-
known hospital, at the same time, I was sad about leaving my
friends, especially Sewa Singh and Professor Buchan.

Of all my friends, Sewa was the saddest to see me leave.
Together, we participated more actively in American social life
than most Indians. We enjoyed going to American parties and
drive-in restaurants, and we liked to sit on the side of the road
at an intersection in front of his apartment, drinking beer and
talking. During those times, we felt the way we did back in India
when nothing else was going on. I would miss all the laughs and
good times we experienced together.

On the day of my departure, Sewa helped me load my
belongings into my sky-blue, 1965 Catalina convertible. On
weekends and most evenings, Sewa and I drove the Catalina
with the top down to drive-in restaurants, blasting Indian music
on a portable record player we borrowed from another Indian
student. The guys and girls at the drive-in restaurant would look
around, wondering where the crazy music was coming from. We
ordered cheeseburgers and drank Old German or Pabst Blue
Ribbon, the cheapest beer we could buy in six packs at the time.

As Sewa and I drank beer and ate curried chicken with

rice at his house, we reminisced about the good times and shared plenty of laughs. When it came time for me to leave, we both became emotional. After saying our goodbyes with heavy hearts, I drove toward Nashville, wondering what the next stage of my life would be like.

❀ ❀ ❀

The next morning, as I walked into Vanderbilt University Hospital a little before 8:00, I felt like a million bucks. My hair was combed neatly, and I wore a suit and tie, a light blue shirt, and Florsheim shoes. The secretary at the front desk showed me to Jacob Walker's office. He was the department head of data processing within the Programming Department, and he gestured for me to sit down. As he explained the functions of the Programming Department, I nodded politely, wondering how this information related to me. I was an engineer, not a programmer.

Once he finished speaking, Mr. Walker showed me to my office, which turned out to be a dim corner in the back of the room, sectioned off by a wooden panel. *What is this?* I thought. After spending so much time imagining my own office, this was a punch in the stomach.

Next, I met the assistant administrator, Mr. Clark. After talking with him for several minutes about his responsibilities and the hospital's organization, it was apparent that I would not have much to do with Mr. Clark, and when I met Mr. Greathouse, I knew I would rarely see him either. I came to like Jean Brown the most. She was the methods analyst and an enthusiastic, friendly person. Previously, she had worked as a registered nurse in the Infection Control Department. She knew the ins and outs of the hospital, and during the next few days, she told me everything she knew about the hospital and its personnel.

At the end of my two-week hospital orientation, I began my first project: investigating the shortage of clean linens on the patient floors. The Laundry Department manager was not enthusiastic about having an outsider come into his area to show him what to do. I needed to win his trust and let him know I was there to help solve the problem, not to show him how to run his department.

After shaking his hand and introducing myself, I asked him questions. It was crucial to get to know him as a person first. I'd learned this from reading articles on my new profession and also from witnessing the positive effect of it on my work at the UT Hospital. What were his likes and dislikes? How long had he worked here? What was his educational background? Seeing a picture of his family on his desk, I asked about them. Soon the manager's face began to soften, and he talked more openly. Now I could approach him from a professional standpoint, collecting data and making observations.

The following week, I began looking for an apartment. Mrs. Brown told me about the Executive House apartment complex fifteen minutes outside of Nashville. I liked that it was in the country, away from congested city traffic. The rent was the lowest I'd seen so far—only $125 a month. The landlady, Mrs. Olsen, was warm and friendly, and after I completed the application to rent an apartment, she asked me questions about my family and where I was from. She was in her sixties and lived with her adopted daughter, Maelie, who was in her early twenties. As Mrs. Olsen gave me the key to my apartment, Maelie came out to the front and smiled shyly at me. Freckles dotted her face and arms, and her red wavy hair fell slightly past her shoulders. I smiled back pleasantly.

Looking from me to Maelie, Mrs. Olsen smiled. "All right Mr. Bedi, just let me know if you have any more questions. Remember, jiggle the lock, and it will open."

I moved in on January 1, 1969. The apartment was a straight shot to work, a twenty-minute drive with only two traffic lights. For a month I slept on the floor and ate dinner on a sheet spread on the carpet until Mrs. Brown suggested I go to a furniture store near the mall for my bedding needs. I followed her advice and purchased a Simmons mattress and box springs, also at her recommendation.

The next day, when Mrs. Olsen let the delivery men in with my new bed, she saw how bare my apartment was. She invited me to dinner that evening, and we ate baked chicken, green beans, mashed potatoes, and apple pie. She made sure I ate my fill, insisting I take seconds. All through dinner, she and Maelie asked endless questions about my family, India, and me.

At the end of the night, Mrs. Olsen said, "Maelie, you could show Kris around Nashville sometime."

Maelie brightened at the idea. "We can double date with Kay and her boyfriend," she said. "Kay is my friend, and she lives in this complex too."

I could not say no. After all, I was eating dinner at their apartment. Politely, I agreed to the plan.

Over the next few months, I grew accustomed to Mrs. Olsen and Maelie watching me. They lived on the first floor of my building and kept the drape to the sliding patio door partially open so they could see who was coming and going. My parking spot was in front of their patio door, and they could easily see me as I walked to my apartment.

Although work and school kept me busy, I made time to drive to Knoxville every three to four weeks to visit Sewa Singh, have dinner with Paul and Arlene, and discuss my thesis with Professor Buchan. For the winter quarter of 1969, I only signed up for one class, Principles of Organization, which I took at Nashville's UT satellite campus. The professor was a kind, older man in his sixties, and after the first class, I explained to him that I needed to raise my GPA to a 3.0 in order to graduate.

"Okay," the professor said noncommittally.

"I really need an A in this class," I said, hoping for a more sympathetic response. "I am writing my thesis, and I work full time at Vanderbilt University Hospital."

"I understand," he said.

I hoped he did understand. Mr. Clark told me that the hospital would reimburse my tuition if I received at least a B in the course, increasing the pressure to make good grades.

❀ ❀ ❀

A number of things bothered me about my job at Vanderbilt University Hospital. I secretly resented my tiny desk in Jacob Walker's office in the Programming Department, and I only saw Mr. Clark when he attended the meetings to discuss my project. To my disappointment, he never contributed to the subject. *The meetings are a waste of his time,* I thought. *Why should he come at all if he does not intend to provide any feedback?*

Most of all, I could not stand working for Mr. Walker, a guy with a physical education degree. He became director of programming because of his data processing experience, and I couldn't help feeling superior to him since I was almost finished with my master's in industrial engineering and had experience at the UT Hospital. I wanted to improve every aspect of Vanderbilt University Hospital, and I could hardly wait to "change the world." They were lucky to have me. I didn't hide the fact that I thought I deserved more, and Mr. Walker started calling me "hot shot" when talking about me to other staff members. There was nothing I could do about the situation, and my work always remained on the back burner, because Mr. Walker's secretary always gave preference to his work and instructions, leaving my notes to be typed up last.

In a way, I blamed Professor Buchan for placing me at this hospital. After discussing my concerns with him, he apologized and said he had not been aware that Mr. Clark would treat me so poorly. He had assumed I would report directly to the assistant administrator.

"Kris, once you receive your degree, I will help you find a better job," he said. "For now, stay where you are until you finish your degree requirements. It is beneficial for you to stay in this job at least a year."

Reluctantly, I accepted his advice.

Soon the time came to present to Mr. Clark and Mr. Walker my study findings for the laundry project. During my observations, I discovered the Laundry Department did not keep inventory for the linen, nor did they keep records of discarded torn linens. They also purchased new linens sporadically. Happy with my report and recommendations, Mr. Clark told me to proceed.

One summer day, as I was washing my car and had begun to wax it, Maelie saw me through the patio door and came outside to ask if she could help. I gave her a rag and let her wax the hood of the car. She seemed to enjoy it and acted as if it were her own car. It took a long time to apply the paste, let it dry, and then rub it into the car with a clean soft cloth. After a while, we grew tired. It took longer than I expected, and the sun was already low in the sky before we even finished half the car. As I folded the rags and put the lid on the paste, Maelie said, "Kris, I can finish waxing your car while you are at work."

"I don't know," I said, hesitant to accept her offer.

"Please let me, Kris," she said. "I would love to do it, and it would save you time."

I couldn't say no to her, and for the rest of the week, I hitched a ride to the hospital with a guy from Franklin, the nearest town to the apartment complex, while Maelie waxed a portion of the car each day of the week. Knowing she had a crush on me, I was amused.

At work, I often talked to Mrs. Brown, and she enjoyed telling me about her daughter. One day, while she helped me look at furniture for my apartment, she mentioned her daughter was coming to Nashville to attend a formal dinner.

"There will be good food and dancing," Mrs. Brown said. "Would you be interested in going with her? She just graduated from an out-of-town university and doesn't know anyone in Franklin or Nashville."

"Sure," I said. "But I'm not a good dancer."

"Oh, that doesn't matter. Since we are near the mall, I'll help you pick out a suit to wear."

With Mrs. Brown's help, I chose a formal, black, double-breasted suit with a bow tie and a pleated, sky-blue shirt with French cuffs.

Later that evening, I mentioned my dinner date to Mrs. Olsen. "Hmm," she said quietly, looking thoughtful. Maelie was in the room, and her eyes flashed. "Oh really," she said. Her voice choked, and her face showed a strange mixture of anger and disappointment. Then she muttered under her breath, "Who is she to go out with you? You were mine."

Maelie couldn't look me in the eye after saying this and quickly went to her room. Mrs. Olsen watched Maelie leave, and I could tell she was dissatisfied about something. I went back to my apartment, deciding to ignore Maelie's comments. We were friends, that's all, and only because we lived in the same apartment building. Unfortunately, Maelie wanted us to be more than friends, and as the months passed, her feelings for me became clearer.

The evening of the dinner, I picked up Mrs. Brown's daughter in my Catalina. At the party hall, we enjoyed dinner and conversation with the other guests. Afterward, there was dancing to several slow songs as well as more upbeat tunes. I watched while everyone did the twist and a few other popular dances. Peggy Sood had taught me the twist, but that was years ago, and I did not feel comfortable attempting it in front of Mrs. Brown's daughter and a bunch of strangers.

At the end of the night, we drove back to Franklin, stopping at my apartment on the way so she could see the furniture her mother helped pick out. I offered her a cup of hot tea or coffee, and after a few minutes, I drove her home. Before entering her house, she gave me a light hug and a kiss on the cheek. As a courtesy, I wrote down her phone number, but I never called her.

Later, when talking to Mrs. Olsen, she said casually, "Oh, Maelie and I saw you and your date coming and going last night. Pretty girl. Didn't stay very long, though."

I sensed resentment in her tone, but with other things on my mind, I didn't think much about it.

❀ ❀ ❀

When I'd worked at the UT Hospital the previous spring, Mr. McFarland and Professor Buchan often talked about a big national convention for the Hospital Management Systems Society (HMSS) that was to take place in Tampa, Florida. They came back with many stories about the good times they'd had. I hoped one day I could go to the convention too.

When I started my job at Vanderbilt University Hospital, I became a member of the HMSS. In May 1969, the HMSS held its convention in Houston, Texas. The hospital administration encouraged me to go and paid for my travel expenses. The convention lasted five days and five nights. One night, the society held a formal dinner with a keynote speaker, and every other night, Professor Buchan and I wined and dined at a different restaurant. My favorite was Trader Vic's, where we sat in a tropical island atmosphere and drank mai tais. The trip was a continuous party for five days.

When the convention ended, I was sad to go. I flew back to Nashville, and Maelie picked me up at the airport. I swaggered to the gate, a straw Texas cowboy hat hanging at the back of my neck and a small glass flask in my hand. I wasn't drunk, but I was still in high spirits from the excitement of the trip, and I spoke loudly and with more enthusiasm than usual. Maelie looked at me with a shocked expression. I was not the same Kris, and she stared at me as if I had sprouted two heads. She drove me back to the apartment in silence, not even asking about my trip.

While refusing to let Maelie bring down my spirits, I focused on doing well in my satellite course. On the last day of class in June, I reminded the professor that I had taken his class in order to improve my GPA. "Yes, I understand," he said in the same tone as always, not giving me any clue whether I would pass or not. In the end, I received an A in the course.

❀ ❀ ❀

In July, I met an Indian at the mall named Mr. Talele. He lived in Columbia, Tennessee, thirty-five miles west of Franklin, and he taught physics at Columbia State Community College. He was taking a break from his PhD program at the University of Wisconsin in Madison to teach and earn more money. Before parting, he invited me to a party at his apartment. At the party, Mr. Talele served moderately spiced Indian dishes so everyone could taste them. Because it was so late, he let me sleep at his apartment, and the next morning, he told me that an astronaut was attempting to land on the moon.

We settled in front of the TV and watched until late in the afternoon as the rocket circled the moon and finally landed at approximately 4:17 p.m. "The Eagle has landed," the man reporting from the Houston airbase announced. Six hours later, Neil Armstrong emerged from the *Apollo 11* to take his first step onto the moon. The announcer stated, "That's one small step for a man, one giant leap for mankind." The date was July 20, 1969, a historic and joyous time in history, because an American was the first to land on the moon, a great victory over their Cold War enemy, the USSR.

One day, Mrs. Olsen called. "Maelie isn't feeling well," she said. "Can you come talk to her, Kris? She has been in bed the whole week."

"What is the problem?" I asked. "Has she seen a doctor?"

"She is just down, a little depressed, that's all."

When I entered Maelie's bedroom, she was propped up on some pillows and looked like she hadn't left the bed for days. She smiled at me weakly. I noticed her face was pale, and her thick, wavy hair was a mess.

"How are you doing?" I asked as I sat on the edge of the bed.

"I've been better," she said in a soft voice. "How was work?"

I told her about my project, and how it was going, but as I talked, Maelie looked at me tearfully. "I love you, Kris," she said softly.

I stared at her, completely taken aback. She *loved* me? Knowing she had been in bed for almost a week and hoping to cheer her up, all I could say was, "I love you too." Besides, my American friends told me that if a girl says she loves you, you are supposed to say it in return.

Immediately, Maelie perked up. Her voice changed from speaking softly to a normal tone, and a bright smile lit her face, almost like a sigh of relief. Leaning forward, she gave me a hug and a kiss on the cheek. "Oh, I am so glad!" she said.

Now that Maelie was feeling better, I got up to leave. She followed me into the living room where her mother was sitting, and before I knew what was happening, Maelie said, "Mother, we are engaged!"

Stunned, I stared at Maelie with my mouth hanging open. I did not know what to say. I'd just told her "I love you," so I couldn't contradict her in front of her mother. Besides, she seemed happier than I had seen her in a long time. Mrs. Olsen congratulated us. "I am so happy for both of you!" she said, as if she'd hoped this would happen all along.

I could not think straight. All I knew was that I could not contradict Maelie, so I accepted it, not wanting to hurt her feelings and cause her to go back into a deep depression. Besides, it happened so fast, and I didn't know how to stop the excitement. Maelie rushed to the phone and began calling people, saying, "I'm engaged to Kris!" I couldn't stop her, and my mind seemed to accept the situation. *I guess this is how it must be,* I thought. *This is it. How am I going to tell my parents?*

As Maelie made phone calls, Mrs. Olsen said, "Oh Kris, she loves you so much."

After a few minutes, I returned to my apartment feeling puzzled and under tremendous pressure. *What has happened?* I wondered. *How am I going to break this news to my friends and family back in India?* My parents were supposed to arrange and plan a marriage for me, and up until that point, I had planned to fulfill their wishes and marry someone from my culture.

Apparently, in Maelie's mind, saying "I love you too" meant we were in love. She had hoped for this, and most of all, as I learned later, it was her mother's wish that she marry me. I was educated, had a full time professional job, and always wore a suit. In Mrs. Olsen's mind, I was a perfect match. I also learned that Maelie had cautioned Kay, her best friend, to stay away from me. "Kris is mine," she warned. Kay was a flirtatious girl, and Maelie feared that she might try to date me.

When I shared the news with Mrs. Brown, she acted surprised, because she hoped I would call her daughter again when she was back in town. In any case, she congratulated me, and soon the news spread among the Programming Department employees.

That weekend, when I visited Sewa Singh, I reluctantly told him the news. "I'm engaged, Sewa." He took one look at my face and started laughing. "How did that happen, man? Who is this girl you haven't told me about?" I wanted to laugh along with him, but I couldn't. It wasn't what I wanted, but I thought I had no choice. Part of me was being polite, not wanting to hurt Maelie and Mrs. Olsen's feelings. At the same time, they were trying to manipulate me. I found myself trapped in their fantasy, and not having experience in such a situation, I went along with it. Why didn't I speak up and say I had no wish to marry Maelie? It may have been the easy way out, but thinking back to that time, I wonder if I simply didn't want to disappoint Mrs. Olsen. She was a mother figure to me, and I desperately missed my own mother after eight years away from home. In a way, Mrs. Olsen filled that gap in my life. Nevertheless, I spent many sleepless nights hoping the relationship would not mature.

❀ ❀ ❀

While I tried to figure out what was happening with my life, my thesis became my primary focus, as well as, completing my final course requirement—Managerial Planning and Control. I passed my last two classes with As, and with only one course left,

I could spend more time writing my thesis. I began writing it by hand, working hard to write a significant amount so I wouldn't fall behind the timeline indicated by the Industrial Engineering Department.

The thesis writing process overwhelmed me. I needed to compile one hundred typed pages, yet I could not exceed a certain number of words. I did not own a typewriter, nor did I know how to type, so I needed to hire someone to type the thesis for me. After searching around, I found Belinda, a pregnant woman experienced in typing the thesis in the required format. She charged $450 to type my thesis. Since she lived between Nashville and Franklin, three times a week I delivered my handwritten notes to her on my way home from work. Every other weekend, I drove to Knoxville and reviewed my thesis with Professor Buchan.

One evening, two weeks before my thesis submittal date, Belinda gave me the bad news. "I can't do it anymore, Kris. I'm sorry. These typing deadlines are putting too much pressure on me. I'm in my eighth month of pregnancy, and my husband doesn't think all this pressure and tension is good for the baby. I don't want the baby to come prematurely because of this."

I couldn't believe what was happening. Graduation was just around the corner, and without someone to type for me, I didn't know if I would finish in time.

In the end, I found a woman in Knoxville who promised to give my thesis first priority over the other work she was doing. I accepted her charges with no bargaining, gave the thesis material to her, and drove back to Nashville, relieved a solution had surfaced so quickly. However, it meant I would need to drive to Knoxville twice a week instead of twice a month. In addition to the extra driving, I needed to study for my final exam. The only thing keeping me going was the fact that I was almost done. I celebrated every little success, knowing that the big one was closer than ever.

Chapter 10

The committee for my oral exam consisted of three professors from the Industrial Engineering Department:
Dr. Hutchinson, the department head, known to be tough on
students; Dr. Snyder, who came to my parties with Professor
Buchan; and my trusted advisor as well as good friend, Professor
Buchan. I wasn't worried at all about Professor Buchan, and I
was comfortable with Dr. Snyder; although, as the saying goes,
"You never know." However, I was concerned about whether or
not Dr. Hutchinson would give me a hard time.

The night before the exam, while I studied my thesis at
Sewa Singh's apartment, Professor Buchan showed up at the
front door. "Tomorrow I'm throwing a party after your oral
exam to celebrate your graduation," he announced. Then, looking at Sewa, he added with a big grin, "And Kris is cooking!"

"But Professor Buchan," I began with wide eyes. "What if
I don't pass the exam? You will have to cancel the party, and I
will look like a fool."

"Just be yourself," Professor Buchan said, as if that were
the easiest thing in the world. "Answer the questions directly
and to the point."

The next day, I arrived early to set up my thesis materials.
It was a labor of love, and I had not worked so hard on anything
in all my years at college. For the graduation requirement, I
printed five soft covers and three hard covers. On the dedication
page, I wrote: "This thesis is fondly dedicated to two wonderful
people—Father and Mother." My eyes filled with tears when I
came to this part. I felt my parents had been with me all these
years, guiding me along the path of my dream to receive an
engineering degree.

As the hour of the examination approached, I waited anxiously outside the room. One by one, the committee members arrived and took their seats on one side of the conference table. After a minute, Professor Buchan stuck his head outside the door and waved for me to come in. "We're ready for you," he said.

Upon entering the room, I greeted each of them with a handshake, saying, "Dr. Hutchinson, sir. Dr. Snyder, sir. Professor Buchan, sir." Then, I stood in front of them and waited for their permission to start.

Professor Buchan took the lead. "Kris go ahead and explain your thesis to us."

Launching into a brief background of my topic, I described the methods I'd used to collect information, conduct research, form an analysis, develop staffing formulas, and create a methodology for other hospitals to use my formulas. Each committee member was required to ask at least two questions. Dr. Snyder asked the first question.

"Explain the previous research on the staffing formula and methodology for the hospital's Lab Department," he said.

Once I explained, he followed up with another question regarding the staffing formula. "Explain using the blackboard," he said.

Suddenly, I became inexplicably nervous as I walked to the blackboard and tried to explain in greater detail. At one point, when I became confused between the workload formula and the staffing formula, Dr. Snyder grew huffy and impatient. "Damn, Kris, just write the formula," he said in a frustrated voice.

My mind went blank as I tried to think what to write on the board.

Thumping his fist on the table, Dr. Snyder commanded, "Kris, please just write the damn formula on the board."

Flustered by his behavior, I couldn't think at all.

Just when I started to think my industrial engineering degree was about to go down the tubes, Professor Buchan spoke up. "Kris, write your staffing formula and explain the parameters and limitations of the formula."

Immediately, it clicked in my mind what I needed to write. "Okay," I said with renewed vigor and inspiration.

Effortlessly, I wrote the staffing formula and explained it.

"Now, Kris, that was not so difficult," Dr. Snyder said, leaning back in his chair.

I was sweating a little, chalk powder sticking to my clammy hands, as Professor Buchan asked his two questions and Dr. Hutchinson wrapped up the exam by asking about the conclusions and recommendations. I answered quickly, and then they asked me to wait in the hall while they made their decision.

After a while, Professor Buchan asked me to join them. The moment I entered the room, I saw a smile on Dr. Snyder's face. Then Professor Buchan gave me the news. "Congratulations, Kris. You passed."

Relief surged through me. Not knowing what to do or say, I simply thanked all three of them. They congratulated me and shook my hand before I left the room. I was halfway down the hall when Professor Buchan called after me, "Don't forget to go to my apartment and get the food ready for the party!"

Joyfully, I drove to Sewa Singh's apartment. Everything was filled with light and happiness. Birds sang in the trees under a cloudless sky, and the traffic in the streets seemed to open up for me as I maneuvered past the houses up the hill and the remaining few blocks to Sewa's place. He sat on the porch, waiting anxiously to see how I'd done.

I jumped out of the car and shouted, "I made it, Sewa! I passed the orals! Let's celebrate with beer!" Leaping up the porch steps in bounds, I went straight for the kitchen. Sewa and I pulled back the tabs on our beers, clicked the cans together, and said, "Cheers!"

"Here's to no more studying!" I exclaimed, tilting my head back and taking a large swig.

Five minutes later, Sewa and I drove to Professor Buchan's

apartment to prepare the big feast. Sewa was playing hooky from work so he could be at this party, and while cutting onions and cleaning the chicken, we drank more beer. Professor Buchan joined us at around 5:00 to help prepare food. We set up the bar with scotch (Chivas Regal), bourbon, gin, vodka, and two types of beer, all of which Professor Buchan bought on his way back to the apartment. "Kris, this is all for you," he said. "Especially the scotch."

"Enough of beer!" I said. "Let's switch over to scotch."

At seven o'clock, people began to arrive, and the party started. Dr. Snyder and his wife showed up, and we all sat down wherever we could find a spot while Dr. Snyder relayed what happened four hours earlier.

"You should have seen the look on his face when I said 'Damn, Kris!'" Dr. Snyder laughed. "And when I slammed my hand on the table and said, 'Put your damn formula on the board,' he looked like he wanted to run out of the room!"

We all laughed, and what had seemed so awful to me hours earlier now seemed like a big joke. Dr. Snyder took a swig of beer and said, "Kris, I just wanted to see the formula, so we could get it over quickly and come to your party."

Graduation was set for August 25, and up until then, Sewa and I threw small parties with a few friends, enjoying food, beer, whisky, and good conversation. Everyone teased me about Maelie because, by that time, they knew she was the one who'd announced the engagement. "Oooo, Kris, is in love," they said. I kept quiet, careful not to share my true feelings. *Let us see what will happen,* I thought.

The morning of August 25, to my pleasant surprise, Billo arrived with her three-year-old son, Yusuf. While I'd invited her to come, I didn't think she would travel all this way. Together, we went downtown to the Knoxville Civic Auditorium and Coliseum where we met Mrs. Olsen, her sister, and Maelie. When

Billo heard that Maelie and I were engaged, she raised her eyebrows. Later, she pulled me aside. "Kris, what is going on? You did not tell me this." Billo wanted to know all about Maelie, but I told her I would explain later. "For now, just enjoy my graduation," I said.

When the time came, I sat near the back with the College of Engineering grad students. While waiting for the ceremony to start, I could not help thinking of my parents. I missed them tremendously, and seeing all the parents and relatives at the graduation made the absence of mine only more noticeable. These parents had come to witness their sons or daughters receive their degrees and share the joy of the occasion, along with many relatives. My parents did not have the luxury to travel so far.

The ceremony began exactly at 11:00 a.m. As the president of the university gave his speech, I flipped through the program booklet, gratified to see my name printed with the other engineering graduates. I would save the booklet and send it to my parents. They would be proud and would have something to show our relatives, friends, and the whole village.

When it was my turn to walk across the stage, a sense of anticipation and excitement filled me. The faculty members flashed me wide smiles and shook my hand, saying "Congratulations." It was one of the biggest moments of my life, to stand on the stage and receive my long-awaited, hard-earned master's of science degree in industrial engineering, which I'd paid for with my sweat and tears. All the nights I'd fretted and cried, buried my head in books and notes, and now I could finally say, "I did it."

Clutching my diploma, I walked back to my seat, again, wishing with all my heart that my parents could be there. I felt tears come to my eyes as I watched the rest of the ceremony. I had succeeded. I had not embarrassed my parents, and now I could go back to India.

After the ceremony, I walked back to Sewa, Billo, and the others, crying loudly with tears flowing down my cheeks. Sewa and Billo understood I was missing my parents, and they hugged me, saying, "It's okay. You made it. Congratulations!"

Mrs. Olsen, her sister, and Maelie congratulated me, and Mrs. Olsen held me close. "I'm proud of you, Kris," she said, her eyes crinkling. Maelie looked at me shyly, kissed her index finger and pointed it toward me. She did not like to kiss or hug in public.

As we walked to our cars, I looked up at the sky and said to my parents, "Here it is, what we all have been waiting for. Thank you for all your prayers and faith in me."

Mrs. Olsen, her sister, and Maelie drove back to Franklin, and Billo drove to Frankfurt, Kentucky, to visit friends, after a late lunch, leaving only Sewa and me to celebrate.

As soon as I returned to Nashville, I wrote my parents a letter, saying, "You all will be glad to know that I have received my master's degree due to your blessings and prayers. Mother, thank you for all your support, encouragement, and blessings." I laughed to myself as I remembered the previous letters I'd written, praising my mother so much that my brother wrote back angrily, saying, "Why don't you ever say much about me?"

My parents replied immediately. "We are very proud of you and glad you have achieved this. But Krishan, it is all your hard work. You have done a good job. And you have made our name shine in the US. To share our happiness, we distributed sweets to the Malaudh residents, especially to the poor." Much later, I learned that the poor people would come to my mother and say blessings—"Your son Krishan has succeeded in Amrika and will come soon." Their words made her happy, and she would feed them snacks.

My mother only wanted to know one thing. When would I be coming back? Sadly, I could not give a definite answer. I needed more work experience in the US before I would return. In the meantime, the VU Hospital raised my salary from $9,000 to $10,000. As I progressed on my projects at the hospital, one uncertainty hovered over me wherever I went.

Maelie.

Whatever my own reservations about our relationship, Maelie had no doubt in her mind. In fact, she had practically moved in. Although we weren't living together, she brought her dishware to my apartment, and one afternoon, she lugged over two cushioned, high-back chairs and a large painting of a horse, which she hung above my music system.

As Labor Day approached, Mrs. Olsen suggested that Maelie and I visit Maelie's stepsister in Jacksonville, Florida. She insisted that her sister would love to see us, and we would enjoy their big house by the lake, where we could go boating. Mrs. Olsen often talked about her elder stepdaughter, Galina, who was fifteen years older than Maelie and had several children of her own. Mrs. Olsen said in her motherly voice, "It would be so good if you both went there."

As I had no plans to visit Knoxville for Labor Day weekend, I agreed to go.

The evening before we left, I returned from work, planning to pack so we could leave early the next morning in Maelie's car. Maelie came to my apartment and fixed a cup of hot tea for me. We sat on the couch she had brought over several weeks earlier, talking and listening to music. All of a sudden, she moved closer to me and laid her head on my shoulder, the closest she had gotten to me since we met. When she looked up, straight into my eyes, I could tell she wanted me to kiss her. In an instant, we wrapped our arms around each other and started kissing heavily. I felt no romantic feelings, but I figured if we were engaged, we should kiss sooner or later.

Suddenly, Maelie gasped, pushed me aside, and hurried from the apartment. As she slammed the door behind her, I didn't know what to think. I just sat there, feeling I hadn't said or done anything to upset her.

Even though the evening did not end well, I finished packing, under the impression we were still going to Florida. The next morning, I walked over to Mrs. Olsen's apartment to see if Maelie was ready. Mrs. Olsen opened the door and asked me to come in, her voice low and broken as if she had been crying. With tears in her eyes, Mrs. Olsen said, "I am sorry to tell you that Maelie left for Florida this morning." In a heavy voice, she added, "I'm so sorry, Kris. She did not talk much. After coming back from your apartment, she went straight to bed and ate very little."

Not knowing what to say or whether I should ask any questions, I just sat at the kitchen table feeling confused. *What is going on?* I wondered. *How could she do this to me?*

"I don't know what happened, Mrs. Olsen," I said. "I was nice to her. We drank tea, listened to music, and kissed. That's all. Then she just got upset."

"I understand you didn't do anything wrong," Mrs. Olsen said. "It is how Maelie behaves sometimes."

I thought, *If that is how she behaves, then why are we engaged?*

Mrs. Olsen did not know what else to tell me except that Maelie had been emotional and depressed before she left for Jacksonville alone. I returned to my apartment, feeling ashamed and not wanting to share this episode with my friends. They all knew I was supposed to go to Florida with Maelie, so I did not call anyone that day.

That same afternoon, Mrs. Olsen called and asked me to come to her apartment. "Maelie has reached Jacksonville," she informed me, cheerfully. "She is sorry she left without you. She was not thinking straight and would like you to come down to Florida."

Perhaps I looked astounded because Mrs. Olsen said, "I know, I know, Kris. I realize your feelings right now, but it would be so good for both of you if you flew to Jacksonville, and you both can drive back together. How does that sound?"

I was completely shocked that Mrs. Olsen and Maelie expected me to fly to Florida after what just happened. Mrs. Olsen wanted me to go more than anything. "Kris, Maelie loves you very much. She has high regard for you. It was not your fault. Maelie just gets depressed sometimes, and her behavior can be erratic."

Not wanting to hurt either Maelie or Mrs. Olsen's feelings, I flew down to Jacksonville the next day. Maelie picked me up at the airport, and we drove to her sister's house. Galina and Charlton welcomed me into their home and showed me to a room where I could set my suitcase.

When Maelie and I were alone for a moment, she apologized for leaving my apartment so abruptly and for going to Florida without me. "It was not you, Kris. You did not do anything wrong," she said. "It was just me. That is all I want to say right now. But oh! I am so happy you have come. Thank you!" She smiled her sweetest smile, kissed her finger, and pointed it at me.

Later that evening, after Galina and Charlton treated us to a delicious home-cooked dinner, they shared their good wishes for Maelie and me, saying how they hoped we would make a good couple. I simply sat on the couch for a long, uncomfortable moment, not saying anything. However, Maelie seemed happy to hear it. She grinned and looped her fingers through mine.

When the weekend was over, I was ready to get back to Franklin. On the drive back, I found that I didn't know what to say. Maelie was not a big talker either, resulting in a long, mostly quiet trip. Besides, I worried that if I said one wrong word, she'd ditch me at a gas station a hundred miles from Tennessee. I had no idea what was going on in her head.

Ten hours later, we pulled into the Executive House parking lot. Mrs. Olsen greeted us with her usual cheer, noting Maelie's hand in mine and that we seemed to be a little closer. The news of our engagement spread quickly among Maelie's relatives and my friends. When Maelie started talking about the wedding date and wedding preparations, I decided it was time to break the news to my parents. I wrote them a letter, saying I met a nice American girl named Maelie, detailing the sort of things parents in India would like to hear about a girl's background and social status—she has a sister, her mother is a nice lady, she does not have a father, and she works at a bank. In this way, I prepared them for the possibility of a wedding.

My parents responded quickly, surprising me with their neutral feelings. They had always hoped I would follow my country's tradition and marry a nice Indian girl with their consent, but now they accepted my decision because I had succeeded in receiving my degree after almost eight years of hard work. They knew that many Indians who study in America often marry American girls, and now their fear was coming true. At the same time, they wrote, "Whatever you are happy with, it is okay with us. We want to see you both. When are you coming back?" I still did not know, but I hoped it would be soon.

In the meantime, I began teaching an Industrial Safety course at Columbia State Community College fifty miles away. I had come to the US to learn, and now here I was teaching Americans. It didn't matter that I knew nothing about industrial safety.

The fall semester began the third week of September. Once a week, I drove fifty miles to Columbia State Community College as soon as I got off work at the hospital, so I could make it in time for class at 6:00. The class lasted two and a half hours, and eight students attended. The course helped take my mind off Maelie and her strange, inappropriate behavior. Each week, I read the chapters and made notes so I could act as though I were the expert in front of the students, learning and teaching at the same time. The job brought in an extra $150 per month, a nice amount to go toward rent or to cushion my savings account.

Meanwhile, Maelie continued bringing small items to my apartment. We were not romantic with each other, and I didn't dare kiss her again. Perhaps she loved me, but I couldn't find any such feelings for her. I didn't know what to do, so I busied myself with work and my teaching job. However, it seemed like everything was coming to a boiling point, and I didn't know how much longer I could stand it.

Then came Diwali in mid-November—the Festival of Lights. The joy and radiance of Diwali was magical, and it was my favorite time of year. My friend Randhir Chopra—called Randy—invited me to celebrate Diwali with him and his wife, Dulari, in Knoxville. Not sure if I had told him yet, I informed him about my engagement to Maelie

"What?" he said. Then after a brief pause, he added, "Okay, bring her as well."

I was excited to see Randy and his wife. Randy had been my friend during my early years in Knoxville, and we didn't get to see each other often, but when we did, it was like a homecoming.

I invited Maelie to come with me, and on the day of the festival, we left for Knoxville in Maelie's car, which was newer than mine. We arrived at Randy's house after 6:00 p.m., and I introduced Maelie, leaving out the part that she was my fiancé, but it seemed I made a mistake by not saying it.

She shook Randy's hand, saying, "We are engaged," and shooting me a sideways glance.

"A drink or hot tea?" Randy asked me, oblivious to the tension.

"This is drink time," I said. "Tea time is over at 5:00 p.m."

Randy and I drank scotch while Maelie sipped a cup of water. Then, Randy told me about the Dean's Hill Country Club not far from his house.

"It is a very prestigious club, Kris, and it is not easy to join," he told me. "The membership fee is $3,000. I made a reservation for us to eat there tonight."

Randy and I couldn't wait to celebrate with a glass of whiskey. Once seated at a table in the club, we ordered Randy's favorite scotch, Ballantine's Eighteen-Year-Old, considered a little better than Chivas Regal. I drank quickly, gulping down each glass and looking forward to more, hoping to drink away my situation—the fact that I was engaged, and it had happened without my proposal. After drinking three shots of straight Ballantine's, I felt in high spirits, having let go all the tension of the past months. Maelie sat next to me, her back straight and her lips pursed as she eyed me nervously.

I didn't eat much, just kept wanting more scotch, and each time I finished one glass, I looked toward the waiter to ask for more. The alcohol ran down my throat and set my stomach on fire, numbing away my feelings. *I'm engaged.* I set the empty glass on the table harder than I meant to. *How did I get into this mess? I never asked her to marry me, and I never gave her a ring.* I watched the amber liquid fill my glass again as the waiter poured with a steady hand. My hand seemed not so steady. Randy and Dulari exchanged looks. Maelie's eyes darkened, and her face turned red to match her hair, then nearly as pale as the white table cloth. She fidgeted with her silverware, and her fingers tapped on the table. She did not talk, only moved her food around on the plate, leaving most of it untouched.

After dinner, we returned to Randy's house. I don't remember much of what happened that night, but I am told that Randy directed me to one room and Dulari took Maelie to another. Sometime in the middle of the night, I woke up to go to the bathroom. By mistake, I opened the closet door and tried to urinate there. Randy came out and directed me to the bathroom, which caused a great commotion since I was still half asleep and partially drunk.

The next morning, I woke up at around 9:00 a.m. with a pounding headache. We all waited for Maelie to come out of her room, but after more than an hour, she did not appear. Finally, we went in and saw the room empty and the bed made.

We could not believe it.

"Hey Kris, what is this?" Randy said. "Your fiancé left you here."

Dulari, new to the culture and customs of America, was surprised and teased me, "Hey Kris, your girlfriend has run away from you. What did you do?"

Completely embarrassed by Maelie's behavior, I couldn't even speak. The rest of the day, Randy, Dulari, and I enjoyed ourselves, and I began to feel better about the situation. *Hopefully this is over,* I thought.

After spending all of Saturday and Sunday morning with the Chopras, I took a bus to Nashville, feeling upset, relieved, and confused all at once. Monday evening, Mrs. Olsen apologized, saying Maelie had rushed back in a frenzy. She was not used to seeing me drink and told her mother I was a completely different person when I was not at the Executive House.

"It was not Kris," she kept saying. "That was not the Kris I know."

I could not tell Mrs. Olsen the real reason I drank glass after glass so quickly. Maelie was in her room, lying in bed, so I did not see her. Frankly, I did not want to see her. But Mrs. Olsen looked on the verge of tears, and I tried to console her.

"Mrs. Olsen, it is okay this has happened," I said in a calm voice.

Then, Mrs. Olsen started crying, and I comforted her as best I could.

"It is fine," I said. "It is okay with me. Perhaps this is best for both of us."

Mrs. Olsen only cried harder and apologized again.

"I wish Maelie very well," I said, finally.

I returned to my apartment and stared at the bare walls. Maelie had taken all of her belongings from my apartment before I returned, and she never exchanged any words with me, either to apologize or to tell me the engagement was off. Regardless of the way the situation ended, I felt a sudden freedom. For some inexplicable reason, I could never say no to Mrs. Olsen. She was a picture of kindness and generosity toward me. Now I did not need to worry about hurting her feelings. Feeling like a new person, I put the kettle on the stove and made myself a cup of tea.

Chapter 11

In January 1970, I started thinking about when I would return to India. As much as I wanted to see my family again, I realized I had become comfortable in America. What if going back to India, marrying there, and settling down did not work out so well? Not wanting to turn my back on my new American lifestyle, I thought it would be a good idea to bring my wife to the US once I married, so she could experience the culture. After she became familiar with it, we could both go back to India.

In order for that to work, I needed a permanent visa to return to the US. As I also needed my employer to sponsor me, I approached Mr. Clark and told him I would like to apply for a permanent visa; otherwise, I would have to leave in six months. Mr. Clark agreed to help, and after filling out the required documents, I wrote to my parents and told them that as soon as I received my permanent visa, I would come to see them. The excitement started building. After eight years, I expected to find many changes. In my absence, my brother's wife had given birth to five sons and one daughter, and my elder sister had two daughters and one son, all under the age of nine. I couldn't wait to see my nieces and nephews for the first time and to start searching for my own wife.

Toward the end of January, I received a letter from my parents. "Good news," they wrote. "There is going to be a telephone installed in Malaudh at the post office."

Most houses did not own a telephone because not only must you apply to the government with a deposit of one thousand rupees ($175 in the 1960s), but it might take a year or two to get the phone and a connection. Usually, the phone service was set up through a telephone exchange for the entire city, and until that point, it had been possible only in big cities.

My Indian friends warned me it was complicated to make a phone call to India, but I decided to surprise my parents anyway. First, I subscribed to AT&T—the only phone service at the time—for international calling, which required an extra monthly fee. Next I booked a call with the international operator in New Jersey. Since the time difference between India and the US is about eleven hours, I booked the call for the evening, so I could reach my family during daytime hours.

Indeed, as my friends warned, telephoning my parents in India seemed to be nearly as difficult as earning a master's degree. Just as at one point I thought I would never finish college, I now thought I might never speak to my parents on the telephone.

For three nights I tried, but the operator continually failed to make a connection. Frustrated, I spoke to the supervisor who explained that the New Jersey operator must call the New Delhi main telephone exchange. Then the New Delhi operator would call the exchange in Ludhiana city. From Ludhiana, the call would go to Mandi Ahmed Garh's telephone exchange. Finally, the operator at Mandi Ahmed Garh would call the post office in Malaudh. The second night, every time the New Jersey supervisor placed the call, the New Delhi operators either would not pick up the phone or they would say, "Wait a minute," and never come back to the phone. And no wonder. It was a lot of work to call the Ludhiana exchange and wait for the Mandi Ahmed Garh exchange, then wait for the Malaudh post office to pick up the phone, and finally, to wait for my parents to come to the post office. The operators in New Delhi wanted no part of it.

On the third night, I spoke to the manager of the New Jersey operators. "I have been in the US for almost eight years and have not talked to my parents even once," I explained. "Our hometown village has just installed a phone, and I need to talk to them so that I can hear their voices and so they can hear mine."

Sympathetic to my story, the manager could only say, "I am truly sorry, Mr. Bedi, but we are helpless if the New Delhi operator does not pick up the phone."

For three more nights I tried to reach Malaudh. Each night, I emphasized my story to the New Jersey operator, who would relay my story to the New Delhi operator. Still no luck. Later, the operator told me that sometimes the New Delhi operator goes to sleep or is on break so they just don't pick up the phone. That could be the story in Ludhiana as well as Mandi Ahmed Garh.

On the seventh night, as my patience was running thin and I pleaded my case yet again, all the while praising the operators for trying so hard, we finally made it through all the exchanges. The phone rang at the Malaudh post office, and the operator at the Mandi Ahmed Garh exchange said, "Hello, there is a call from America for Shree Mukandi Lal Bedi." The man who answered the phone knew Mr. Mukandi Lal's son was studying in the US, and he ran to my father's shop to tell him that his son was on the phone—"Please hurry and come!"

When my father heard this, he immediately sent a message to my mother that I was on the phone at the post office. "Come in a hurry," he urged. My parents ran to the post office. At the same time, our neighbors next to the shop also ran, passing the news along that there was a phone call from America. Around twenty-five people gathered at the post office to hear my voice. I could hear my father saying "Hello, hello," and I answered, saying, "Hello, hello. *Pari pana*," meaning "touching your feet," a gesture of respect in Indian culture used when greeting an elderly person on the phone. That was all I could say and all I could hear due to the poor connection and the voice delay. Still my heart jumped with excitement when I heard my father's voice. The connection was not clear, and I strained to hear him through the phone's static.

"Krishan, our neighbor's son, Bhushan, wants to talk to you," my father said. The battery to the post office telephone was going low, and when he handed the phone to Bhushan, all I could hear was "Hello, hello," before the connection became fuzzy and I could only hear static and faint noises in the background. I slumped back in my chair, frustrated that I could not talk to my mother. It was 3:00 a.m.

Meanwhile, the man at the post office suggested to my parents that if they were willing to travel to Mandi Ahmed Garh, the connection would be clearer, and they would be able to hear me better. The operator from Mandi Ahmed Garh was still on the line and could hear what was going on. He relayed the message to Ludhiana's operator, who told New Delhi's operator, who repeated it to the operator in New Jersey. "Will you wait for your parents to travel to Mandi Ahmed Garh?" the New Jersey operator asked me.

"Yes, I will wait."

Even though Mandi Ahmed Garh is only fourteen miles away from Malaudh, I knew it would take my parents about forty minutes to reach the town by bus. Later, I learned that someone offered to take them on his scooter.

An hour later, the New Jersey operator called. "Let's try the connection now," she said.

Putting me on hold, she repeated the long process of getting through to the New Delhi, Ludhiana, and Mandi Ahmed Garh operators. Finally, they reached Mandi Ahmed Garh. When the line connected, I could hear many voices clamoring in the background. Besides my parents, there must have been ten to fifteen people from Malaudh crowding around the phone, anxious to hear my voice.

"Hello," "Hello," my father and I said at the same time. Because of the five second voice delay, we continued to talk over each other. Even still, I was happy that I could hear my father, and then finally, my mother. We didn't say much, just kept repeating hello and simple greetings. *"Pari pana,"* I said to her, and my mother showered blessings on me.

"You stay happy and healthy, and may God give you lots of money." Then my mother said in a heavy voice, "Krishan, when are you coming back? It has been eight years that I have not seen you."

She started crying, and hearing her, I felt the tears in my own heart. "Soon," I replied. "In a few months, once I get my visa."

"Your three minutes are up," the operator interrupted. "Do you want an extension?"

"Yes, yes," I said quickly.

My father and I said "Hello," "Hello" again, but before I could get another word in, my father said, "Here is someone who wants to say hello to you."

The other people wanted to hear my voice, and while I said "Hello" to each of these people, I kept thinking, *I have made the call to talk to my father and mother, and here the whole neighborhood has come to say hello.* After spending so much money—seven dollars for the first three minutes and two dollars per minute after that—I felt I should get to talk to my parents more.

After nine minutes, the maximum two extensions, the operator cut me off. I went to bed and stayed awake the whole night thinking about my parents and visualizing the scene at the post office and the Mandi Ahmed Garh exchange. It made me laugh, knowing my parents would give the phone to the neighbors, and I felt good after hearing their voices. However, I did not try calling my parents often after that. The battery at the post office was always low, and calling was a long and tedious process—staying up late all those nights waiting for a connection, and my parents needing to travel to Mandi Ahmed Garh on someone else's scooter.

The year 1970 brought about several major changes in my life. With the help of Professor Buchan, I landed a job earning $15,000 per year at a 450-bed hospital in Covington, Kentucky. As the director of management engineering at St. Elizabeth Hospital, my career took a turn for the better. Mr. Gilreath, the hospital administrator, showed me a great deal of respect. I was more than happy to leave my job at Vanderbilt University Hospital and my apartment at the Executive House. Relieved to be out from under the watchful eyes of Mrs. Olsen and Maelie, I did not stay in touch with them. I looked forward to this new chapter in my life.

My first day was more than I could have asked for or imagined.

"Welcome to St. Elizabeth Hospital, Mr. Bedi," Mr. Gilreath said when I arrived at his office. He grinned and shook my hand with a strong, enthusiastic grip. At once, he threw an arm around my shoulder and led me along the hallway and down the stairs. "We've got your office all ready for you. You've got your own secretary too, by the way." I was moments into my first day, and it couldn't be going any better.

The office was good-sized with an oak desk and matching chair. As we entered, a girl stood to greet us, flashing a pleasant smile.

"Mr. Bedi, this is Susan Moore, your secretary," Mr. Gilreath said. "She is an English major at Thames Moore College in Crestview Hills, Kentucky, seven miles from here."

As I shook her hand, I smiled to myself, knowing I would have many reports for her to type up and proofread. Already I could see I would get much more done here than at the previous hospital. Nodding at Susan politely, I followed Mr. Gilreath back to his office.

At nine o'clock, Mr. Gilreath called a meeting in the board conference room next to his office. He ordered donuts, coffee, and orange juice for the thirty department heads and administrative staff members filing into the room to greet me. The room contained only twelve to fourteen seats, so many of the managers stood. I sat next to Mr. Gilreath, drinking my coffee and smiling politely while Mr. Gilreath addressed the room.

"Mr. Bedi is from India and has studied at the University of Tennessee in Knoxville, where he received his master's degree in industrial engineering," he began. "He has work experience at the Vanderbilt University Hospital in Nashville. Today he is starting his position as director of management engineering, and he will be reporting to me. I ask all of you to extend your cooperation and help Mr. Bedi with whatever he needs to know."

During that time, not many people could say they were experienced in management engineering in the healthcare field. After all the studying and working dozens of jobs to pay for school, I felt I should enjoy the attention. I had driven all night and reached my new apartment at 4:30 a.m., only sleeping for a few hours in my car. Now I wished I had arrived the day before so I could feel more rested for my first day. Even though I was tired, I made an extra effort to show how happy I was to be there.

After the reception, I followed Mr. Gilreath around the hospital while he explained its organization and his vision for the facility. I admired his eye for improvement and his determination to make changes. His confidence in my skills and knowledge gave me a renewed sense of purpose.

❖ ❖ ❖

One late evening, while drinking hot tea after work and walking around in my undershirt and underwear, I heard a knock on the door. *Who could this be?* I wondered. *I just moved here, and I don't know anyone.* Another knock sounded, and still in my underwear, I opened the door.

"Hi there," said the tall, broad-shouldered man with a friendly face. "My name is Bob Vanherpe. I'm here to invite you to a get-together at my place this Saturday night."

For a moment I just looked at him. *I don't know anybody here,* I thought. *He must have the wrong apartment.*

"You are trying to invite me?" I asked. "Are you sure you are not at the wrong door?"

"Oh no," he said. "Are you Kris? You just moved in?"

"Yes, I am."

"I am inviting you Saturday evening for beer and snacks," he repeated. "The apartment complex manager told me you just moved here from Nashville."

Pleasantly surprised, I invited him in for a beer.

"Sure," he said, walking in while I pulled on my pants. When I opened the refrigerator, I found there was only one can of beer.

"You can have it," I offered.

"Oh no, we will share," he insisted.

I popped the tab, and we each drank half the beer.

As I set the empty can on the counter, Bob said, "Why don't you come to my place for a beer if you are not busy this evening?"

"Sounds great," I said, not having anything better to do.

At his apartment, Bob introduced me to his girlfriend, Evie, who lived with him and worked as a registered nurse in Cincinnati.

"She is from a small town near Lexington, Kentucky, farther south of here," Bob told me. He affected a thick southern accent, and said, "She's my hillbilly."

Evie groaned and rolled her eyes. "He's always making fun of my accent," she said. "Nice to meet you, Kris."

It was the beginning of a great friendship. We both enjoyed social outings and drinking beer with friends. I liked to try new things and meet new people, and as the weeks went by, Bob enjoyed bringing me with him everywhere he went and introducing me to everyone he knew.

Almost every day at around 4:30 p.m., Bob would call and say, "Hey, Kris, what's going on?" Somehow he would convince me to meet him at the Press Club, the local bar, for a cold beer. One or two people always met us at the bar, and they would buy a round. I was a novelty that Bob wanted to show off to all his friends, the "new kid on the block."

Sometimes on the weekends, Bob and I would go to the local brewery, Hudepohl Brewing Company in Cincinnati, and buy half a keg of beer. Bob knew everyone in the sales office there and introduced me to them. A keg, about fifteen gallons, cost thirty-eight dollars, and lasted the entire weekend and sometimes into the week.

One Sunday afternoon in late June 1970, I went to Bob's place for a social gathering. As people arrived, I poured beer into cups from the keg tap and handed it to them. Bob had bought the keg on Friday and kept the beer iced so it would stay cold. There were about ten or twelve people standing in Bob's living room. George, a state senator, sipped his beer and watched me out of the corner of his eye. I had met George at Bob's place a while back, and he knew I was from India and was close friends with Bob. It seemed he did not like me as much as everyone else did.

"Hey Kris," he said as I poured another beer for one of Bob's friends. "The beer tastes flat."

A complete silence fell over the room. Everyone watched me to see what I would say. George looked at me with a challenging expression.

Turning around, I replied, "George, how can a free beer be flat? It is cold, it is free, and someone is serving you. How can it be flat?"

Everyone laughed and looked at George. He looked embarrassed and didn't know how to respond to my remark. Later, he tried to make a comeback.

"Hey Kris, can I ask you a question?" he said.

"Sure," I replied. "It's a free country."

Other people were listening with interest. Knowing this and hoping he would embarrass me this time, George asked, "Is it safe to go to India?"

"Hell, no," I exclaimed. "The moment you get off the plane you will find people with knives, swords, and guns slaughtering each other and then coming at you!" I imitated the high-pitched noise an American Indian would make by clapping my hand back and forth over my mouth.

Now everyone was listening.

"George, you don't need to go to India to look for trouble," I said. "Just go to the northern part of Covington, Kentucky, and there you'll find it."

Everyone laughed and stared at George for asking such a question. Bob, happy with my comeback, raised his cup of beer to me while everyone resumed their conversations. This story was told many times to newcomers to Bob's apartment, and no one ever dared to say the beer was flat again, even if it was.

✤ ✤ ✤

I loved my new job, and most of all, I liked my new boss. He was a man to be respected, and I felt honored to report to him. For my first project, Mr. Gilreath asked me to evaluate the laundry equipment for a replacement plan to meet the demand for clean linen supplies and to provide timely service. The flatwork ironer needed constant repair and was causing an overflow of laundry needing ironing, meaning more overtime pay to the staff.

At the end of June 1970, Mr. Gilreath invited me to attend the annual convention for the American College of Hospital Administrators (ACHA) in Houston, Texas, along with the other hospital administrative staff and their wives. Once we reached Houston, I flipped through the telephone directory to find an Indian to call, preferably a Singh since there were quite a few of them in the US at the time. If he were willing, perhaps he could show us around Houston. To an American, making such a request to a stranger, even a fellow countryman, would seem odd. At the time, this was my way of doing things.

I contacted Mohinder Singh and told him who I was, that I was from Punjab and was in Houston for a conference. I mentioned that several members of the administrative team and their wives wanted to explore the night life in Houston. Mr. Gilreath could not go with us because of a meeting, but he told us to have a good time.

Mohinder agreed, and he picked us up at our hotel.

"Would you like to go to the Body Shop?" he asked everyone.

"Sounds good," we all replied, having no idea what a Body Shop was.

It turned out the Body Shop was a bar, and not an ordinary type of bar either.

Not long after we sat down and ordered drinks, several girls wearing bikini tops and G-strings came to our table. Everyone's eyes widened, and the wives stared at each other in shock. We didn't know what to do. We couldn't leave after already ordering drinks. One of the girls set a container of brushes and some paints on the table. Apparently, we were supposed to paint the girls' bodies. The wives of the older gentlemen were fuming.

Walter, the Director of Finances, however, was having a good time. He picked up a paintbrush and began painting one of the girls. The other girl eyed us seductively. "Anyone else want to give it a go?" she offered. The older man's wife kept shooting him angry stares. Mrs. Gilreath, sitting next to me, thought it was the funniest thing, and neither of us could stop laughing at the shocked looks on the older ladies' faces. Mo sipped his beer, smiled, and nodded at us, seeming oblivious to the tension between the women.

A few nights later, while Mr. Gilreath was getting his ACHA certification, I stood in line with Mrs. Gilreath for a steak dinner and rodeo show. We wore name tags on our wrists, and as we handed our tickets to the woman sitting at the ticket table, she looked at Mrs. Gilreath and asked, "Where is Mr. Gilreath?"

Mrs. Gilreath gestured to me and said, "I am with him."

The lady glanced at my name tag, which clearly said, "Krishan Bedi."

Mrs. Gilreath repeated with a smile, "I'm with him." Then, linking her arm through mine, she gave a little laugh.

The lady looked confused and finally threw her hands up in the air. "Whatever you say, honey. If it's okay with you, it's okay with me!" Mrs. Gilreath and I grinned at the lady's reaction, and I was amused that Mrs. Gilreath was so comfortable with the notion.

Once back in Covington, Walter Albrink talked constantly about Mo and the Body Shop and the "good time" he gave us. Everyone had plenty of laughs from that week in Houston and thanked me for finding Mo.

Chapter 12

In August 1970, I received my green card, the permanent residency visa I applied for while I was at the Vanderbilt University Hospital. I wrote to my parents right away: "I am making plans to come to India in a few weeks," I said. "Please start looking for a suitable girl."

My parents wrote back immediately, overjoyed to know I was finally coming. They said that once I arrived they would put an ad in the *Tribune* regarding a suitable girl.

I wrote back that I would not have that much time, so they should have the ad prepared by my brother-in-law, Vijay Kaura, and put it in the newspaper before my arrival so the girls' parents could send their biodatas, which were a simple description of the girl's personal and family background. Then my father could go through the biodatas and pick the ones most suitable for us. Once I arrived in India, we would send my biodata to the parents of the most suitable girls and go from there.

My father liked the idea. He and my brother-in-law prepared the ad. It said: "We require suitable match for handsome, smart Kshatriya boy. Master's degree from the US, good-paying job as director. Girl should be educated, willing to travel to US, from a respectable family. Send biodata to P.O. Box XYX *Tribune*."

While my excitement grew, Mr. Gilreath called me to his office to let me know he felt uneasy that I would be taking time off so soon. He wanted to know if I would be submitting my final report and recommendations for the laundry study before leaving. I assured him I would.

Not knowing if he approved of my leaving three months after joining his hospital had weighed on my mind. Mr. Gilreath indicated as long as I finished the laundry project, he was fine with my taking time off. In the end, my report showed a savings of $40,000 per year in the processing of laundry following my recommendations. Mr. Gilreath was pleased with the results.

The list of items to take to India grew long as my departure date approached. The general impression in India was that money hangs on the trees in the US. You just shake the tree and gather the fallen money. Through my letters, I communicated that this was not the case. But the perception of easy money in the US was so strong that if I did convince my relatives that I didn't have this kind of money, they would say I might not have found the right tree. People would say that so-and-so has sent lakhs (hundreds of thousands) of rupees, and so-and-so has constructed a huge house with money sent by his son in the US. True, there are such cases where some Indians in the US might have sent significant amounts of money, but people in India do not know what kind of lifestyle those Indians are living in the US.

Although I tried to convince my parents that money didn't fall from trees, I did not want to give them the impression that I did not have any money. Because I had worked for almost two years after receiving my degree, I should have saved plenty of money. In reality, I did not put money in my savings account, although I was living a good life with a good-paying, respectable job, nice clothes, a good place to live, and a healthy social life. I justified to myself that although I did not save much money, I had worked hard during all those summer jobs and the tough first year at UT. I deserved to live a good life. I wasn't spending lavishly or throwing money away on foolish items, but I was living comfortably, and that much I thought I deserved.

Included in the list of items, my parents asked me to bring clothing for my nieces and nephews. My father wrote, asking for a two-in-one, which was popular in the seventies because it was a radio that also contained a tape recorder. One day I received another letter from my father, stating, "Please purchase a .32 caliber Smith and Wesson revolver for your brother. It is popular item among a somewhat elite group of people."

Not thinking much of it, I left the letter on the table and went about my usual business. Then my brother pleaded again through my father's letter: "Your brother says he has not asked for anything. This is only one thing. He would be very happy to have it."

Ever since my brother was a young boy, he had the ability to convince my parents to get him whatever he wanted. On the other hand, if I wanted something, it didn't matter how small or large, there was always a big discussion about the matter, and then my brother must also give the okay. It took almost two years to convince my father to buy me a bicycle. I started asking for it in the beginning of ninth grade, and finally, my father purchased it right before I finished tenth grade.

It seemed my brother would get his way once again. Even my mother pleaded, saying, "Krishan, do bring the revolver for your brother."

I could not say no to my mother.

That night, I talked to Bob about buying a revolver. He knew all about guns, and he couldn't wait to help me pick one out. In the end, we chose a .32 caliber Smith and Wesson snub nose with a wooden handle for $90, as well as a cartridge box for $8.50.

Shortly before my departure date, I bought and shipped a refrigerator and air conditioner to my parents. Although $650 was the most I had ever spent on any purchase at one time, I told myself that these items would be long lasting and would give my parents comfort during the sweltering hot summer months. In addition to purchasing items for my family, I purchased most of the items that my parents requested on behalf of family members. However, with all the demands I received, my mother did not ask for anything. Her message was simple: "Krishan, just come home. You have been away from me for nine years. I just want to see you, hold you close to me, and hug you for a long time."

❋ ❋ ❋

My flight arrived in New Delhi on September 28, a day later than expected. My family members, who had been waiting for me so eagerly, finally returned home thinking something terrible must have happened to me. I called them from a payphone as soon as I got off the plane, and my parents and two uncles rushed to meet me. My parents paid the excise duty of sixteen hundred rupees for the gift items I brought, but unfortunately, customs confiscated my brother's revolver because I did not have an Indian Arms License.

The moment I passed through customs, I bent to touch the feet of my parents and uncles. They all stopped me right before I reached their feet and said, "No Krishan, it is okay." My mother and father placed garlands of marigold flowers around my neck and hugged me, joyful tears etching their faces. Before we got into the taxi, my mother attached garlands to the front and back of the car so everyone in India would know we were celebrating. Then, she hugged me tightly once more for a long time.

That night, we stayed in New Delhi with my cousin Ved, and the next morning, our taxi bumped along the road toward Malaudh. I sat squished between my mother and uncle. My mother held my arm tightly, her head resting on my shoulder, and every few minutes she would look up at my face as though she couldn't believe I was really there.

As we approached the outskirts of Malaudh, I could see the area had been expanded with more shops, and the dirt road had been paved. It just so happened there was a wedding celebration in Malaudh that same night. A band stood outside with their instruments, waiting to go in and play for the gathering of people. They saw the taxi coming toward them, and knowing that Mukandi Lal's son was returning soon, they realized it must be me. The men jubilantly began playing their instruments, walking in front of us while we drove down the street. Hearing the music, the guests came out of the house to see what was going on. There were not many cars in Malaudh, so the people usually became anxious whenever one came to the village. I rolled down my window as people pointed at us, talking in excited voices. Kids ran out into the street to get a closer look, and they followed behind the car.

"Krishan! Krishan!" voices shouted. In the week since I'd notified my parents of my arrival date, the news had spread quickly through the town. The whole village of Malaudh waited in anticipation of my return. Now that I was finally there, the excitement spread like wildfire. A crowd of people lined the streets to watch me. Children continued to follow behind us, yelling excitedly. The taxi driver stopped in front of my father's shop, and we all clambered out of the car, stiff from hours of sitting. The band continued playing joyful music as more than fifty people surrounded us, clapping and watching me with big smiles on their faces.

Hearing all the noise, my brother rushed out of the shop. The moment he saw me, he ran and gave me a hug. Others drew closer, some to look at me, some to greet me with hugs. My brother placed garlands around my neck, grinning at me and the commotion around us. My chest was bursting with joy. After nine years of hard work, I had returned to Malaudh a successful man with a degree and a respectable, well-paying job.

My parents' faces beamed with joy and pride. I had never seen my father so happy, and my mother smiled through her tears. My brother brought sweets outside, and we distributed them to the people crowded around me. From all sides people hugged me, shook my hand, or patted me on the back, saying, "Welcome home."

❀ ❀ ❀

So much was the same here in Malaudh, and for once it was comforting, even though it felt like a culture shock to be back in my own country after adapting to the US lifestyle. I spent my first few days back in Punjab getting accustomed to the slower pace of life and not having all the amenities readily available as in the US. One day, I helped my father in the cloth shop, folding fabrics and bringing tea or lemonade to the customers.

Instead of the traditional white pajamas, I wore a long-sleeved shirt and a pair of regular pants. The people from the villages said to my father, "Has your son come back from a foreign country?" They could tell by my clothing and my light skin unused to the omnipresent sun. My father grinned proudly and said, "Yes, he has come from Amrika after nine years."

"Very good," they said, looking at me approvingly and imagining the load of money I must have brought.

During my first few days in Malaudh, my father gave me a stack of one rupee and two rupee notes. He was so happy to have me back that he continually gave me money to give to the poor and well-wishers.

Close to thirty girls answered the ad about me that appeared in the *Tribune*, an English newspaper in Punjab. My father, brother, and two brothers-in-law helped me select fifteen suitable girls to send detailed responses to, giving my qualifications such as height and weight, appearance, job title, and my family background.

Based upon these details, almost all the parents responded, asking to meet me. My parents did not own a phone, so we corresponded solely through letters. The process was taking too long, but it was out of my hands, so I tried not to get frustrated. After we met each girl and her parents, my father and I told them we would think it through and discuss the matter with my mother. Then we would contact them at a later date.

A few meetings did not go as planned. One day, while my father and I waited at a restaurant for a girl and her father, the father showed up fifteen minutes late without his daughter. "I am not sure why my daughter is not here yet," the girl's father said. "She is coming from out of town and said she would be here. Would you like to reschedule the meeting?"

"This will not be appropriate," my father explained. The girl's behavior was insulting. "Krishan will be in India for a short time, and he is planning to go back in two or three weeks. It would not work to reschedule."

The girl must have been reluctant to come, I thought to myself. My time in India was short, and I needed to keep moving forward.

On another occasion, a girl's parents invited us to a luncheon at their house in Ludhiana. We managed to reach their house on time, despite the difficulty of locating it in an area with no street names. After some conversation in the drawing room, the father stated that his daughter was taking the train from Bhatinda, and the train was late. "Let us start lunch," he said. "She will arrive any minute."

An hour later, the girl had still not arrived. The parents seemed shocked, not knowing why their daughter did not come. My father and I felt our time had been wasted, and I suspected the girl might have a boyfriend her parents were not aware of. Dating was not common, but people did meet secretively.

On our way back to Malaudh I told my father not to be disappointed. If we did not find a suitable girl, I would come back the following year. He frowned, displeased with my statement.

When five weeks had passed, I told my parents that I might have to go back soon because I had taken leave from work for only six weeks. My parents were frightened that I might go back alone. They had been fortunate that in the last nine years I had not married an American girl, which was unusual for being in the US so long. *If I go back now,* I thought, *who knows what might happen?*

In the meantime, my brother-in-law Vijay Kaura told a family in Patiala about me. They were good friends with my father and thought it would be a good idea to approach my father and me about a relationship with their daughter. The family was well-respected in Patiala and well-to-do financially. Vijay felt good about a relationship maturing with them.

My father and I arrived in Patiala at 8:00 p.m. The family lived in a huge, two-story house. Since the late October weather was not too hot, we all sat in the courtyard. The girl's father served us Johnnie Walker Black Label scotch, not commonly available in India except among affluent families. I drank it with delight while the girl's younger sister sang songs for us. After a couple of drinks, we all felt good, and the courtyard transformed into a festive environment. We feasted on *pakoras*, enjoying the savory fritters of vegetable dipped in spicy chickpea batter, and everyone laughed, told stories, listened to songs recited by the girl's sister, and did their best to entertain me. I was impressed by this family and enjoyed myself immensely.

After drinks and snacks, the girl joined us for dinner. I tried to catch discreet glimpses of her while trying not to stare in front of her parents and sister. She was slightly on the heavy side. It was hard to get a good look at her, and I was not sure, but it seemed she had a crossed eye. I wondered about this and wished I could get a better look at her without the scrutiny of her parents.

It was midnight by the time we finished dinner and dessert. The girl left right after dinner, and her parents looked at me as if to say, "So what do you think?" As usual, I replied, "We will discuss it with my mother once we get back, and then we will let you know."

The situation was tricky. Vijay wanted this relationship to develop since he also lived in Patiala and was close friends with the family. Back at Vijay's house, we discussed the matter of her crossed eye with him. I wanted to see her again, alone, and Vijay felt it sounded appropriate. He agreed to arrange another meeting.

The next day, the girl and I met at the park. My sister Santosh, Vijay, and the girl's mother accompanied us. We sat on a sheet beneath a large shade tree, and this time I felt more comfortable to look at her closely. As I asked basic questions about her education, I could see that one of her eyes was indeed crossed.

How would I settle this matter? I felt great pressure to please both her father, who was a close friend to my father, and Vijay, who acted as the matchmaker. The relationship between my family and my brother-in-law was a delicate one. We must keep him happy, so in return, he would keep my sister happy. I decided to prolong my decision and discuss it further with my parents. Once back in Malaudh, I still did not know what to do.

❀ ❀ ❀

One evening, my father and I traveled to Mandi Gobind-Garh to visit my uncle. We were having a drink and pakoras when a knock sounded on the door at around 8:30 p.m.

"Who could that be this late?" my uncle wondered as he went to the door.

Moments later, he returned. "Krishan, there is a man here to see you," he said. "It is urgent."

Taken aback, I went outside. The man introduced himself as Yash Verma. He had ridden his scooter forty miles from Nabha to Malaudh, and when he learned I was at my uncle's home, he rode another forty-five miles to Mandi Gobind-Garh. Altogether, it was a three-hour journey. He had learned from a relative of Vijay Kaura that I was back from the US for a short stay and was looking for a girl to marry. "I want you to meet my niece," he said. "She is very qualified and well-suited for this relationship."

"What are her qualifications?" I asked.

"She has a master's in zoology, which she has completed with honors at Punjab University in Chandigarh," he replied.

Yash saw the confused look on my face. "It is the study of animals," he explained.

I raised my eyebrows, impressed and intrigued by this girl who completed her studies with honors in such a unique subject.

"We are interested in discussing further a marriage between you and my niece," Yash said. "Would you like to come to Nabha to meet her and the family?"

I agreed to go to Nabha the next day. Happy, Yash got on his scooter and rode off into the dark.

❀ ❀ ❀

The next day, my father and I rode a bus twenty-four miles to Nabha. As soon as my father and I stepped off the bus, Yash Verma and several other relatives came forward to greet us. They had been waiting at their family-owned petrol pump which happened to be right next to the bus station. They ushered us into their car, and the chauffeur drove us to Yash's house, where the rest of the family was waiting to meet me.

As soon as my father and I entered the house, the girl's parents, her brother, and her grandmother crowded around us, offering warm greetings and friendly smiles. When they introduced me to the grandmother, I immediately bowed my head and made a gesture to touch her feet, a customary practice to show respect to the elderly and get their blessings. Later, I learned she approved of me just from this gesture, thinking, *This boy has come from America after so many years and still remembers the Indian culture.*

The family watched us closely as we sat in the drawing room, drinking tea and warm milk, and chatting politely. At two o'clock, we gathered around the table for lunch. The women of the house served a large meal of vegetables, rice pilaf, yogurt, and chapatis. The girl's name was Raj, and she joined us at the table, sitting several places away from me. I tried to talk to her in the presence of her mother, brother, and aunt, but whenever I asked her a question, someone else answered for her. She looked at me a couple of times without much expression, and while I didn't want to stare in front of her mother, I felt pleased with her overall appearance and demeanor.

After about ten minutes, Raj left the table, and everyone else returned to the drawing room. Her father and uncle wanted to know my decision.

"My father and I will discuss the matter with my mother, and we will let you know," I replied.

We shook hands, and her other uncle gave me a big hug, once again impressing me with how friendly and sociable this family was.

When we returned to Malaudh, I told my mother about Raj and her family in Nabha. She was so overjoyed to hear about the girl from Nabha that she couldn't stop smiling and exclaiming how wonderful it was. I did not find out until much later why she was so joyful about the meeting with Raj.

It turned out that my mother already knew about the Nabha family. One day, a customer from the village of Kheri had stopped by my father's shop. He was well-known to our family, and my mother had invited him in for a cup of tea. They got to talking, and the man told her about the Vermas, saying that they had four or five daughters. "This family is well-respected in Nabha," he told her. "And their daughters are well-educated and eligible to be married."

"Oh," my mother had exclaimed. "Why don't you tell this family in Nabha about my son Krishan who will be coming from the States."

"Oh, Mrs. Bedi, that will not be possible," the man said. "This family is too good for your family. Socially and financially, they are better known in the community than your family. It would not be a suitable match."

At these words, my mother felt small and insulted. After the man left, she prayed, "Oh God, somehow bring that family's daughter to our house in Malaudh. Cause a relationship to develop between one of their daughters and Krishan, so that they should be married."

Not knowing these details, I mulled over my options while my mother kept this story to herself, only choosing to tell me about it at the end of my visit.

Days passed as I thought about which girl I should choose. There were many factors to consider, the biggest one being that while I wanted to know more about Raj Verma, I felt pressure to consider the girl from Patiala. What would happen if I chose Raj in the end? My brother-in-law, who had invested so much attention in the match between me and the Patiala girl, would be angry. The father of the girl, also a close friend of my father's, might never want to see us again. The relations involved were a delicate matter to be handled with care.

While I considered my predicament, the Nabha family came to Malaudh to talk to us. "What is your decision?" they wanted to know. "What do we need to do in order to make this happen?"

"I would like to see the girl again," I told them. "This time no big lunch or social gathering, and this time at her house, not her uncle's." They agreed happily.

On the day we arrived at her house, the family insisted we eat a small lunch with them. My father and I sat around the table with Raj and her parents, brother, and grandmother. This time there were no uncles or other family members to watch the ordeal. When we finished lunch, everyone left the table, leaving Raj and me to talk by ourselves, although her mother and grandmother sat barely seven feet away.

Raj looked at me, waiting, and I was at a loss about what to ask. I started by inquiring more about her degree and where she'd earned it.

"I studied at Chandigarh," she said, "where I pursued my interest in science and animals with a master's in zoology."

I remembered a letter sent to me by a professor from Chandigarh. Professor Mehra had expressed an interest in a match between one of his daughters and me. He would be returning from Paris in a couple of weeks and wanted to pursue the matter.

"Do you know Mehra?" I asked, thinking Raj might have taken classes with him.

It seemed that Raj felt there must be some talk going on between the professor and me because she said, "Oh yes, I do know him. He has six daughters, and the ones I have seen are very pretty and well-educated."

Surprised at how quickly she picked up on my connection to the professor, I felt awkward and dumb for mentioning him. It did not seem appropriate to bring up a connection with another man and his daughter to a girl I might someday marry. I did not know what else to say, and we ended the conversation. It lasted about ten to fifteen minutes, and her mother, seeing that we were done, gave Raj an indication to leave. Now, she wanted to know my decision.

"I will need to discuss the matter with my parents first," I said.

Normally, it is the tradition for the parents to advise or make the decision about which girl is the most suitable to marry. But in my case, I had studied abroad, finally returning after nine long years, and my parents wanted me to have the final say.

One night, while staying in New Delhi with Ved and his wife, I explained my predicament in great detail, speaking openly and honestly with them.

"On one side," I told them, "it is my father's close friend and distant relative, whose daughter I saw twice, a girl who is a little on the heavy side with one crossed eye. On the other side, it is Raj, who seems very intelligent and good-looking, having a master's with honors in zoology, who comes from a good family, and whose sisters and brother are well educated."

Ved's wife advised me, "Krishan, you should do what your heart tells you to do. *You're* the one getting married, and it's *your* life, and *you're* going to live with her, and it's *you* who will take her back to the US."

I thought it over. What would my friends in the US and my boss, Mr. Gilreath, say if I married the girl from Patiala? I imagined them saying, "Kris, is that the girl you went there for?" I didn't feel comfortable with this thought and realized, as my cousin's wife said, I must please myself and go with the decision that made me the most comfortable.

After thinking it through, I said, "I am leaning toward the girl in Nabha."

My cousin's wife smiled at me and said joyfully, "Go for it with great confidence."

Chapter 13

Since I was back in India after such a long time away, I was particular about going through all the marriage traditions, even though time was running short. During the first week of November, I sent Mr. Gilreath a letter stating: "I have taken six weeks time off, and it is already six weeks that I have been here. I hope you will understand it is a matter of my lifetime companion, so it is taking a little longer than I anticipated. Please grant me a little longer—another three weeks' leave. I will appreciate it very much, and I will also keep you informed with the progress of finding a suitable girl in India."

With my request for an extended leave settled, we turned our attention to choosing the best engagement and wedding dates in line with the astrological signs. However, while we were staying with my sister in Patiala, my uncle brought a halt to our planning stage by raising an issue.

"This girl must be older than they are saying," he said. "We are told she is twenty-three, but if she completed her master's in 1967, based upon my calculations, she should be closer to twenty-four or twenty-five."

We all paused to think about this. It was normal for girls to get married in their early twenties, and twenty-four seemed to be the cut-off age. A girl of twenty-five was considered rather old to be unmarried.

I sighed. Now my marriage process would take even longer. In the Indian tradition, if any elder, such as an uncle or an aunt, brought up a point or made a suggestion, it must be taken seriously.

To uncover the truth of the matter, we contacted the Verma family and asked to see Raj's matriculation certificate. To our dismay, they said they could not find it. We insisted they find it as soon as possible because normally all the documents should be there, and we needed to see her certificate.

That night at my sister's house, we all went to bed early because her children needed to get up for school the next morning. At around 10:30 p.m., a knock sounded on the door. *Who could it be at this time of night?* My brother-in-law picked up a large hockey stick and went to the door. Annoyed at being disturbed at such a late hour, he opened the door to find Yash, Raj's brother Satish, and her other uncle standing outside.

"We want to talk to Krishan," they said.

Hearing this, I came into the room. My brother-in-law let them inside, and we all sat in the drawing room. My brother-in-law sat in the corner of the room with his hockey stick, and glared at the three men from Nabha.

Turning to me, Yash said, "Whatever we are telling you about age, that's what it is, and we cannot locate the matriculation certificate, so it is up to you whether or not to continue this relation and set a date for the engagement."

I was taken aback. My father was staying at my uncle's house, forcing me to make the decision on my own. In that moment, all that mattered to me was that I liked the girl, and I liked her family. I felt sure she was a good match for me.

"It's okay with me," I told them. "I do not want to call off the relationship."

They asked me again, not wanting to have any doubt about the matter.

"Yes, I am ready to finalize the marriage," I said.

Relieved, the three men stood up to leave.

"Do you want tea or anything to eat," I asked.

"No," they said, glancing nervously at my brother-in-law in the corner. Still clutching the hockey stick, he watched them with an angry expression. Later, Raj's brother told me that the whole time they were there, he was afraid somebody was going to get hit with that stick.

Shortly after our late-night meeting, we set the engagement date for November 18 and the wedding date for November 26.

❋ ❋ ❋

A few days before the wedding, my mother and several ladies carried a clay pitcher of water and walked around the village at around ten o'clock at night, singing traditional wedding songs, such as, "Jaggo Aiya," meaning, "Wake up people! The wedding celebration has started."

The day before the wedding, several female relatives applied turmeric and sandalwood paste to my body. My relatives from villages far and near began to arrive for the *sehra bandi* ceremony. The house bustled with people greeting each other, setting down luggage, giving me hugs, wishing me the best for my big day, and drinking tea. Cooks hired by my father prepared large quantities of food on makeshift stoves set up in the courtyard near the kitchen. Amid all the excitement, my nerves were on edge. Soon I would be a married man. How different my life would be!

After dinner, the sehra bandi ceremony began. I sat on the floor while my father and brother tied an orange turban around my head, and around the turban, they tied a veil of small golden flowers which draped in front of my face like a curtain. Around my neck, they placed a garland of shiny silver tinsel. My relatives approached me one by one and presented me with *shagun*, cash money placed in envelopes or small cloth pouches to wish me good luck and blessings. At the end of the ceremony, someone read a poem, and everyone shared a prayer that all would go well with the wedding and the future of the bride and groom.

After the ceremony, my brother helped me get on the horse, decorated with gold and silver-colored artificial jewelry that made a jingling sound when it walked. Orange marigold garlands hung around its neck. A band began to play, and they walked in front of our procession. Children followed them, skipping and dancing to the music. I followed behind on my horse, and my relatives walked behind me. The villagers of Malaudh came out of their houses and shops to watch us pass by. My parents and relatives waved money over me and dropped it for the poor people to pick up. The villagers scrambled to retrieve the coins, calling out blessings for my future marriage as we passed.

The next day was a whirl of nonstop activity. After we arrived in Nabha, followed by a busload of more than fifty of my relatives and guests, the *baraat*, we spent most of the day partaking of an endless array of snacks and drinks provided by the Verma family. Then, at around 8:00 p.m., the local band escorted us to the park where the wedding would be held. Once again, I rode on a mare decorated with garlands and jewelry, sparkling golden and silver even in the dark of night. The groom riding a mare to the bride's home symbolizes that he is a warrior coming to take his bride. I carried a sword on my left side, a sign that I would always protect her.

On either side of me, servants held kerosene lamps, and in front of me, a dozen boys did the *bhangra* dance to the rhythm of a *dhol* (drum). The band played old Hindi songs from the most popular Hindi movies. All the while, my horse moved slowly forward. My brother, uncles, and other relatives danced around me, waving money over my head and throwing it on the ground or giving it to the dhol player and the bandleader. In this manner, we proceeded slowly, covering barely one-sixth of a mile in an hour. Many spectators came out of their houses to watch.

Standing at the entrance of the park, the Verma family eagerly awaited our arrival, but our baraat took its time. This was my baraat's only chance to celebrate with me and have a good time. Also, it was customary to keep the bride and her family waiting anxiously. Everyone sang, danced, and shouted with great enthusiasm and joy. In a way, my feelings were similar to what I felt when I left India for the first time nine years earlier. As I stood on the boat pulling away from the dock in Bombay, I realized, with an overwhelming sense of gratitude and excitement, that my dreams were truly in motion, my many days of prayer and preparation had come to fruition, and the long-awaited day had arrived.

This same feeling washed over me as I sat on the mare and allowed myself to be escorted with much fanfare to the entrance of the park. I had spent many days in search of a suitable match, and before that, I waited many years until I could return home to find a girl to marry.

The moon gleamed above me in the dark sky, and for a moment, I felt as if it were reflecting its light in my heart. The stars were lovely, and at first I thought they must have come down from the sky, because as we came to the entrance of the park, I saw that all the bushes and trees flickered with thousands of lights. Hundreds of fresh marigolds and roses decorated the entrance, and on each side stood tall banana trees.

The procession stopped at the entrance, and the band played even more vigorously. The boys danced and twirled until someone put a stop to it so we could start the *milni* ceremony. My father and Raj's father exchanged garlands while the priest said a prayer. Then Raj's father presented my father with a gift of suit-length material and a strip of wool material. It is hard to keep several hundred people quiet, but the noise level was at its lowest since we set out.

One by one, my uncles went forward to meet the bride's uncles, followed by the maternal uncles, and then finally, the brother-in-laws, and any other elderly male considered to be a close relative on the groom's side.

Once Raj's relatives had been escorted into a huge white pavilion, I stood in front of a couch and waited as Raj walked toward me, flanked by her sisters on both sides. Raj wore a beautiful red sari embroidered with gold, and a veil hid her face from the view of my male relatives. Gold jewelry adorned her wrists, red *choora* bangles decorated her arms, and long gold earrings dangled from her ears. In her left nostril, she wore a gold *nath*, a nose ring, which was hooked to her earring. She wore a glittering gold necklace studded with diamonds, and silver ankle bracelets, and intricate henna designs decorated her hands, arms, and feet. I could not take my eyes off her for a moment. It was a sight that I will never forget. Raj looked just beautiful in her wedding sari and jewelry.

Raj stood next to me, her eyes lowered as everyone smiled, admiring her beauty. The *jaimala* ceremony was a difficult moment for Raj because it meant she would be leaving her parents. The priest came forward and said a few prayers in Sanskrit. Then, he handed Raj and me each a garland of fresh marigolds, and while the priest said more prayers, Raj and I placed the garlands around each other's necks to signify our acceptance of each other. The people surrounding us cheered and clapped, calling out wishes of good luck and making all sorts of noise. With jaimala finished, we sat on the couch so the relatives could give us gifts of shagun money.

After an elaborate meal, the processional band led my baraat and me back to the guest house, playing jubilant music. This time I did not ride on the horse, and we all reached the building in much less time. The baraat members fixed their bedding and went to sleep, but my close relatives and I prepared to stay awake. The *phere* ceremony, the most important ceremony of all, would begin at 2:00 a.m., the time determined by the priest.

Raj and I sat side by side on two cushions in the courtyard of her house, our legs crossed. I could only imagine what was going through her head. She was about to marry a stranger, one she would travel across the ocean and live with in a foreign country. Her face was composed, graceful. The *mandap* we sat beneath was a type of canopy with a net covering four pillars decorated with banana trees and flowers.

The priest from Malaudh and the priest from Nabha were taking turns reciting prayers in Sanskrit. Our parents and relatives sat on the ground, forming a circle around the mandap.

One of the priests lit the sacred fire in the middle of the mandap. Raj and I poured ghee into the sacred fire and dropped fresh flower petals, shavings of coconut, and rice into the flames. After the priest dabbed red vermillion paste onto our foreheads for good luck, the Nabha priest performed the *kanyadaan*, the giving away of the bride. Raj's father placed her right hand into mine, asking that I pledge my enduring love and dedication in caring for his daughter. At that moment, Raj's father was overcome with tears, and her mother, sisters, brothers, aunts, and uncles grew teary-eyed as well. Raj's eyes filled as she tried not to cry at this most crucial moment of the ceremony. My heart went out to Raj and her family, understanding how hard it is to leave one's family to go to an unknown place and live with an unknown person. We both were wondering what our lives would be like and what the nature of the other person would be.

The priest recited more prayers and asked Raj to place her right foot on a stone. He gestured for me to say my part, and I told her to be as firm as a stone so that we could face the difficulties of life together.

Guided by the priests, Raj and I performed ceremony after ceremony for the next three hours. Raj and I struggled to stay awake as the priests recited prayers for everything that could be thought of. At five o'clock, the priests ended the phere, and Raj and I were officially a married couple. It was a somber moment compared to the festive atmosphere of the night before. Everyone was half asleep, and someone shook my brother awake to let him know it was over.

Unfortunately for me, when we returned to the guest house, there was no time for sleep; I needed to freshen up for the day because the members of the baraat were already waking up to bathe and get ready for breakfast provided by Raj's family.

❁ ❁ ❁

A few hours later, I stood with Raj in front of her house. Women were chanting songs in tearful voices. Amid the clamor of Raj's family and friends crowding around her to say goodbye, I caught one of the lines the women repeated over and over as Raj's parents, sisters, and older brother said their goodbyes. "Our daughter is leaving. Her parents took care of her and loved her before she left the house."

Servants were bustling in and out of the crowd, carrying trays laden with tea and sweets.

Raj's eyes filled with tears as she and her parents embraced one final time. After Raj and I touched the feet of her elder family members (parents, grandmother, aunts, and uncles) to receive their blessings, I led Raj to the car decorated with orange, red, and white flower garlands. Fastened to the back window, a sign read, "Krishan weds Raj."

Raj's brother escorted her into the seat next to me, a gesture that signified, "I am giving you away to your husband. He should take care of you."

Raj shook with sobs. Close to fifty of her relatives pressed in close around the car, crying loudly and calling out farewells. The local band began to play jubilant music which strangely contrasted with the sadness of the moment, and as the band escorted us to the outskirts of Nabha, the noise of the relatives followed us until everyone dropped back to watch us go. A few minutes later, the car left Nabha, and the band waved after us, leaving Raj and me in a sudden silence.

I will love Raj and take care of her the best I can, I thought to myself. *I will make her happy and will never give her a reason to cry.*

When we reached my parents' house in Malaudh an hour later, there were more ceremonies to perform, each of which a held special meaning for the groom to bring the bride to his parents' house for the first time. Then, for the remainder of the day and night, everyone ate and drank. Since nothing was planned ahead, there was much confusion as everyone jostled each other and the cooks hurried to finish the food preparation. At 9:30

p.m., the servants served a huge meal. I ate with my male family members at one end of the room, while Raj ate at the other end surrounded by my mother, sisters, and aunts. Although I enjoyed the conversations and laughter with my relatives, I couldn't wait to go to bed. I could tell Raj felt the same way.

It was nearly midnight by the time I said goodbye to my relatives and climbed to the roof, entering a room containing two beds. Raj was already in bed with her eyes closed. She had changed out of her wedding sari and was buried under the covers since it was cold and there was no heat in the room. Going to the other bed, I lay still for fifteen minutes, wondering if she was still awake.

"Raj?" I said after a while.

"*Gee,*" she replied, using the respectful form of yes.

Moving to her bed, I took off the gold ring my parents had given me and held it out. "This ring is for you, a token of my love for you," I said. My initials were carved on the outside.

She took the ring and, smiling slightly, put it on her finger. Then, exhausted from the long two days of countless ceremonies, celebrations, and no rest, we both fell into a deep sleep.

Chapter 14

After Raj acquired her visa, and after we made numerous trips to visit our closest relatives in other towns one last time, we were ready to leave for the States. On the day of our departure, our family members took us to the airport, and we all stood together to say goodbye. With so many emotions overflowing, it was hard to leave. After hugging everyone tightly, we passed through customs with heavy hearts and waved at our parents and relatives for the last time. I held my head down as we boarded the plane. An overwhelming tightness filled my chest and throat. I did not know when I would see my parents again, and thinking of my mother, tears streamed from my eyes. I wondered if this was the last time I would see her face. Just a week earlier, my mother became so sick at the thought of my leaving India again that she started spitting up blood, alarming me and my entire family. I delayed my trip again, wanting to see her healthy before I left. Once I'd reassured her that I planned to return to India after getting more work experience, her health gradually improved.

The evening of our return to Covington, Bob and Evie invited Raj and me to dinner, knowing we would be exhausted from the long flight and the equally long drive from New York. Regretfully, I realized I had forgotten to mention Raj did not eat meat. I could smell the steak as we walked up to their door. Once inside, I introduced Raj to Bob and Evie, and she gave them a shy smile. Evie admired Raj's sari and made small talk while she set the food on the table and Bob popped open a few beers. I did not mention to Raj that Bob and Evie were living together even though they were not married. It would have been a shock to her, and I thought it best she learns the culture gradually.

While Bob, Evie, and I ate steak, Raj picked at the cheesy cauliflower and ate a few pieces of bread. She didn't care for the taste of the cauliflower without spices, but she managed to eat most of it. After I drank a few beers with Bob, Raj and I returned to our apartment at around ten o'clock.

The next day, Raj watched me get ready for work. Normally, we drank our tea in bed, but I had forgotten to buy milk, so we could not make tea. During my student life, I was particular about keeping things a girl would like in my apartment, and here I had no milk for my own dear wife who was so new in this country. As I left for work, I promised Raj I would send my secretary to bring milk, juice, and bread to the apartment.

At eight o'clock, I strolled into St. Elizabeth Hospital, only to be greeted by surprised reactions from the administrative staff. When three months had passed and I still had not returned, they'd all placed bets with Mr. Gilreath, saying, "Kris is not coming back from India. He's decided to stay there." Then, when they heard I would be returning to work on Monday, January 18, they bet each other that I would not come to work at 8:00 a.m. "Oh, he will show up at noon," they said, "being a newlywed, and since it's the first night in his apartment."

Mr. Gilreath told me he'd had faith in me all along and kept telling them that I would be coming back. He was keen to know all about my wedding. We sat in the conference room, eating donuts and drinking coffee, while I filled him in on the basic details. Bill Poll, the assistant administrator, joined us, as did other administrative staff members. It was not every day that someone left their hospital to go to India and marry a stranger. Before I left the conference room, Mr. Gilreath and I discussed my work and the upcoming projects he planned for me.

Once in my office, I sat at my desk, basking in how good it

felt to be back. Suddenly, I remembered Raj needed milk for her tea. Just then, my secretary came in.

"Oh, Mr. Bedi!" she said. "It's good to see you back! How did your trip go? How was your wedding? You must tell me all about it. What is your wife like?"

Susan was talkative, and while I would have liked to answer her questions, I needed to make sure Raj had milk for her tea.

"Susan," I said, "would you please buy some milk and take it to my apartment for my wife, Raj?"

Susan's eyes widened. "Would I? You bet I would!"

She jumped up from her chair and snatched her purse from a hook on the wall. I scrawled my address and apartment number on a scrap of paper as well as several other items for her to buy. Then I gave her some money, and she was out the door.

Reaching for the phone, I called Raj. After a few rings, Raj answered hesitantly.

"Raj, it's me, Krishan," I said. "I just sent my secretary to buy milk for your tea. She will be there in a few minutes."

After I hung up the phone, I started planning the details for my next project, thinking Susan would return in half an hour. However, an hour passed and Susan still did not return. After two hours, I really started to worry and struggled to concentrate on my work. Finally, after nearly three hours, Susan walked into the office with a smile on her face.

I stared at her. "Susan, what happened? What took you so long?"

"Oh, Mr. Bedi," she exclaimed. "I was talking to your wife. She is just beautiful. I couldn't leave! It was so interesting to listen to her. I asked her all about your wedding, and she told me everything I wanted to know. It was so interesting that I completely forgot about the time."

At this, Susan laughed, but I just stared at her in amazement. What did Raj think of Susan? It never occurred to me that perhaps it was not a good idea to send a young, attractive secretary to my apartment. I did not think of Susan as anything but a friendly secretary, but Raj barely knew me, and she knew nothing of my life in America. There were stories circulating in India about successful Indian men returning to India, allowing their parents to arrange a wedding merely to please them, and then bringing the new wife back to the States. Once there, the poor girl would find this stranger already had a wife, a nice American girl he'd fallen in love with. Now, this traditional Indian girl would fall by the wayside with no choice but to return to India a disgrace or find some way to stay in the States on her own and keep the news from her family.

At around five o'clock, I came back to the apartment. Raj made a pot of hot tea, and we drank it together, sitting on the sheet in the living room. She did not mention Susan's visit, and when I brought up the subject, she simply stated how thoughtful it was for me to send my secretary to bring her milk. She did not seem upset, and we did not speak any further about my secretary.

One evening, we invited Bob and Evie to come over and taste the pakoras Raj had prepared. Once Bob tasted them, he became so obsessed that it was practically all he would talk about. Bob went on and on, praising Raj to no end. Raj only smiled and nodded her head as she formed the potatoes and cauliflower into small balls, coated them with a paste of chickpea flour mixed with spices, and deep fried them in cooking oil.

Any time I invited Bob to come to our place instead of us going to his, he would ask if he could bring along a friend so he could try the pakoras. "They go great with beer," he would tell his friends.

For about a month and a half, Raj fixed pakoras three to four times a week. She did not object once, and after a couple of months, almost all our friends had met my wife and eaten her famous pakoras.

❧ ❧ ❧

In January 1971, a reporter named Connie Remlinger asked to meet my wife and me so she could write a story about us for *The Kentucky Post*. The next day, she sat in my office and asked me all about my wedding from start to finish. An hour later, she asked if she could take pictures of us.

"Let me talk to my wife about it first," I said.

I called Raj right away. "Raj, there is a lady from the newspaper here who wants to do a story on our wedding. She would like to take a picture of us."

"What?" Raj exclaimed. "Why?"

"I don't know. She just wants to take some pictures."

Raj sounded hesitant, but she agreed.

"You have such long beautiful hair," Connie said as soon as I introduced her to Raj. "Would you like to go put on a good sari? Then I will take a few pictures of you two. It won't take long at all, I promise."

Raj changed into her best sari, and we followed Connie outside into the early afternoon sunlight. Connie took out her camera and began giving us directions on how to pose. After snapping a few shots, she looked at us thoughtfully and said, "You know what I'd really like to see? Kris, have you carried Raj across the threshold yet?"

"No, what do you mean?"

"Oh, it's an old tradition where the husband carries his wife in his arms into the house."

Raj stared at the reporter in shock. Then she looked at me in disbelief. "Kris," she said. "How are you going to carry me to the apartment on the second floor? I am too heavy!"

"Kris is good and strong," Connie encouraged. "He can do it."

As I bent to pick Raj up in my arms, she couldn't stop laughing, her dark eyes shining as she smiled. I carried her to the building, looking toward her face and she looking toward mine with Connie several feet in front snapping picture after picture.

The story appeared on the front page of *The Kentucky Post* on January 23, with the title, "Want Ad Bride Didn't Read It."

Long-awaited journey starts with Shagun of Good Luck from the family at my home in Nov. 1961

To the right of me, my sister-in-law with her brother and my younger sister

My mother and maternal grandmother at the railway station

Railway station, with my father and his friend who helped with depositing the money

Boarding the train to Bombay, a 1,200-mile journey over 34 hours

Boarded the ship on Nov. 26, realized truly leaving my family, tears start flowing

Ship sailing away to take me far away from home

Getting off the boat in 1961, reaching for my passport

At the residence of The President of the University of Tennessee, trying to score with his daughter, 1962

My first job at McDonalds in the summer of 1962, posing with Cherokee Indian children

Achieving hard-earned goals with sweat, tears, and blood: my Masters degree in 1969

My mother, pumping the water for our water buffalo in 1970. This is a task I used to do before leaving India

Marriage ceremony in 1970: My three sisters at the shop where I folded the cloth bolts during my high school years

Carrying my wife, Raj, across the threshold to my apartment in Covington, Kentucky in 1971

Promoted to Assistant Administrator at Providence Hospital in Cincinnati, Ohio in 1972

Visiting Kashmir, India in 1981, dressed as Kashmiris

*Celebration of 10ᵗʰ anniversary of
Providence Hospital in 1981*

*Enjoying the National American Institute of
Industrial Engineers Convention*

*Mr. Gilreath, the administrator, awarding me
a plaque of Excellence Service with Providence
Hospital. I then accepted the position of Executive
Director at a 500-bed complex to be built in New
Delhi, India*

Last goodbye kiss from Kathy, 1983

I partnered up with OSCAR television
and appeared in a TV ad after achieving
number one in sales at Gwalior Annual
State Mela (Fair) in 1987

Awarding OSCAR TV to a winning athlete at the ceremony in 1988

It was a constant source of amazement to the people of Covington that I would search for my wife by placing an advertisement in the newspaper, and after going to all this trouble, the woman I chose in the end never saw the ad. A few weeks later, the St. Elizabeth Hospital publication, *Stethescoop*, reprinted the story with the heading, "Mr. Bedi Finds a Wife."

Two to three weeks after bringing Raj to the US, I took her to Coppin's department store to buy American clothes. It was the beginning of February 1971, and Raj did not have many warm clothes. While Raj browsed through a rack of women's pantsuits, I stood several feet away browsing through a selection of sweaters. Just then, two girls got off the elevator. One of them was a girl I'd met the previous year while barhopping with Bob. Never having met anyone from India, she got it into her head that I was an exotic prince from the Middle East. She showed me off to her friends, saying, "I want you to meet my husband!" It turned into a huge joke, and I went along with it.

As the girl and her friend walked toward the women's clothing section, she saw me right away.

"Kris, I haven't seen you for so long!" she said, rushing over and wrapping her arm around me. Turning to her friend, she said, "I want you to meet my husband."

I froze at these words, and Raj turned around to look at the girl who was still holding my arm and smiling at me.

Feeling embarrassed, not only for myself but for this girl, I said, "I would like you to meet my wife." I turned to Raj, and she came forward, her dark eyes passive and unreadable. She gave a slight, tight-lipped nod at the two girls, who stared at us in shock. We all were speechless. The girl's mouth dropped open as she backed away.

"I am so sorry," she said to Raj. "It is very nice to meet you."

We all stood there for a moment, feeling awkward and not knowing what to say. Finally, after a few more words, the girl and her friend walked away.

Raj continued looking at clothes, and the entire time, I wondered what that must have looked like to Raj. I often left Raj alone at the apartment so I could party with Bob and his friends after work. Perhaps she thought I was with my other wife.

Raj never shared her thoughts on this subject with me. At the time, it was not the nature of our relationship to tell each other what we were thinking, and it was such an awkward situation. It was easier to pretend it never happened, and Raj did not press me for any explanation.

On February 27, 1971, Bob and Evie hosted a wedding reception for Raj and me so we could introduce Raj to our friends. Bob was excited about planning the event, and he asked me to tell him what food and decorations to buy for the party. I made a list and began reading it to him.

"Fifty pounds of onions," I began.

Bob's jaw dropped, and Evie almost had a stroke. She dropped the pan she was cleaning and stared at me.

"Kris, what in the world are you going to do with fifty pounds of onions?" Evie exclaimed.

"We need 3/4 pound of onions per person," I answered. "We are going to chop and sauté them for the curried chicken, dal, aloo gobi, and the mater paneer (peas and ricotta cheese)."

They stared at me incredulously.

"Okay, Kris," Evie laughed. "Whatever you say."

The day of the reception, Bob, Evie, and my Indian friends decorated the party room. Quite a few of my friends came from out of town, and we made arrangements for them to stay at Bob's place and with Ravi Chopra and his wife who also lived in our apartment complex. Several other couples chose to stay at a hotel. Sewa Singh and his girlfriend, Gail, would stay at my apartment that night.

Shortly before 5:00 p.m., I put on an Indian record. Raj, my Indian friends, and I fetched the rest of the food, which we had taken turns making in my apartment. As my friends arrived, I greeted them and introduced Raj who looked beautiful in an orange silk sari embroidered with gold thread. She wore her waist-length hair in a braid draped over one shoulder. Evie, wearing the green sari Raj gave her, helped Bob mix cocktails for the guests. Fifty to sixty people crowded into the room, conversing as they sipped cocktails from plastic cups. I led Raj around the room to meet everyone, and she greeted them with a shy smile, accepting their congratulations with a nod of her head and a small thank you.

After some formal introductions and a toast, Bob explained the food to the guests and told everyone to help themselves. He felt happy that he knew the names of the Indian dishes and felt great about showing off to his American friends how intimate he was with Raj and me.

At one point, Bob and Evie stood in line behind the owner of Coppin's department store, Mr. Franklin and his wife. Mrs. Franklin spooned at least six Bedekar peppers onto her plate. These are spicy pickled peppers that look a lot like green beans. I bought them mostly for the Indians because we liked to eat hot peppers with our spicy food.

"Those are very hot," Bob warned Mrs. Franklin, knowing from experience.

Mrs. Franklin gave him a reproving look. "Oh come on, Bob," she said. "I can handle it. These are just beans."

Bob and Evie finished filling their plates and went to stand with the other Americans who formed a small group at one end of the room. Mrs. Franklin, standing only a foot away from Bob, took a few bites of the curried chicken and lentils.

"This is very good," she remarked to Mr. Franklin.

Then, forking a couple of Bedekar peppers, she took a big bite. Immediately, she let out a loud yelp, grabbed Bob's mug of beer and gulped it down.

"Oh my God, this stuff is hot!" she exclaimed between drinks.

After the dinner, Raj served the Indian sweets she had made, while Bob and Evie brought out a cake. Most everyone brought presents, which Raj and I opened at that time. The evening was a huge success, and by ten o'clock, the last of the guests had said their farewells, leaving only Bob, Evie, and several of my Indian friends to clean up. I was happy that most of my friends had met my wife. More than anything, I wanted Raj to feel welcome in America.

Chapter 15

On March 8, 1971, Raj and I climbed into the back of Bob and Evie's VW van. We were on our way to Knoxville to celebrate Sewa Singh's birthday, and Bob did not want to waste one second in getting to the party. He pulled onto the highway, driving seventy-five miles an hour, looking out for cops along the way. Bob had put in a table so passengers could sit across from each other and play cards, and he had also installed new carpeting, which he was proud of, constantly telling us to be careful and not make a mess with dirty shoes or any food we brought in. Half a keg of Hudepohl beer sat in the corner, and Raj held a container filled with hot *aloo prantas*, flat bread cooked over the stove with potatoes and spices between its two layers. We would eat the prantas and drink beer while Bob drove. At that time, the laws were not as strict about drinking beer in the back of a vehicle while someone else was driving.

An hour into the trip, I glanced at Raj and noticed a strange look on her face. Suddenly, she leaned over and threw up all over Bob's new carpet.

Bob whipped his head back to see what happened. "No, aw, no," he groaned over and over. "The new carpet! Hurry, someone clean it up."

Evie turned around in the front passenger seat. "Raj, are you okay?" she asked.

"Kris, clean it up," Bob said. "Do something!"

"There aren't any rags back here," I said, frantically looking around for something to wipe up the mess.

"Look in the very back," Bob said, almost yelling now.

He had slowed the van down, and we all were staring at Raj. She wiped her mouth on a corner of her sari and took a few swigs from a can of soft drink Evie gave her. Glancing at Bob and me with a worried look on her face, she said, "I'm so sorry, Bob."

"It's okay, Raj," Bob said, realizing how bad she felt. "We'll pull over at the next gas station and let you get out for a bit."

"Bob," Evie said, "maybe you should drive slower the rest of the way."

The next day, as we drove back to Covington, Raj leaned over and whispered to me, "I think I need to see the doctor. I think I'm pregnant."

Raj had mentioned she'd missed her period in February, so I should have known what was coming, but still, I felt surprised and a little bit hopeful at the same time.

The next day, I took Raj to see an obstetrician. After the doctor examined her and ran some tests, he confirmed Raj's suspicions.

"You are pregnant," he said. "You are about three months along."

Raj and I left the doctor's office feeling happy. Would the baby be a boy or a girl? How would we take care of it? There was so much to learn. At the same time, we felt a little scared. I did not know much about babies or pregnancy, and while Raj knew a little from witnessing births in her hometown, there was a lot she didn't know.

As the months passed, I still lived like a bachelor. Whenever Bob called me to come down for a beer, I went right away. Also, when my friends invited Raj and me to a social gathering, I was always ready to go. Raj, on the other hand, was reluctant. In some cases, she did not go, preferring to stay home to knit or to prepare supper. I always went out anyway, coming home late and not thinking much about how Raj felt about my behavior. Looking back years later, I realized I should have paid more attention to Raj and what she wanted, but at the time, I was unaccustomed to having another person to look out for. Now, in a matter of months, I would have a second person to care for. This news sobered me up, if not right away, then eventually.

If there had been a book on the subject, maybe that would have helped me when it came to understanding how to be a better husband or to understand my wife's needs. However, even if there had been hundreds of books written on the subject, I wasn't seeking them out, and no one was giving any of them to me, saying, "Look, read this." Marriage was seldom discussed in those days, and the matters between a husband and wife were mostly kept private.

As Raj's due date approached, we began preparing a room for the baby. We did not have any baby furniture, so one day, while Billo Cheema was visiting with her sons, Billo mentioned that she could give us her baby furniture as she did not plan to have any more children. Raj and I drove up to Morristown, New Jersey, on Saturday, and I drove home with the furniture on Sunday, letting Raj stay with the Cheemas for a few extra days to talk to Billo about pregnancy, giving birth, and parenting.

A few weeks after Raj returned from the Cheemas' house, she went into labor and gave birth to a beautiful baby boy. This was good news for our families back home. In Indian culture, it is a great celebration if the firstborn child is a boy, especially in those days. Now things are changing, but in some parts of India, a firstborn baby girl is still not welcome.

The hospital personnel wanted to know what name we chose for the baby. Since Raj and I didn't know the gender until the moment of his birth, we hadn't thought about it. "I don't know," I said. "We are still thinking about it."

"You *have* to have a name," the personnel insisted. "We have to prepare the certificate."

Even though I worked there, it was a difficult task to persuade them to give us a few extra days to decide on a name. Finally, they agreed, and on the fourth day of Raj's stay in the hospital, just before she was discharged, we decided to name our son Subhash after a great man of India who had played a huge role in helping India free itself from British rule. His middle name would be Jony, an American name that we liked.

I took Raj and the baby home at around 2:00 p.m. There was a lot to carry: Raj's things, the baby's things, and several vases of flowers. We did not have the car seat yet, so Raj carried the baby in her lap.

Raj warmed to the role of mother right away. She sang to the baby in Hindi and bathed him lovingly each morning in a small tub Billo had given her. Raj seemed happy in those days, content to finally have the baby with her and to take care of him. Part of me felt anxious because taking care of such a tiny person seemed like a huge responsibility. But Raj was a good mother, and she seemed to know what to do right from the start.

I took the first couple days off to stay with Raj and the baby. Once back at work, I couldn't wait to go home to see how Raj and the baby were doing. Sometimes I would call Raj from my office to ask if there was anything she needed. I felt so proud to have a son that for a whole month I was walking on air.

Subhash's arrival in our lives proved to be a great learning period. We were unaware of certain aspects of caring for a baby. For instance, at night we would feed him milk from the bottle then put him to sleep. However, ten minutes after putting him in his crib, he would start crying. Raj and I would go to his room, pat him on the back, and try to put him to sleep, but he would always wake up again with a cry. We fed him, so why was he crying? We did not know what to do. One day, Mr. and Mrs. Gilreath came to see Subhash at our apartment, and while Mrs. Gilreath held Subhash, she noticed that he was crunching his legs towards his stomach. Mrs. Gilreath, a nurse, mentioned that he had colic. "Does he cry in a low short scream?" she asked. We confirmed this. "Yes, he definitely has colic," she said.

"What is colic?" I asked.

"It is something that happens when a baby has too much air going into his mouth from sucking on the bottle. The air has to come out, which causes him to cry. Don't you know you are supposed to burp him?"

"No, what does burp mean?" we asked.

"Well, it is very common for a baby to burp, Kris. After you feed him, you hold him close to your shoulder and pat his back until he burps. This helps him get the excess air out."

"Gee, we didn't know," I said.

Mr. Gilreath just laughed. "That's very common. Call Subhash's pediatrician, Kris. He may prescribe medicine."

Subhash was quite chubby, but he loved to eat and was always smiling. Raj, strict with his feeding schedule, would always scold me whenever I tried to feed him too much. I was lenient, and whenever he cried, I would feed him. "No!" Raj would correct me. "This is not his feeding time."

When he was around ten months old, Subhash weighed close to thirty pounds. Mr. Gilreath just died laughing when he saw how chubby Subhash was.

"Look at this double-breasted guy!" he said.

Indeed, Subhash looked as if he had breasts. Once, during a visit to the pediatrician, the doctor said, "Boy, your son is growing so well. Maybe you need to put him on a diet."

We all laughed and joked about it, but Subhash just loved to drink his Similac milk and to eat the baby food whenever Raj or I fed him. He always wanted more and more.

A few years earlier, I'd learned that a person only needed a four-year degree relating to the sciences to become a medical technologist. Much of Raj's coursework from her zoology degree matched the medical technology program requirements. She only needed to complete a one-year internship in a hospital lab, which offered a stipend of $200 a month. She agreed to try it, and in September 1972, she started her rotation in the pathology lab at St. Elizabeth Hospital after dropping Subhash off at the Toddler's Inn daycare managed and staffed by the hospital.

Raj's first assignment was to draw blood from patients, yet she did not feel comfortable sticking patients with the needle. It was especially difficult for her to draw blood from the little children in the Pediatrics Department. They would cry, and it reminded her too much of her own son. Within two weeks, one of her supervisors started giving her a hard time. Raj had requested to be assigned to a different department instead of Pediatrics because she was uncomfortable drawing blood from the little ones.

The supervisor said, "It is not your job to direct me what to do. In the lab, you are Raj. You are not Mrs. Bedi. You are not going to get any preferential treatment because of Mr. Bedi's position."

This statement hurt Raj. She did not expect special treatment. She was only trying to do her job, but she was new in the work environment and sticking children with needles bothered her. Raj said no more about it, but the supervisor continued giving her a hard time. Raj did not share her troubles with me then, but I noticed she was unhappy when I picked her up at the end of her shift.

"What's the matter, Raj?" I asked one day. "What's going on?"

We were in the convertible on the way back to the apartment, and for a moment Raj didn't answer. Then before I knew it, tears began to roll down her cheeks. She shook with loud, heart-wrenching sobs. When we reached the apartment complex, I tried to comfort her so she could calm down and tell me what was wrong. After ten minutes, Raj quieted down and explained the situation.

"Don't pay any attention to that lady," I said. "You will be just fine."

There was not much I could do about the situation, and I hoped the problem would go away.

It surprised me when Mr. Gilreath walked into my office one afternoon to discuss Raj with me. The supervisor had reported to the chief pathologist about Raj not feeling comfortable with drawing blood from children.

"Perhaps this program is too much on Raj," Mr. Gilreath said.

"Raj is a very smart girl," I responded. "She completed her master's in zoology with honors. Perhaps she just needs to keep drawing blood, and she will get used to it."

"Okay, that's fine," Mr. Gilreath said, noting my determination for Raj to keep the internship.

The first week of October, I was driving Raj to work at 6:15 a.m., Subhash sat in his chair in the back seat, and Raj sat quietly, wearing the white dress which was her lab uniform, her long hair wrapped in a bun. As I stopped at a stop sign, all of a sudden, a car hit us from behind, causing us to jerk forward. I was holding onto the steering wheel, but Raj didn't have anything to hang onto, and the impact shook her head so hard that her bun came out and her hair flew forward across her face. She started crying, and we both turned around to make sure Subhash was okay. He was crying too, and at that moment, Raj said, "I'm done with the internship!"

Once the police came, wrote a report, and ticketed the person who hit us, we were so shook up that I simply turned the car around and headed back to the apartment. On the way, I tried to change her mind, saying, "It's your decision, but it will be good if you can continue this. You will have a degree from this country, and if need be, later you will be able to get a good job easily in a hospital. It's a decent job to work in a hospital lab."

"No, I'm done with it, Kris," she said in a firm tone. "I'm done. I'm frustrated with that supervisor and her constant taunting. And most of all, I am not happy leaving Subhash at Toddler's Inn. He is only a year old, and I don't like to see him cry when we leave him there."

I told her that if she didn't want to do it, that was fine with me. Later, I informed Mr. Gilreath, and he seemed relieved the situation worked out in the end.

❖ ❖ ❖

In May 1971, a new facility named Providence Hospital opened in Cincinnati, replacing St. Mary's Hospital which was ninety years old. The sisters (nuns) who started the planning of Providence had hired a consultant, Gordon A. Friesen, from Washington, DC, to design Providence Hospital based on new concepts he developed. Since there were only a small handful of hospitals across the country built on his concepts, it became well-known that Providence was built upon the Friesen concept. However, within ten months, Providence had lost one million dollars. Seeing that St. Elizabeth Hospital was making good money under the leadership of Mr. Gilreath, in March 1972, the chairman at Providence approached the board at St. Elizabeth to request the expertise of Mr. Gilreath for six months. The board agreed and assigned Mr. Gilreath to oversee the operations at Providence Hospital as well.

Within one week, Mr. Gilreath fired the administrator of Providence Hospital and began managing that facility. It was exciting for the administrative staff at St. Elizabeth, especially when Mr. Gilreath asked any of them to come with him to Providence so they could observe and become familiar with its setup. A few times, he asked Bill Poll, his assistant administrator, to come with him. If any of the administrative staff were asked to go to Providence, it was like a feather in their cap because it meant they were considered experts. Each time Bill Poll went with Mr. Gilreath, I felt disappointed. The whole time I hoped Mr. Gilreath would ask me.

Then, one day in April 1972, Mr. Gilreath asked me to accompany him to Providence Hospital. He had encountered several problems in the support service departments, especially with the Supply Processing and Distribution (SPD) Department.

"Kris, your expertise would be great in this area," Mr. Gilreath told me. "I would like you to observe the operations in the support departments, especially the SPD, and then, I would be glad to hear your recommendations."

I felt excited to be considered an expert in the eyes of the

Providence Hospital staff, even though I knew nothing about the Friesen concept. The first step I took was to read Friesen's manual and familiarize myself with the hospital's design.

The Friesen design, a modern concept, meant that all the handling and delivery of supplies was automated. The carts moved on a monorail system which functioned by turning knobs to set what floor the cart should go to. Also, there were no nurses' stations. On the patient floors, the nurses would do charting in the rooms, and they also used a cabinet, called a "nurse server," built into a wall of each patient's room. The cabinets could be opened from the hallway as well as from inside the room. The patient's chart was kept in the middle part of the nurse server. The upper part of the nurse server contained clean supplies while the lower part contained the soiled linens that the housekeeping department could pick up from the hallway, consequently reducing the traffic going into the patient room. At least, this is how it was supposed to work. But the more time I spent observing operations at the hospital, the more I saw the employees struggling to make this work efficiently. The nurses always complained about running out of supplies and clean linens.

In short, I was impressed by the automated system's ability to save labor costs, but the hospital faced several problems. Sometimes the equipment did not function properly, and the mechanics were not trained to fix it. Second, the employees found it difficult to adapt to the automation. The previous administrative staff had not been able to make the Friesen concept work because all the staff members came from an old facility and either could not adapt or were resistant to change.

After familiarizing myself with how Friesen's concepts *should* work, I began observing the SPD Department, which centralized all of the hospital supplies. In a traditional hospital, each department has its own storage area where it kept supplies, but at Providence, all of the supplies were stored in one place and distributed throughout the different departments on the monorail system. Even the instruments for the surgery department were kept in the preparation and sterilization section of the SPD Department where all dirty instruments were transported on monorail carts to be reprocessed and sent back out, based on the number of surgeries scheduled for the next day. Again, at a traditional hospital, the instruments would be washed, sterilized, and packaged directly within the surgery department. However, at Providence, the reprocessing section was centralized for all soiled material, regardless of whether it was trash, linens, dietary trays, or instruments.

Within two to three months, I had made my observations and developed recommendations that I discussed with Mr. Gilreath. One change we needed to implement involved the way in which the instruments were being transported from the Surgery Department to the centralized reprocessing area. Currently, the instruments were not being soaked in saline solution while transported on the carts, so that by the time the instruments reached their destination, the blood on them would be so dried out that they took much longer to clean, and sometimes when they were sent back to the operating rooms, they would come out of the packages still dirty.

Of course, the preparation and sterilization personnel were blamed, but based on my academic background, I knew that I needed to further analyze the issue and get to the root cause of the problem. "Why don't we try placing the instruments in the saline solution while they are being transported to the reprocessing section" I suggested to Mr. Gilreath one day. He accepted the recommendation, but we also needed to discuss it with Dr. Thomas Wright, the assistant administrator, who also headed the SPD and Pharmacy Departments and had a PhD in Pharmacology.

When Dr. Wright heard my recommendation, he became obstinate. "We cannot do it that way," he said. "I am doing it the best way I know, and if we place the instruments in saline while they are being transported on the carts, the saline will splash all over the place. I think it is better to do it the way we have been doing it."

A long discussion took place with Mr. Gilreath trying to persuade Dr. Wright to at least try my suggestion for a while to see how it worked. Finally, Dr. Wright agreed to test my recommendation. We set a date and time for Dr. Wright and me to meet so we could both observe my recommended method. Mr. Gilreath indicated that he also would like to be there to oversee our experiment.

On the scheduled day, I happened to arrive earlier than the set time. As I walked into the SPD area, I saw that Dr. Wright was already there, and he was testing my recommendation without me, hoping that he'd be able to prove that it didn't work. Also, he did not want to be embarrassed if we both gave it a try and found that the new method did work.

I communicated what I saw to Mr. Gilreath who became furious and called Dr. Wright into his office. "Why did you try this process alone when we decided it would be done in the presence of Kris and you both?"

Dr. Wright felt terrible and did not have a good answer. Instead, he began crying. Mr. Gilreath's expression softened. "Excuse us, Kris," he said.

I left the office, and later, Mr. Gilreath told me that Dr. Wright cried his heart out and kept saying, "I can't take this anymore."

"Kris, I realized that Dr. Wright does not have the expertise to make the new design of this hospital work," Mr. Gilreath said. "That is why I brought you here. Your background is in analyzing hospital systems and finding solutions. The Friesen concept for this hospital is putting too much stress on Dr. Wright."

It turned out that Dr. Wright and Providence Hospital Staff were not the only ones experiencing this problem. Of the five or six hospitals adopting Friesen's concept, only one or two could make it function successfully according to design.

Later, in October 1972, Mr. Gilreath explained that he and Dr. Wright had talked in great length about the best course of action regarding Dr. Wright's position. He clearly did not have either the appropriate education or experience to handle the SPD Department which, due to the centralization system, branched out into nearly all areas of the hospital. He and Mr. Gilreath came to a mutual decision: Dr. Wright would step down from being assistant administrator, and instead, he would simply be the Director of the Pharmacy Department.

"The memo appointing you as assistant administrator over the SPD department will go out tomorrow," Mr. Gilreath informed me.

I was happy to hear this, although at the same time, I was sad for Dr. Wright. Mr. Gilreath explained that this was best for the hospital and the patients.

The next day, many people congratulated me on my promotion. It was one of the happiest days of my life. I would have a tremendous amount of responsibility and authority, something I thrived on. I loved the challenge and eagerly anticipated the high level of respect I would have in such an important position. I had steadily worked my way up from the bottom rung of society, picking up trash in the McDonald's parking lot, and here I was, only one step away from being the head of a hospital. This was a pivotal moment in my life, one that I would treasure for a long time.

That same day, Bob called. When he heard about my promotion, he invited me to come to the Press Club to celebrate. Feeling high on excitement, I agreed and called Raj to give her the news about my promotion. "I'm going to be home a little late since I'm going to stop and have a beer with Bob," I added.

Once at the bar, things got out of hand. People were buying me drinks left and right. I felt that after so much hard work, I deserved to relax and let go. When I finally returned to the apartment late that evening, I stumbled through the door, laughing and singing drunkenly.

Raj glared at me.

"You're gone all day, leaving me to take care of Subhash all by myself, and then you come home like this?" she snapped.

I stopped in my tracks. Raj had never raised her voice before. In the next moment, Raj broke into tears.

"I'm so sorry, Raj," I said. "I'm so, so sorry."

She continued to cry and wouldn't look at me.

"We were celebrating," I explained. "Things got a little crazy."

I kept apologizing, but it didn't matter what I said. For the rest of the evening, we sat quietly at opposite ends of the room. I had anticipated celebrating my promotion with Raj, but I did not realize my actions would make her so angry.

Chapter 16

As assistant administrator over the SPD department, it became my responsibility to make sure that SPD provided efficient services to the patient floors and other departments. SPD, located on the basement level, had a bad reputation in this regard. All the upper departments referred to it as "Stupid People Downstairs." Since I was in charge of SPD, I did not like this term. Although there was not much I could do about it, I was determined to change its image by making as many improvements to SPD as I could. Once we started giving timely, more efficient service, the image would correct itself.

First and foremost, I tackled "Mount Hopeless," the giant mound of soiled laundry that perpetually sat in the reprocessing section. There was so much backlog that the reprocessing employees could not keep up with it, and one employee, a slightly mentally challenged person but still a good worker, put a sign near it on which he had written, with creative spelling, "Mount Hopless."

Due to the enormous backlog, the nurses constantly yelled at the Laundry Department because they continually ran out of clean linens. Having experience in this area from my laundry project at St. Elizabeth Hospital, I began observing the reprocessing section's methods right away. Currently, they utilized a specific formula for all the various types of linens that came through the reprocessing section, the area that contained the laundry washer and extractor. This formula had been set to a sixty-minute cycle required for heavily soiled linens. After studying how many pounds of laundry were to be reprocessed on a daily basis, I realized there would always be a backlog, and the employee who ran the machines during an eight-hour shift Monday through Friday would never catch up.

I set a goal to shorten the laundry washing time and still provide clean linens to the patient floor. Working with a sales rep from the American Laundry Company (who designed the formulas for the machines), we were able to incorporate three different formulas by classifying the linens into three groups: surgical linens, heavily soiled linens, and moderately soiled linens. I noted that not all of the linens were heavily soiled. By washing these separately, we could reduce the washing time for each load, meaning we could redistribute these linens to the patient floors more quickly. By implementing these formulas, we would be able to wash all the soiled laundry on a daily basis in an eight-hour shift Monday thru Friday.

However, there was still the matter of "Mount Hopeless." Mr. Gilreath approved my request for employees to work overtime to wash the entire backlog of laundry. Once people saw the results of my changes, the nurses and reprocessing employees began to have confidence in me.

Yet there was one more issue in the reprocessing section that bothered me. In the entire time Providence Hospital was open, the laundry bags holding all the soiled laundry had never been washed. They looked dirty and bloody, and whenever I went into that area, the room would have a strange, musty odor. There were around seventy to eighty bags, and I calculated that if we washed ten to fifteen bags a week over a five-week period, all the bags would be clean. The reprocessing supervisor agreed with me, but some of the employees didn't.

One day while I was making my rounds, one employee said, "Mr. Bedi, why do we wash these laundry bags? They are only going to get dirty again."

"Gee, you have a point," I said. "But now let me ask you a question. I hope you wear underwear. And probably, you are changing it every day and washing it. Why wash it if it's going to get dirty again?"

The employee just looked at me and said, "Mr. Bedi, you have a point."

Later, when I told this story to Mr. Gilreath, he could not stop laughing.

"Kris, what a question!" he laughed, tears in his eyes as he tried to control himself. "Very good example. Very good!"

One Saturday while out shopping with Raj and Subhash, I decided to stop by Providence Hospital to see what was happening in my departments. As I entered the reprocessing area, I was stunned to see four college students playing baseball with a broomstick, while the soiled laundry, dirty dishes, and contaminated instruments were piling up in each section.

Another weekend, I found them sitting on the floor playing a game of cards. The supervisor had trouble being strict with them. She felt like a mother figure, and she often said, "These are my kids."

I could only shake my head. "That is not how your relationship should be," I explained. "You are their supervisor, and you need to make sure they do their work."

One day, an employee came to my office to tell me he could not work Monday nights because it was football night on television. I couldn't believe my ears. At the same time, I realized that he was a college student, and since I had been a college student once, I tried to be helpful, talking to him as an equal. Yet, when it came down to it, I told him, "While you are at work, *do a good job.* This job is providing you the means to carry on your college studies and to achieve your dreams. The football game is not going to do it." He left my office, not happy, but realizing it made sense.

It was a challenge to get these college students to improve their work ethic at Providence Hospital. One day, Mr. Gilreath invited a consultant to help design the office space layout, and while giving him a tour, Mr. Gilreath brought the consultant to the SPD Department. He pointed out the bare concrete floors in the reprocessing area and explained that he wanted to create a more aesthetic feel to the area by installing a covering that would give the floor more traction, since it often got wet. All of a sudden, someone threw a glass toward them while their backs were turned. The glass crashed against the wall. It was an act of rebellion, as the employees were unhappy with some of the changes Mr. Gilreath was implementing.

Alarmed, Mr. Gilreath demanded to know who threw the glass. No employee came forward because they all were protecting each other. After the tour, the consultant expressed amazement at how the employees behaved and how chaotic the department functions were. Needless to say, once it was determined who threw the glass, that employee was fired.

After I had been assistant administrator for four or five months and had made significant improvements in reprocessing, Mr. Gilreath asked the consultant to take another look at the floor. This time he encountered no incident with the reprocessing employees, and after the tour, the consultant commented to Mr. Gilreath, "I don't know what Kris has done, but today those chimpanzees behaved like adults."

I felt strongly about creating a good image in the reprocessing area of the SPD department. As assistant administrator, it especially reflected on me. I kept telling the employees, "Just because you are working with soiled items, it doesn't mean it should look dirty or smell soiled, and it doesn't mean that your job is not important." Over time, the employees began to cooperate, as they realized I was genuinely interested in them.

At the same time, while making my rounds, I observed that the reprocessing employees were washing the vacuum containers, referred to as "vacutainers," that the pathology lab used to draw blood specimens. I was sure that vacutainers could not be used again, since they did not have their tabs anymore and were only a single-use item. Yet it took the employees hours to wash the vacutainers by hand so they could send them back to the pathology lab.

One day, I asked an employee, "Hey, why are you washing these?"

"This is what we have always done ever since the hospital opened," the employee replied.

The reprocessing supervisor said the same thing.

At the end of the day, I mentioned this incident to Mr. Gilreath. He just laughed. "Kris, let me handle that," he said.

Immediately, he went to the pathology lab and spoke to the lab manager in charge of operations. "What do you do with these vacutainers when they are sent back to you?" Mr. Gilreath asked.

"Oh, we just throw them away," she said.

Mr. Gilreath could not believe it. The reprocessing employees were spending so much time washing these containers, and the lab employees had never taken the time to inform the reprocessing supervisor that they only threw them away.

"What a discovery you are making every day!" Mr. Gilreath told me.

❖ ❖ ❖

In 1973, Raj and I bought a house in Anderson Township southeast of Cincinnati, an area with a good school district, since Subhash would be starting preschool soon. Located on Sunderland Avenue, it was a four-bedroom, ranch style home on a peaceful cul-de-sac.

One day in early June 1973, Raj woke up with a sinus headache and a stuffy nose. After feeding Subhash, she decided to go out on the deck to see if the sunshine would make her feel better. As usual, she closed the sliding door behind her so Subhash would stay inside. After a few seconds, Subhash came to the door and pushed the latch down. Hearing the click, Raj turned around and saw Subhash grinning at her, his face pushed up against the glass.

"No, Subhash!" Raj called out, rushing to the door and kneeling down to Subhash's level. "Unlock the door, Subhash. Please! Push the latch back!"

He did not understand her, and with her fingers, Raj mimed touching the latch and pushing it up. Subhash only smiled, thinking, *Mommy is playing with me.* Raj made another attempt to communicate with him, but Subhash only laughed and rapped his hands on the glass.

Determined to find a way to get inside, Raj went to the deck railing, hoisted herself over, and jumped fourteen feet to the ground. Barefoot and in her pajamas, she walked to our next door neighbor's house and rang the bell. Belinda came to the door and looked at Raj in surprise.

"I'm sorry for being in my pajamas," Raj began, "but I am locked out of my house, and my one-and-a-half-year-old son is inside."

"Oh, dear. Come in, come in," Belinda said. "I will call the locksmith and see if they can send someone over right away."

She made several phone calls, but the locksmiths said the soonest they could come was the next day, and the last one said he could be there in the afternoon.

"That is too late," Raj said, nearly in tears. "I need inside right away."

"You could break the small ventilation window in the basement," one of the locksmiths suggested. "That would be the quickest way to get in, and it's not expensive to repair."

Raj nodded. "Let's do that."

Belinda called her son downstairs, and they all went to the side of our house. Her son picked up a big rock and used it to break all the glass from the window. Carefully, he climbed through the window and unlocked the front door. As soon as Raj entered the house, Subhash ran to Raj to give her a hug. He was happy to have his mother back, but there were no words to express how joyful Raj felt to be back inside with her son.

When I came home from work that evening, Raj told me, "We need to get the basement window repaired."

"Why?" I asked. "What happened?"

She told me everything that had happened, and I stared at her in alarm.

"Raj, all that you went through!" I exclaimed. "Why didn't you just call me?"

"I didn't want to interrupt you at work. You could have

been in a meeting. And it is forty-five minutes to get here. I didn't want you to drive all this way, and then drive back."

The next day when I told Mr. Gilreath about Raj's morning, he said, "Boy, Raj is very brave to jump off the deck like that, and she sure is considerate of you, Kris."

As time passed, my foremost goal was to change the SPD Department's image from "Stupid People Downstairs" to "Super People Downstairs." This department was the most difficult to improve. With eighty-five employees at the bottom of the totem pole, most of them lacked motivation to do well in their work. They did not consider their jobs important, and they knew they were looked down on by the employees on the upper floors.

One day at the weekly staff meeting, I looked at the employees, some of them slumped in their chairs, arms crossed, most of them looking bored. I knew I had to do something drastic to get their attention. "Just so you know," I said, "all this equipment you guys are working with—the washers, the sterilizers, the distribution system—is all fixed. It's not going to move anywhere. Only people are replaceable."

The employees were taken aback by my boldness. Right away, my comment caught fire, and in the following weeks, people began saying that I was not sensitive to the employees. Mr. Gilreath also heard of my comment. "Kris, that was quite blunt," he said. "Perhaps you should have stated it differently, even though it is a fact."

After that, I became more sensitive to the way I stated things and tried to choose my words more carefully. However, the perception that I was not sensitive to employees simply was not true. I made a point to learn everyone's name, and when I spoke to people, calling them by their first name, they would look at me in amazement because I could remember eighty-five people. As I made rounds, I spoke to the employees about their personal situations. If someone was in the middle of a divorce or became engaged or had a new grandchild, I would listen and ask questions, showing concern or interest about their lives outside of work. If someone went on vacation, I would ask where they were going, and once they returned, I made sure to ask them how they enjoyed their trip. If a family member was sick, I made certain that I followed up with the employee to see how that person was doing. I tried to be nice to the employees and show that I genuinely cared for them, but at the same time, I expected them to work hard and to know their purpose at Providence Hospital was to provide good service.

As time went on, one other problem weighed on my shoulders. The surgical instruments were still not being redistributed in a timely manner. It was a life or death matter if a surgeon did not have the appropriate instrument to continue a procedure. I began developing a case cart system (CCS) for the preparation and sterilization section which involved getting a list of instruments, supplies, and stainless steel bowls and trays needed for each individual case. Then, the case cart with the requested items would be prepared from the processed stores section and sent to the designated area of the operating room, so the carts would already be there for the next day's case. The Surgery Department used thousands of different instruments, and it soon became clear that I would need help if I were to make any valuable contribution to this area.

Mr. Gilreath suggested that his wife, an operating room nurse, could help me with the project. With Mrs. Gilreath's assistance, I could better understand the terminology and issues relating to each surgery.

In the SPD department, I began holding monthly meetings with the eighty-five employees. Sometimes Mr. Gilreath joined us, and once, he announced, "Hey, as staff members, you need to work with Kris so we can make all these improvements. Once we implement them, and once you guys start showing improvement, I will treat you all to an evening at the Beverly Hills Club."

A buzz went around the room at the prospect of being treated to a night out. An outspoken black woman raised her hand.

"Yes, Annabelle?" Mr. Gilreath said.

"Oh, you are going to take us to Beverly Hills, California?" Annabelle asked in a hopeful voice.

Amused, Mr. Gilreath smiled and answered, "I would love to, Annabelle. But I meant the Beverly Hills Supper Club in Newport, Kentucky."

Everyone laughed at this, but now, with a motive to improve their department, they began to work harder.

In October 1973, Raj found out she was pregnant again. Once again, we kept this news to ourselves, not sharing it with our parents because we did not want them to worry. Raj seemed to be getting along well. She rested much more, and I also took extra pains to remind her not to do so much work around the house. Subhash was walking by this time, so Raj did not have to carry him as often, and the young ladies in our neighborhood were a great help to her, often visiting the house while I was at work to see how Raj was doing and to let their children play together.

In June, our neighbor Nancy Hollinger threw Raj a baby shower. The other ladies from the neighborhood gathered at Nancy's house, bringing gifts for Raj and the baby. They played games, drank tea, and ate snacks. Raj seemed to enjoy herself and appreciated this gesture from Nancy. It was a great comfort to her to have a woman close to her own age to confide in and to take an interest in her baby and her wellbeing.

One summer evening in June 1974, Providence Hospital hosted the quarterly medical staff dinner meeting at the Crosley Mansion Courtyard, which was part of the hospital campus. I volunteered to cook the steaks, and I spent most of my time in front of the flaming grill with Mayer Kray, the assistant administrator of maintenance and engineering. I wore a tall white chef's hat, and with my experience in cooking, I enjoyed flipping the fresh steaks high into the air, catching them expertly on the spatula, and throwing them back on the grill. I put on quite a performance, and as the doctors arrived, they watched me at the grill.

With dozens of steaks to cook, Mayer and I had no time to get our own drinks. Eniko, the food service director, made routine rounds to fill our glasses.

"Kris, drink up!" he'd say, filling my glass to the brim.

I did drink up, and before long, I was in high spirits, flipping the steaks even more exuberantly. Sometimes I accidentally dropped a steak on the ground. Grabbing it with the tongs, I placed it back on the grill. "No harm done!" I called out.

At around 8:30 p.m., my citywide pager beeped. Having such a great time drinking and cooking the steaks, I ignored it. About ten minutes later, Mr. Gilreath came over and said, "Kris, Raj has been trying to call you. I think you need to go home."

I set down my drink and turned over another steak, examining it to see if it was nearly finished. "No, she is okay," I said. Raj had been in labor with Subhash for 24 hours so I figured I had plenty of time.

"Kris, *go home*," Mr. Gilreath said in a firm voice, leaving no room for argument.

When I saw how serious he was, I sobered up. "Okay, okay, I'll go home."

I called Raj from the phone in the lobby and told her that I was coming.

"I'm not feeling well, Kris," she said. "Please hurry."

I was not about to go without taking a steak with me. I went back to the grill, cooked two more steaks, finished my drink, and put the steaks on a plate.

When I walked in the door, our neighbor Skip was sitting with Raj. I said, "Skip, what are you doing here? Go home."

"Raj called me," Skip replied, looking concerned.

Raj felt embarrassed at my rudeness, and she could also tell I had been drinking. She gave me a hard look and turned to Skip. "Take Subhash with you. I'm going to the hospital."

As Skip left with Subhash, I took the two steaks out of a bag along with a bottle of steak sauce.

"Let's sit down and have steak first," I told Raj.

Raj stared at me. "No, I have to go to the hospital!"

"You'll be fine," I said as I went to the kitchen for a fork and a steak knife. "These steaks are all the way from Chicago Stockyards. It's not every day you get to eat one of these!"

Raj looked at me in astonishment. "Kris, I have already called Dr. Brunsman. He is getting everything ready for me at the hospital. You must take me right now!" Her voice rose to a high pitch, and her eyes flashed angrily.

I cut off a chunk of steak, slathered it in the sauce, and put it in my mouth. "Mm, this is good. You should try some, Raj," I said, cutting another smaller piece and pushing the plate toward her.

"Kris, I have to go right away! Maybe we should call the ambulance." She started to walk to the phone.

"No, no. I will drive you."

"Do you know the way to the hospital?" Raj asked.

I forked another bite of steak into my mouth, and chewed with great enjoyment. It was perfect, it was juicy, and it was everything a steak should be. Raj watched me, tears forming in her eyes as she waited for an answer.

"Of course I know how to get there," I said.

Raj's delivery would take place at Christ Hospital in downtown Cincinnati, since Providence Hospital did not have a labor and delivery unit. I sped toward the hospital as fast as I could, hoping a cop would pull us over, so I could explain the situation and he would escort us to the hospital. No such luck. Instead, after driving for 30 minutes, we ended up right in front of our driveway. By this time it was around 9:30 p.m., and Dr. Brunsman had been waiting for us at the hospital for more than an hour.

Raj burst into tears. "You are too drunk to drive!" she cried. "You took the wrong exit. We should have called the ambulance."

"Stay calm," I said. "I will take you to the hospital."

This time we made it to Christ Hospital, and immediately, the nurses whisked Raj away to labor and delivery.

Several hours later, as I sat in the waiting room, Mayer and Eniko showed up with a bottle of Chivas Regal and some steaks. The dinner meeting was over, and knowing I would be here, they wanted to celebrate with me. It was close to midnight, and Mayer and Eniko were pretty drunk by this time.

"Kris, Kris, let's have another drink! To celebrate your new child. May it be a son!"

I agreed, thinking, why not? We all started to pass the bottle around when a nurse came over to us. "You can't drink that here," she scolded. "This is a hospital."

"But his wife is giving birth to a child!" Eniko yelled, slurring his words. "He is going to be a father again!"

We all were laughing and speaking loudly. The nurse looked embarrassed, and seeing that we weren't going to cooperate, she told us we could move to the nurse's lounge. "But you still cannot drink here," she said. "This is a hospital."

"Who gives a shit?" I slurred. "I am the assistant administrator at Providence Hospital!"

Mayer and Eniko hooted encouragement, but the nurse was appalled. Knowing that my wife was in labor, she didn't make a big to-do about it, but only shook her head and left us in the nurse's lounge.

Our second son was born at 1:30 a.m. on Tuesday, June 26, 1974. As with Subhash, we wanted to pick a name with a strong history of leadership behind it. We decided to call him Christopher, after Christopher Columbus, the great explorer and discoverer of America.

Looking back, I realized that it was not a good decision to ignore the page from my wife, to come home in that condition, and to drive after having drunk so much. But at the time, I did not think I'd had much to drink. I felt horrible about my behavior during a time that was urgent and stressful for Raj. I apologized to Raj afterward, telling her that somehow Eniko doctored the drinks and that I did not realize how strong they were. Raj would not accept my explanation. "You drank it," she said. "Do not blame Eniko."

Later, I also apologized to Skip for telling her to go home. She just laughed and said, "That's okay. I knew you were not yourself."

Chapter 17

In April 1974, Mr. Gilreath and I hosted a dinner for the eighty-five SPD employees at the Beverly Hills Supper Club in Newport, Kentucky. We had reached our goal. The soiled reusable items were being processed and distributed according to procedures, and the department looked clean.

The employees wore nice suits and dresses, and we all enjoyed cocktails and an excellent dinner. Mr. Gilreath and I gave short speeches and then went around to speak with the employees and their spouses. The dinner did wonders for boosting their morale. Before, they had been referred to as the "Stupid People Downstairs," and now they were being wined and dined at a posh club, and the hospital administrator was taking an interest in them.

During my speech, I told them, "You are the ones making this department work. It's not the system, not the automation. It's the people who make things happen. It is due to your hard work that we are having this wonderful evening."

In the meantime, Mrs. Gilreath and I developed a case cart system, making sure that there was a cart loaded with supplies and every surgical instrument needed for each scheduled surgery case. The surgeons would have everything they needed right at their fingertips, whereas before, they might be missing instruments. Also, a lot of instruments were being thrown away in the linens instead of being sent to SPD for reprocessing. The new system would cut down on loss of instruments, saving the hospital money in the long run, and it would also capture the lost revenue from not charging the patients for all the supplies. It would also save the surgeons the hassle of sending their operating room technicians in search of supplies in the middle of an operation.

Unfortunately, the employees did not adapt well to the new system. One day, the nurses took matters into their own hands and refused to transport patients to the surgery department. They did not like all the changes we were making to their supply system, and they decided that this would be the most effective way to get our attention. At 7:00 a.m., while the surgeons were waiting for their patients to arrive for the first surgeries of the day, the nurses walked out on them.

"We're not going to do anything until our demands are met," they said.

Mrs. Monahan, the Surgery Department manager, immediately called Mr. Gilreath.

"I'm on my way," Mr. Gilreath said, slamming down the receiver and immediately calling Mr. Prater, the director of personnel.

"You get your ass over to the hospital," he growled. "The surgery staff has walked out. They are refusing to transport any patients to the operating rooms."

After hanging up the phone, Mr. Prater became sick to his stomach and was so nervous that he was struggling to pull himself together.

Meanwhile, Mr. Gilreath sped ninety miles per hour to the hospital. The nurses and operating room technicians stood together in clusters, talking in low voices, and when he stormed into the hallway, a hush fell over the group.

"Who wants to talk to me?" Mr. Gilreath demanded in a loud voice. "You guys have a problem? Who wants to talk to me?"

At first, no one volunteered to speak, but finally, three employees came forward, one of them an OR technician named Robert, who seemed to be the self-appointed ringleader of the surgery staff. He was from a country in Africa and spoke in a British accent.

"We want to meet with you to tell you our demands," Robert said. "There is a lot going on here that we don't like."

Mr. Gilreath was not in the mood for any nonsense. "I'm willing to listen to you at the end of the day, but right now, you get your asses in the OR suites and work with the surgeons to perform surgeries on the patients," Mr. Gilreath demanded. "Mrs. Monahan, I want you to tell the transportation technician to start transporting patients right now. Line them up in the hallway, and we will see if they will not go to surgery suites to prepare for surgeries."

The nurses and technicians still would not have it. "We aren't going to work until we know that you are going to negotiate with us," they said.

Mr. Gilreath turned on them fiercely. "You walk out on these patients lined up in the hallway, and I will see to it that you get jobs nowhere in the entire country!"

The employees opened their mouths to argue, but the look on Mr. Gilreath's face silenced them. Seeing that he was not going to back down from his statement, they reluctantly agreed to do the surgeries and to wait until the end of the day to meet with him.

By the time I arrived at work at 8:30, the news about the walkout had spread through the hospital, and the atmosphere was tense. Mr. Gilreath stopped by my office and shared with me what happened. "I'm meeting with them at 3:30, when all the patients are finished," he said. "They have some nerve to do what they did this morning. If they think I'm going to let them take over the hospital, they are dead wrong."

At 3:30, all the nurses and technicians came downstairs to the SPD conference room. While Mr. Gilreath went into the room to talk to them, Mr. Poll and I waited anxiously in our offices. An hour and a half later, Mr. Gilreath stopped by our offices.

"It's done," he said. "I heard all their complaints, and I've gotten them to understand."

Their chief concern was: "Who is Mrs. Gilreath to make changes, and what are her qualifications? What is she doing with Kris?" This was a sensitive subject with them, and Mr. Gilreath answered "Mrs. Gilreath is a surgical nurse. She has more than fifteen years of experience in the surgery department. She is working with Kris and the preparation/sterilization supervisor to develop the instrumentation, and she has volunteered her service to help the surgery department."

They accepted this reluctantly, and at one point, someone said, "We know the SPD personnel and Kris Bedi are trying to make things happen, but we prefer going back to the system as it was at St. Mary's."

"That will not be acceptable," Mr. Gilreath said sternly. "Let them finish this study, and let's see what they come up with. We will discuss the recommendations, and then they will be implemented. All of these changes are for the sake of improving patient care."

At one point in the meeting, an employee who was slouched in his chair tried to shift his position, getting up slightly so he could sit up straight. Mr. Gilreath, in the middle of speaking, suddenly pointed his finger at the employee and yelled, "Sit down! I'm not done yet!"

Shaken up, his face turning red, the employee stuttered, "Sir, sir, I was not getting ready to leave."

Mr. Gilreath, Mr. Poll, and I laughed about this later. "You should have seen his face. He looked so scared," Mr. Gilreath said with a laugh. Then, more seriously, he said, "But it is necessary to put some fear into the employees. If you let them have their own way and take advantage of you, they will be running the hospital, not you."

At the end of the meeting, the employees felt a little relieved, although not completely satisfied when they realized that Mr. Gilreath wasn't going to let them go back to the traditional way of doing things. They each shook his hand as they filed out of the room, having promised that from that point on they would cooperate with my efforts to improve their operations.

Later, Mr. Gilreath and I talked about involving people from the Surgery Department in the study. We both felt it would be great to get the ringleader on our side so one day I approached Robert, the OR technician.

"Robert, since you are so concerned with these changes and with patient care," I said, "we would like you to become a member of our team to work on the surgery study."

Robert stared at me, stunned. "Me? You want me to help you guys?"

"Sure. We think you would be a great asset to our study."

"Okay, that would be great," he said.

I also asked Belinda, an outspoken RN, to join our team. She was always speaking her mind about how the department should be improved, and we thought she would be a good person to have on our side as well.

In September 1974, my team and I finished the report. Mr. Gilreath and the Surgery Department manager helped me present the study to the surgical committee, which consisted of the surgeons and the chief anesthesiologist. All along, the surgical committee had viewed the study negatively. The surgeons wanted to do away with the Friesen concept altogether and go back to the way things had been at St. Mary's Hospital.

During the presentation, the surgeons sat side by side at the other end of the conference table, listening to us with solemn expressions. Dr. Zenni, an orthopedic surgeon and the chief of the committee, sat in the middle. He listened with great interest and asked several pointed questions, but it was difficult to tell what he thought. He had a stern face, and at times, it seemed he would never accept our proposal.

Mr. Gilreath and I were determined. At the end of the presentation, Mr. Gilreath said, "Give us just three months with this new case cart system. Once we implement these changes, we can always go back. I assure you that if these changes do not work as Kris is recommending, I'll be the first one to revert this whole thing to whatever you guys want. Please just give us three months."

Dr. Zenni nodded his head solemnly. After conferring momentarily with the other surgeons, he said reluctantly, "Okay, we'll give you three months. If the system isn't working by then, we go back to the traditional method."

Mr. Gilreath and I left the conference room, exchanging a look that meant "Okay, now we've got some work to do."

We set the implementation date, or "D-day" as Mr. Gilreath and I called it, for a weekend in September. On the big day, I arrived in the surgery department at 6:30 a.m. Mrs. Gilreath and Catherine arrived at 6:00 to make sure everything was set up in the SPD Department. The surgeons turned out to be supportive, and the whole day, Mr. Gilreath sat in his office with his eye on the Surgery Department, hoping he wouldn't have to hear about any problems from the staff.

Overall, the surgery staff was pleased with SPD's effort. Instead of making thirty to forty calls to SPD because of a missing instrument, they only made three to four calls. The revised case cart system also improved the hospital's revenue. Since our lists were more complete, the surgery staff only needed to put a checkmark by the used item. In the past, the staff missed charges because no one knew if an item had been used. After a month of following the new system, we found that the revenue in the surgery department increased by almost thirty percent.

Nearly three months after implementation, Mr. Gilreath told me Dr. Zenni was very pleased, and had said, "Since you put that Indian downstairs, there has been a eighty-seven percent improvement in the instrument, supplies, and case cart system."

Mr. Gilreath and I laughed, wondering how he had calculated such a precise percentage.

Six months after we implemented the changes, Mr. Gilreath persuaded the surgical committee to make me a member. Previously, only physicians were members, and more recently, the committee appointed Mr. Poll, assistant administrator of the Diagnostic Department, as well.

❖ ❖ ❖

As the months passed, word of Providence Hospital's improvement spread throughout Cincinnati, the Friesen concept hospitals in America, and especially the hospitals wanting to implement the case cart system. Providence Hospital had lost close to one million dollars during its first nine months in operation, and its occupancy rate was at approximately eighty percent. After Mr. Gilreath, Mr. Poll, and I were brought to the hospital, we turned things around, showing a profit of one million dollars and an occupancy rate of ninety-nine percent, sometimes even running at full capacity. Although the hospital was a nonprofit organization, this money was used to buy new equipment and upgrade to new technology. As a result of these improvements and an elimination of certain highly paid positions, it was no longer necessary to eliminate 125 employee positions, which Mr. Gilreath felt would have been negative publicity.

The six hospitals in the Cincinnati area were amazed and envious because we were their competition, and now Providence, with its increase in good publicity, was taking some of their business. Providence Hospital gained fame throughout the country, and we started receiving calls from other hospitals wanting to see our operations, specifically the CCS. Since my team implemented the system, Mr. Gilreath asked me to conduct weekly tours.

"This is your pride and joy, Kris," he told me. "The credit should be given to you."

Many hospitals, although not following Friesen's design, were moving to the CCS, which allowed operating room nurses to concentrate on their professional work instead of worrying about supplies, sterilizing instruments, and preparing instrument trays. Even Congressman Tom Lukin visited Providence to see what all the talk was about.

During the tours, I made sure to give my team credit for all their hard work, even praising the SPD staff. "They are working very hard to make this system function," I informed the visitors as we passed through the basement level. "If even one of these sections is taken away, the hospital will fail."

❀ ❀ ❀

"Kris, I have some big news for you," Mr. Gilreath told me one day. "The news of this hospital's success has reached the ears of Gordon Friesen. I talked to him on the phone this morning, and I told him that you are the key person in making all this work."

"Really?" I said, surprised yet pleased at the same time.

"Yes, Mr. Friesen is interested in you. So interested, in fact, that he wants you to come to Germany to consult for a hospital he has designed there."

If I was surprised before, now I was stunned. "He wants me to go to *Germany*?"

"Yes, there is a two-thousand-bed complex in Köln— Cologne —that needs a great deal of work. He sounded eager to have you go there for a consultation visit."

My mouth dropped open at the word "two thousand." That was nearly five times the size of Providence.

"Mr. Friesen sounds very taken with you, Kris," Mr. Gilreath continued, after giving me a moment to register the news. "He didn't even ask *me* if I wanted to go to Germany and help with this hospital. I would have loved an opportunity like this." Then he added with a smile, "I'm happy for you, Kris. You may be going to Köln, Germany."

Several weeks later, Mr. Gilreath walked into my office again. "It's final, Kris. Mr. Friesen has given me the confirmation. You are going to Köln. Just let me know when you will be able to travel."

While in Germany, I would receive $300 per day, and my airfare, food, and living expenses would be covered. On top of that, I would still be receiving my paycheck from Providence during that time. This was typical of Mr. Gilreath's generosity. He told me in confidence, "Kris, you worked very long hours as well as weekends at the hospital, so I will consider these two weeks as compensatory time. You deserve it."

❀ ❀ ❀

My trip to Germany took place toward the end of October 1974, and by the time I returned home near the middle of November, I was mentally exhausted. My first day back at Providence, Mr. Gilreath was eager to hear all about the trip, and I told him everything I could think of. The layout of the hospital was extremely different from Providence Hospital's. Located in a building of its own, the SPD department served several buildings of patients as well as the outpatient clinics. The buildings were connected by a network of tunnels, through which the supply carts were transported by a monorail system. The intricacy of the design was mind-boggling. After a week of observation, asking many questions, and taking pages upon pages of notes, I noted some of the problems were similar to those at Providence Hospital. For one, the supervisory staff did not accept the new design, and any problems that developed were not dealt with immediately. The supervisory staff would simply leave the problems, hoping they would resolve on their own, or the staff would blame the system, saying it simply did not work.

Each day, I spent eight to nine hours at the hospital and then returned to my hotel room, where I would write down my observations and ideas that might lead to possible solutions. I constantly compared the German hospital to Providence Hospital, trying to use my previous experience to help me understand this huge complex. I could hardly wrap my mind around the separate buildings, and the tunnels, and the heartbeat of the place, the SPD building. All the while, the language barrier made communicating with the hospital staff difficult. Many could speak only German, and the few who knew English had thick German accents that I struggled to understand.

In the evenings, I enjoyed a beer and a nice meal at the hotel, but at night, I could not sleep soundly. Though I felt worn out, my mind was swimming with all the information I tried to take in. Also, I was missing Raj and my two sons , especially the baby Christopher.

Although a challenging experience, in the end it was rewarding to say that Gordon Friesen personally asked me to be a consultant for a large hospital in another country. After I returned to the US, I sifted through all my notes, compiled my recommendations into a report, and sent a typed copy of the report to Gordon Friesen at his Washington, DC, consulting office.

Chapter 18

In November 1974, Raj and I enrolled Subhash at Summit Country Day for preschool, paying an extra $150 for his uniform, a grey jacket with blue slacks and a tie. Raj and I were proud to take Subhash to this private Catholic school directed by nuns. Earlier in August, Raj had taken Subhash to a preschool in a church basement, but when Raj and I went to an open house where Subhash showed us all he learned and everything they did there, Raj remarked, "Gee, Subhash knows everything there. Maybe we need to place him at a better-known private school. If he stays here, he may get bored and run into problems."

Summit Country Day was a prestigious school recommended to me by the physicians at Providence Hospital. The fee was $3,000 a year, but Raj and I felt that the high cost was worth Subhash having a good educational foundation. In December, Subhash brought us his report card. We were pleased to see he excelled in all areas, even earning the honorary achievement reward.

"He is doing so well," Raj said. "Do you think it is a good idea to take him out of school for so long when we go to India? I don't want it to affect his reports poorly."

"Yes, it may make it more difficult for him when we come back," I said. "But it is equally important for Subhash to see his grandparents."

We had planned a trip to India in February, and Raj and I were eager for our parents to meet Subhash and Christopher.

On February 15, 1975, our flight landed in Bombay. While sitting in the lounge to wait for our next flight to New Delhi, Subhash became extremely annoyed with the dozens of flies dashing around our heads. One big fly landed on the tip of his nose, and he swatted it away vigorously, hitting himself in the process. He made it his duty to kill as many of them as he could, at first smashing them with his hands, and then hitting them with a rolled up magazine.

We reached New Delhi at around 10:00 a.m. Before the plane landed, I shaved and put on a suit, while Raj changed into a pantsuit and put the boys into a fresh change of clothes. It was our belief that when you come from a foreign country, you should be dressed up and looking your best.

While we waited for our luggage to pass through customs, our family members were waiting anxiously for us outside. It is always a nuisance when you know your family is out there waiting, and you haven't seen them in years, but you must wait for those infuriating customs officials to display the contents of your luggage to the world. When we finally burst out of the airport into the blinding sunshine, the hassle was forgotten. All at once, we were surrounded by Raj's sister and brother, my brother, my cousin-brother Ved Bedi, my maternal uncle, and our parents. With loud cries of delight, they embraced us and draped marigold garlands around our necks until Raj and I were weighed down by at least ten garlands each. Even Subhash was given garlands. He eyed them curiously and flashed a charming grin at whoever patted his head, squeezed his cheek, or bent down to embrace him.

There were tears from Raj and me as we bent to touch our parents' feet. At first, my eyes only watered, but Raj's tears streamed down her cheeks. Our mothers wept joyfully, and soon we all were shedding tears of joy and laughter as everyone began speaking at once. Raj embraced her sister who took a closer look at Christopher, held close to Raj's chest. His eyes were wide, and at eight months, he was getting bigger, more lively, and full of gurgling baby talk.

We all were full of words, everyone asking questions and trying to answer at the same time. Finally, someone suggested we take the party to Ved's house in Delhi where we planned to stay the night. From the airport, Raj's parents traveled to Karol Bagh where they were staying with Raj's aunt.

When we first arrived at Ved's house, Raj and I tried to rest, since we had not slept on the flight. Christopher and Subhash were wide awake, having slept easily on the plane. Ved's son and daughter, a few years older than Subhash, entertained him and played with him. At one point I was talking to Ved's kids in Hindi, thinking they might not know English well enough to converse. To my dismay, the daughter asked in a loud voice, "Uncle, don't you know English?"

I was stunned, and her father corrected her. "You do not talk like this to your uncle."

"Oh, it is okay," I said, and from then on I conversed with her in English. Later this became a joke, and my sister-in-law also made a comment, saying "Krishan, you must talk in English with my kids."

I spent most of the day and evening talking to my parents. As evening approached, Raj took Christopher by taxi to her aunt's house in Karol Bagh where her parents were staying. They would stay the night there, and the next day I would pick them up on the way to Malaudh. Meanwhile, the excitement and chatter at Ved's house did not stop until after midnight. We drank cup after cup of hot black tea, and Ved's wife cooked a meal and snacks for us to enjoy. Subhash, a naturally happy and friendly child, kept everyone busy. He interacted easily with my father and amazed everyone with his intelligent remarks. Like me, he did not act shy around strangers, instead seeming to thrive at this social gathering. The laughter and the stories continued relentlessly until finally, my parents observed how tired I must be after all the traveling. Exhausted from the long day but happy that we were together once more, we all went to sleep, eager for the next day to begin.

In the morning, we left New Delhi at around ten o'clock. We rode in my sister's chauffer-driven car to pick up Raj and Christopher, and then headed toward Malaudh, approximately 200 miles away. On the way, we stopped at Lake Karnal for lunch and some fresh air, as well as to give Subhash a taste of the outdoors in India. We stood beneath the cool shade of the trees and admired the shimmering blue water, pointing out to Subhash the boats floating leisurely and the fishermen waiting for the fish to bite. Raj placed a small blanket on the ground, set Christopher on it, and proceeded to change his diaper, folding it up when she was finished and disposing of it in a nearby garbage bin. Raj's mother watched curiously, but did not say anything. Raj also pulled out a small jar of mashed Gerber carrots and began feeding Christopher.

After leaving Lake Karnal, we stopped in Mandi Gobind-Garh to visit my brother's family, my maternal uncle, and my maternal grandmother. From there, we drove to Samrala to eat dinner with my sister and her family. My sister and her husband received us into their home with great excitement. They could not get enough of Subhash and Christopher, and they played with the two children while we talked. We did not leave Samrala until 10:00 p.m.

It was 11:00 by the time we reached Malaudh. We were tired from the long day and ready to settle down at my parents' house. We began to unload our suitcases, and once inside, Raj rummaged through the baby bag, looking for Christopher's bottle so she could feed him. It was a special kind of bottle with disposable plastic bags we inserted so we would not have to wash the bottle.

"Kris, I can't find the bottle case," Raj said frantically after several moments of searching. "We must have left it in Samrala."

How would we feed Christopher now? He was beginning to cry, and Raj held him on her lap, trying to soothe him, but he only cried harder. I found a cup in the kitchen, and we mixed his Similac formula in that, but Christopher only pushed it away, scrunched up his face, and continued to cry. He was so used to his bottle with the American-made nipple that he would not accept anything else. Raj was getting upset and did not know what else to do. Right away, I told my brother that he needed to go back to Samrala to get the bottle. The car was still parked outside so he left immediately. In the meantime, I asked my father if any shop in Malaudh would have baby bottles.

"It's a small place," my father answered. "All the shops are closed by now."

Looking from Raj's anxious face to Christopher wailing on her lap, he knew something must be done.

"I will be back," he said.

He walked down the street to a neighbor's house, persuaded him to open his shop, paid for a bottle, and brought it home, all within fifteen minutes. However, Christopher still would not accept it. He wanted his own bottle with the American nipple, not these different Indian nipples. Frustrated, Raj and I tried to keep Christopher calm while we waited for my brother to return from Samrala.

In the meantime, Subhash had to go "number two." I took him to the lavatory on the roof, which, having no light bulb, was pitch black inside. Subhash immediately began screaming, "Nooo, nooo, I don't want to do it! I don't want to go in there. Don't make me!"

Ignoring his protests, I carried the struggling Subhash into the lavatory and sat him on the four bricks. Wailing at the top of his lungs, Subhash would not use that dark room sitting on bricks over a dark space. Seeing this would never work, I took him downstairs into the light, and placing him over to an open drain, I said, "Squat and go, Subhash, go!"

He looked up at me for a moment and started crying. "My stomach hurts, Daddy. My stomach hurts," he moaned.

By this time, all my family members were watching. Raj sat across the room with Christopher on her lap, an amused look on her face as if to say, "What will you do now?"

I wondered the same thing. Then, an idea hit me.

"Mother, let me have a bucket," I said.

"What do you need a bucket for?" she asked.

I just looked at her for a moment, and she realized what I meant to do.

"Oh no. I am not having anyone go in my bucket I use in the kitchen. I will never be able to use it again. We will have to throw it away. What a waste of a perfectly good brass bucket!"

"Bibi," I pleaded. "Right now we need to solve this problem. Subhash is having a stomachache and needs to go. I will buy you a new bucket."

My mother sighed dramatically and went into the kitchen to fetch the bucket. I filled it a quarter full with water and held Subhash over it, making believe it was a commode.

"Go ahead, Subhash. *Do it*," I urged.

Miraculously, my plan worked, and Subhash finally went in the bucket.

A short time later, my brother returned with Christopher's bottle at 1:00 a.m. Christopher had quieted down from a screaming wail to a sad whimper, and now he accepted the American bottle right away with no fuss.

"These Amrikan kids," my mother grumbled. "They do not know Indian ways."

It was a phrase I would hear many times during our stay. Raj and I had no idea our first night in Malaudh would be so rough.

On February 27, we attended a wedding of Raj's sister in New Delhi where the groom lived. After the wedding, the relatives on Raj's side returned to Raj's parents' rented home in New Delhi to go to sleep after a long ceremony in the early morning hours. My mother-in-law, whom I called "Biji" according to Indian custom, told the kitchen servants to rest for a few hours and to be ready at 11:00 a.m. to prepare lunch for the family members. The bride and groom also would be returning soon after lunch for their first visit as a married couple, and all must be ready to receive them. However, after everyone went to sleep, Biji received a message from the groom's parents saying the bride and groom would be returning at 9:00 a.m., several hours earlier than expected.

I was awake when the message came, and I observed how tense Biji became.

"Oh, what do I do now?" she moaned. "I have already told the servants to go rest."

Relatives were already waking up and wanting breakfast, while Biji also must begin lunch preparations on her own.

"Biji, don't worry," I said. "I will help with breakfast."

Still wearing my pajamas, I went into the kitchen and began cooking omelets for all the hungry relatives. At first, they were surprised to see me go into the kitchen and start cooking. It must have been a funny image to see the son-in-law, who is supposed to be treated like a king in his mother-in-law's house, cooking eggs in the kitchen. Then they were impressed, especially when I flipped the omelets high in the air the way I learned at the Dorsey Hotel. Biji, while happy I was helping her, was also extremely embarrassed. Her son-in-law, on his first return from America since his marriage to her daughter, was now doing servant's work in the kitchen.

"Biji, it's okay," I assured her. "In the USA, we do things on our own."

My words comforted her, and after a while, Biji seemed pleased. Later, she bragged to her family members, saying, "I have a son-in-law who does not hesitate to work in the kitchen to prepare breakfast for the guests. How lucky can a mother-in-law get?"

For the next four weeks of our stay, we traveled from town to town visiting our parents and siblings as well as other relatives. We also took Christopher to the religious city of Kiratpur for a *mundun* ceremony, celebrating his first haircut. Afterwards, we visited several shrines in the area. On April 6, our last day in Malaudh, I worshipped with my family in both temples. We had practiced a similar ritual in Nabha several days before, worshipping at Raj's house, then going to a temple in town where Raj's mother wanted us to worship and get blessings, as we were traveling so far with our two sons.

After worshipping, Raj and I got into the car with Christopher and Subhash on our laps. A crowd of people surrounded the car to say goodbye. This happened every time we left for a different town or city to visit relatives. It wasn't often that someone came back from the US to visit. No other person from my village left India like I did.

Today, the crowd increased in number. News traveled fast about our departure for the States, and as the car inched forward, the people moved with it, a colorful array of men, women, and children in front, behind, and on both sides, shouting our names and wishing us blessings in "Amrika." Raj and I waved at them, and Subhash waved and smiled in his usual friendly manner. Christopher simply watched with big eyes, taking it all in.

When we reached the outskirts of Malaudh, the crowd fell back, still waving and watching until the car disappeared from view. As we rumbled along the busy road to New Delhi, passing corn and wheat fields, bullock-driven carts, and men herding cows out of the way, I thought about my mother. It had been difficult for me to look into her grief-filled eyes and tell her it would only be a few more years.

"I'm trying to save enough money to live off the interest when we move back," I had explained.

My father understood why I must leave. While he wished I could stay as well, he was not aware of what I would do in order to support my family in India.

My mother had nodded woefully, but in an encouraging voice, she had said, "Krishan, wherever you are, my blessings are with you. Be safe and happy."

In May 1977, I received a letter from the Immigration and Naturalization Department requesting an interview to complete the process of becoming a US citizen. Over six months earlier, at the encouragement of a friend, I had applied for citizenship. Now, as I read the letter, I felt a strange sense of ambivalence instead of the excitement I expected to feel. Getting my citizenship would help me if I ever had the opportunity to become administrator of a hospital, and it would also make it easier to sponsor family members to come to the US, but now that I held the interview letter in my hands, a realization hit me. If I went through with it, I would be giving up the country of my birth. What would my parents think? They were hoping I would take care of them in their old age. I had promised my mother many times that I would return to India one day, and now, here I was one step away from getting US citizenship. The advantages of becoming a US citizen swayed me in that direction, but was I doing the right thing?

In the end, I decided to go through with it. The interview went smoothly and was not as difficult as I imagined it to be. By the time I received my letter of citizenship a week later, inviting me to a ceremony at the courthouse, any ambivalence about giving up my birth country had faded.

On June 20, 1977, I attended the ceremony to receive my US citizenship. Raj, Mrs. Gilreath, and two of my neighbors came for the ceremony. I stood at the front of the room with fifteen other people from different countries, each of us swearing to protect this country and abide by its laws and the Constitution. America felt like my true home, the place where I fit in so well, creating a place for myself and pursuing a rewarding career. Now, with documentation to prove it, I could truly say I belonged here. I was no longer a foreigner just off the boat. I was an official American citizen.

On the evening of July 4, 1977, our third son came into the world amid the sounds of fireworks and showers of color lighting up the sky. We named him Rajan, for my wife, thinking he would also be called Raj as he grew up.

The day after Rajan's birth, his pediatrician, Dr. Cooper, came to examine him at Christ hospital. After examining Rajan, Dr. Cooper said, "He looks good, and his vitals are okay, but he does have abnormalities. One, he was born with club feet. And two, I cannot feel his testes. They have not descended yet."

Rajan was also an unusually large baby, weighing nine

pounds, eight ounces, so Dr. Cooper asked Raj if she or anyone in her family had a history of diabetes. But Raj did not have diabetes (which blood work confirmed), and as far as we knew, there was no history of diabetes in her family. The doctor stated that the abnormalities she'd discussed with us were all she was seeing at the moment, but she would order tests to be run that day for chromosomal studies to see if there were any problems with his brain. She seemed cautious, not overly concerned.

"It is normal," she explained, "that when there are a couple of abnormalities in a child, there may be something else there as well." She also explained that many kids are born with club feet. An orthopedic surgeon could perform surgery to correct the issue. Rajan could also wear corrective shoes with a brace at an early age, which might resolve the issue without surgery. Regarding his testicles, she explained that those could be brought down at a later stage.

Raj and I were concerned about the news of Rajan's health, but after the doctor left, we tried to stay optimistic, telling ourselves that his feet and testes could be corrected, and then everything would be all right.

I drove to Providence Hospital, thinking that work would keep my mind occupied so I wouldn't worry too much about Rajan. On the way there, I prayed that God would bless the situation and that he would take care of our son and strengthen him. I felt so much love for this new baby, and my heart ached for the struggle he was already facing so early in life.

When I reached my office, I reviewed several reports various managers placed on my desk, and then I went to Mr. Gilreath's office to update him on Rajan. I told him about the club feet and also that his testes had not descended.

"Well, he doesn't need those *yet*," Mr. Gilreath joked. "Tell the doctor he has plenty of time."

That evening, I returned to Christ Hospital to be with Raj. The nurse informed me that they had transferred Rajan to the Children's Hospital Medical Center in Cincinnati due to rapid breathing and signs of jaundice. The doctor felt that he may have left upper-lobe pneumonia. After four hours of labor and a C-section, Raj was holding up well, although she was tired. We spoke optimistically about Rajan, assuring each other that, once treated, he would be a healthy, happy baby.

The next day, after working for a few hours, I visited Rajan in the Children's Hospital. When I arrived, the doctors told me that Rajan's rapid breathing was due to a collapsed right lung. They had drawn blood and ordered a chromosomal test, which they were waiting for the results of, and in the meantime, they continued performing tests.

On July 7, the doctors told me they performed an EKG and found Rajan had myocardial ischemia. In other words, the blood flow to his heart had decreased, resulting in reduced oxygen supply and minor damage to his heart muscles. That day, they also began gavage feeding, inserting a tube through his nose which would carry Similac formula to his stomach. (Later, complications developed with the tube, and they put him on an IV.) In the meantime, a congenital anomaly team examined him, but they could not categorize Rajan into a specific syndrome.

Prior to discharge on July 13, the doctors felt that due to Rajan's low blood sugar, he did present as an infant of a diabetic mother, although Raj exhibited no evidence of having diabetes. We all were puzzled about this, and even though Raj was healthy, she felt that she must have done something wrong for there to be so many abnormalities in our newborn son. Yet she did not share these feelings with me until several months later.

On July 13, Raj and I drove home with our new son. His feet were in the casts the doctor had placed a few days earlier. I focused on positive thoughts, assuring myself and Raj that everything would be okay. The three of us were going home together, and for that, we were glad. To have returned home without Rajan would have saddened our hearts, making the reality of his condition seem all too heavy and serious, and perhaps my attitude would not have been so cheerful, so hopeful.

A few days after bringing Rajan home from the hospital, his chromosomal tests came back, showing that his mental capabilities were normal. He seemed to be doing well, and we were glad his breathing returned to normal. After six weeks, Dr. Zenni removed Rajan's casts, replacing them with protective shoes connected by a brace, a metal rod that kept his feet a certain distance apart from each other. Concerned, Raj and I thought, *How is he going to move?* But the doctor assured us, "Don't worry. He will learn to move his legs together."

We were relieved when Rajan learned to move his legs at the same time, but after two months, he became sick again. He drank very little of Raj's breast milk or the Similac we gave him, and on top of that, he began having loose, watery stools ten to twelve times a day, causing him to become weak, dehydrated, and pale. This went on for several days, and after a consultation with Dr. Cooper, we put him on a liquid diet of Jell-O water, which helped with the consistency of the stools and decreased the frequency. We also changed his formula from Similac to Isomil. This change in diet helped for a while, but a week later his stools became loose again. He still refused to feed, always pushing the bottle away, and he began to lose weight. When he developed a sore throat with nasal congestion, Dr. Cooper suggested it would be best to admit him to the Children's Hospital again. There, Rajan would be in good hands. The nurses and doctors would know what to do to improve his health. Raj and I were anxious every day, because we did not know what we were doing wrong or why Rajan's health only persisted in worsening.

We admitted Rajan to the Children's Hospital on October 5, 1977. He was three months old at the time, and although we knew it was best for Rajan to be there, Raj and I felt distraught as we returned home without him. At the same time, we looked forward to having our questions answered. Why did he not want to feed? Why did his diarrhea persist? What were we doing wrong?

We shared the news with the Cheemas on the phone, and at one point, Dr. Cheema said, "Kris, I understand what you guys are going through. But at the same time, you cannot neglect your other two sons."

I knew Dr. Cheema was right, and with my work at Providence Hospital to think about, I trusted Rajan would receive high quality patient care. After all, he was hardly three months old and could not say what he needed or wanted, so they would need to monitor him closely. I believed that the nurses would be with him at all times, as parents are with their child.

Once again, a team of doctors began examining Rajan for signs of a specific syndrome. They analyzed the length and width of his bones, noting his long bones were mildly abnormal, the femurs appearing long and curved, and the radius and ulna thinner than normal. The ribs were also thin, but these findings, among others, did not lead them to any discovery or syndrome that could explain his abnormalities. All signs of myocardial ischemia had disappeared, but the doctors were concerned about his kidneys. When they found he had a urinary infection, they took an X-ray, which seemed to show that the right kidney was absent and the left kidney was smaller than normal.

Next, the doctors did a renal scan and found evidence of both right and left renal function, leading to the observation that the right kidney functioned much less than the left, and the left kidney was displaced. Consequently, Raj and I would have to alter his diet and lifestyle to keep him healthy. To preserve his kidneys, we were determined to make every effort with his long-term diet plan. Hopefully, in the years to come, scientists in the medical field would develop research that would help our son. In the meantime, we would do everything in our power to help him to stay healthy.

Several times when I visited Rajan at the hospital, I discovered he was dirty, and his stool was all dried out. The nurses had not taken care of him for the past four to five hours. When this happened a second time, I spoke to the nurses, and they apologized, saying, "Oh, I don't know what happened. We were supposed to be watching him." Later, Raj and I experienced deep guilt, wondering if it would have made a difference in Rajan's health later on if we had stayed with him at the hospital.

After Rajan was discharged from the hospital, he was a different child than he'd been going in: scared and nervous. We were shocked to see his movements were more stiff and slower than normal, and he was not as playful as before. Displeased with Dr. Cooper, I immediately began searching for a different pediatrician. If Dr. Cooper had seen Rajan while he had diarrhea, perhaps she could have prevented his dehydration and the need for hospitalization in the first place. But that was in the past, and nothing could be done. The neglect Rajan experienced, which put him in such a frightened state, angered me more than anything.

Through Mr. Gilreath, I learned about Dr. Ernst Rolfes. Everyone assured me he was a dependable man who loved children and was excellent at his work. His office was forty-five minutes away, but I heard such good things about Dr. Rolfes that the distance didn't matter to me, as long as Rajan received good medical care.

I made an appointment, and that week, Dr. Rolfes reviewed Rajan's history and examined him thoroughly. Previously, Dr. Cooper recommended that Raj and I feed Rajan PM60/40 Similac formula to take care of his diarrhea, but Rajan did not like the taste of it and drank very little. As a result, he had lost two to three pounds from his birth weight. When Dr. Rolfes heard this, he immediately recommended we give Rajan any type of milk he would drink, whether it be PM60/40 or regular Similac. His main concern was for Rajan to start drinking enough milk and gaining weight again.

I liked Dr. Rolfes's approach, and as soon as we returned home, we switched Rajan's milk to regular Similac. This time, Rajan drank the milk with no trouble. I was happy with Dr. Rolfes, and we continued seeing him. Later, Mr. Gilreath told me Dr. Rolfes said to him in a conversation after our first appointment, "Even though Mr. Bedi's son is doing okay, he is not out of the woods yet."

As Dr. Rolfes did not say anything of this nature to us, his statement shocked me. However, I said to myself, *Rajan is going to be okay, and I am going to continue thinking positive thoughts.* After that, I persisted even more vigorously in my prayers, asking God to bring Rajan "out of the woods."

As the weeks passed, Raj constantly worked with Rajan, taking him for walks and playing with him. Little by little, he showed improvement, becoming more playful, smiling more often, and laughing when we tickled him or bounced him on our knees. By December 1977, Rajan was eating well, smiling often, and acting playful. With all the love and attention we gave him every day, Rajan was no longer the pale, frightened child we had picked up from the Children's Hospital in October.

While we tried to look on the bright side, we felt discouraged that the cast on his feet made crawling difficult for him. Many other questions plagued us as well. Why did our son have multiple anomalies at birth? Why were his testes not descended yet? What could be done about his abnormal kidneys? And then there was the question that the doctors continually asked themselves as they gave Rajan test after test, X-ray after X-ray: *What disorder does this baby have?* The Children's Hospital in Cincinnati happened to be a teaching hospital, and so more tests were performed than usual, and also, more X-rays.

The doctors said Rajan's kidneys were shrunken. Part of me felt his kidneys had been normal, and it was all the X-rays performed on Rajan that shrunk them. I felt this so strongly that I considered filing a lawsuit against the hospital, but Mr. Gilreath advised against it. "As long as Rajan is making good progress," Mr. Gilreath said, "keep devoting time to his care."

I knew Mr. Gilreath was right. Taking legal action would only detract my attention away from Rajan.

That Christmas, Raj and I took the kids to visit the Cheemas in Morristown, New Jersey. When we arrived at their house, Billo and Zafar saw the heartache on our faces. "Why don't you take Rajan to be examined by my brother," Zafar said. "He is an orthopedic surgeon at Saint Barnabas Medical Center in Livingston. His name is Mehmood. He will look at Rajan's feet, and he can refer you to other specialists as well. It's always good to have a second opinion."

Since Livingston was only a twenty-minute drive from Morristown, we all went together the next day. Dr. Mehmood Cheema examined Rajan's club feet right away and suggested admitting Rajan to Saint Barnabas Medical Center, where several of the best specialists could fully diagnose him. So we admitted our son, and every day, Raj and I drove to be with him. The doctors and nurses took samples of his blood and urine to send to the chemistry lab for analysis. Even more X-rays and renal scans were taken. His kidneys were still the same from the previous hospital visit in October, one still smaller and neither one functioning well. The doctors could not find his testes either, much to our disappointment.

Again, the doctors tried to figure out what type of syndrome Rajan could possibly have, but none of the tests they ran brought up any new information. The doctors concluded that his growth development was slow, but neurologically, he was doing fine. Raj and I felt relieved the doctors did not find anything else wrong with him.

Near the end of Rajan's discharge from Saint Barnabas Hospital, Dr. Mehmood Cheema suggested the necessity for surgery on Rajan's feet.

"The surgery is very simple and effective these days," he said. "I will simply lengthen the tendons of his feet so they look normal."

Raj held Rajan on her lap, bouncing him slightly while we all looked at his feet. Despite wearing the cast, they were still bent inward.

"Since Rajan has already been here for almost a week, we can schedule the surgery for February," Dr. Cheema said. "It's not good for a baby at this age to be in the hospital for too long.

He could catch an infection. Postponing the club feet surgery for two months will not make a big difference. For right now, continue changing his cast every two weeks."

Raj and I felt encouraged by Dr. Mehmood Cheema's kindness. We held great hopes that once Rajan's surgery was done, his kidney function would improve with time or with treatment, and the testes could be brought down later. In the meantime, we would treat him as a normal child.

The surgery was scheduled for February 25, 1978, and since I could not take another week off from work, Raj flew alone with Rajan, arriving in Newark two days before the surgery date. They stayed with Dr. Zafar and Billo Cheema, and it just so happened that Mehmood and Zafar's mother was also there for a visit. Their mother was a kind, affectionate woman, and once she learned that her son was going to perform surgery on Rajan, the whole day she prayed to Allah for Rajan's health and for Mehmood to perform the surgery well. Raj stayed with Rajan at the hospital, and, later, Billo informed us that Dr. Cheema's mother continued praying even after Dr. Cheema had completed Rajan's surgery, moved him to the recovery room, and eventually put him in a regular room at the hospital.

Hearing of Dr. Cheema's mother's kindness and devotion, my heart filled with gratitude. I believed in the power of prayer and had prayed the whole day myself. In fact, the first week of October in 1977, when Rajan's problems flared up again, I made a promise to God that I would repeat the Gayatri Mantra 101 times daily. It was the same mantra I had prayed when I lost all my documents as a young man preparing to travel to America for the first time. I also prayed it continuously throughout my years in college when my studies overwhelmed me. My prayer and devotion to God carried me through the difficult times and the obstacles that met me along my path. Now I prayed for Rajan, repeating the mantra 101 times with my entire heart and soul.

Five days after the surgery, Raj returned to Cincinnati with Rajan. Dr. Mehmood Cheema had successfully extended the tendons of Rajan's feet. While Rajan continued wearing casts to train his feet to stay in the correct position, he was one step closer to having a normal life.

❀ ❀ ❀

For a while after Rajan's surgery, life returned to normal. I was so proud of each of my sons, and now that Rajan was making good progress, I could give Christopher and Subhash my full attention.

In 1978, Raj and I decided to sell our house and buy a new one. We settled on a five bedroom house with a walkout basement on the west end of Cincinnati. The house had a huge playroom on the second floor, a family room on the first floor, a three-car garage, and a wine cellar in the basement. Raj and I especially loved the huge private backyard surrounded by trees with a dog run cutting through it.

In August, on the first night in our new home, Raj prepared a traditional sweet dish to be the first food cooked in the house. Before we ate, we knelt with our sons in a small corner set aside for worship and thanked God, praying for a healthy and wealthy start in our new house. Subhash and Christopher especially loved the house with its large playroom.

Raj and I wanted to fill the house with joy and laughter, friends and family, good food and good conversation. At every opportunity, we invited people to cookouts on the deck. For Subhash's seventh birthday, we decided to throw a party in our new house.

"Who do you want to invite?" Raj asked Subhash.

"Only boys. No girls," he answered.

Raj shook her head and looked at me.

"He's saying this now," I said, "but when he is eighteen, he will say, 'All girls, no boys.'"

❀ ❀ ❀

When Rajan was two years old, Mr. Gilreath told me about a priest who was coming to a well-known church in downtown Cincinnati for a hands-on healing service.

"He is very reputable, very well-known," Mr. Gilreath told me. "They say he can cure sickness by prayer and touch. Is this something you would be interested in for Rajan?"

I never heard such a thing before. Laying hands on someone and healing them? But I was desperate, and I also trusted anything Mr. Gilreath said. It wouldn't hurt to try. Rajan was three years old, and his testes still had not descended. Maybe this priest could heal them. That night, I told Raj about the healing service. She looked skeptical too, but like me, she was willing to try anything.

The service took place on a Saturday evening. Raj and I took Christopher and Subhash to a babysitter and arrived at the church early. The pews were already filled, but we managed to squeeze into a pew with our son. Everyone stood to sing, and at one point, the priest asked anyone with a sickness to come forward for prayer. I stood in a long line with Rajan in my arms, wondering what would happen and hoping it would work. The priest moved forward down the aisle, touching everyone's foreheads as he went, and some fell after he touched them. Then the priest reached me, firmly placing his hand on my forehead while praying in a low voice. Immediately, I fell into a squatting position while the priest's associates took Rajan from me to keep him safe. When the priest moved on, I stood up and took Rajan back, feeling strange about the whole thing, I returned to Raj who gave me a concerned look. "Are you okay?" she whispered. I nodded, and we remained seated for the rest of the service.

When it was over, the lady next to us asserted, "Your prayers have been heard, and whatever you came for has been cured."

Mr. and Mrs. Gilreath said the same thing as we were leaving. "That is the way the hands on healing works," Mrs. Gilreath explained.

I turned to Raj. "Let us see," I said.

We took Rajan onto the stage behind the curtain to see if his testes had descended. We both sighed in disappointment. They had not. Raj and I looked at each other, reading the sadness in each other's eyes. Despite our skepticism, we had been so hopeful. While I'm not sure why I fell down or what it meant, I believed strongly in prayer and still believe in it, even though this priest's prayers did not heal our son. I cared deeply for my son's wellbeing, and I would never stop praying for him.

In 1980, we applied for Rajan to attend the preschool at Summit Country Day. Although Rajan still wore a cast on his feet, he was able to walk, and so one day, we scheduled him for an interview at the school. We were nervous, wondering if he would be able to answer all the questions, because he had spent a considerable amount of time in the hospital and in doctors' offices. But since Raj worked with him, teaching him the alphabet and numbers, he did well and was accepted.

During all this time, we treated Rajan as a normal child, disciplining him and asking him to help with house chores appropriate for his age. Raj had taken a pair of rubber thong sandals, removed the top straps, and taped them to the bottom of his cast so he could walk with a flat foot. It gave him confidence to walk more without being wobbly. It seemed that although his body was not growing as it should (he was small for his age), he was progressing well at school. Raj would talk with Rajan's teacher often, and she said he did well in all the classroom activities and was learning at the same rate as the other students. We were thrilled to hear of Rajan's progress and how competitive he was.

Every year, we celebrated Rajan's Fourth of July birthday by setting off fireworks outside our house. In 1980, when Rajan was three, a police officer showed up. As he approached me, all the kids hid in the garage.

"What's going on?" the police officer asked.

"Officer, today is my son's birthday, and we are setting off fireworks to celebrate the Fourth of July, just like the rest of the country."

"I'm sorry," the officer said. "One of your neighbors thought the kids were playing with fireworks."

"Would you like a beer while we set them off?" I asked.

"No thanks," he said. "I'm on duty. You just carry on."

Once the kids realized the officer wasn't going to arrest me, they came back, and Rajan asked him, "Wasn't it fun, the fireworks?"

The officer left after a few minutes when he saw I was the one setting off the fireworks.

As with the fireworks, I enjoyed pleasing Rajan and making him happy. One year, while driving with my family to a hospital management convention in Tucson, Arizona, with my family, I played a book on tape, *Twenty Thousand Leagues Under the Sea*, and Rajan loved it so much he begged me to play over and over. We all grew tired of it after playing it once, but for Rajan's sake, I played it again and again.

As time passed, my career continued to flourish. In February 1979, I was asked to present a paper at a convention in Orlando, Florida. The paper was titled "A Simple Approach to Controlling Inventory Dollars," and I was thrilled to walk around the convention center wearing the prestigious name tag and blue ribbon indicating I was a speaker.

After my presentation, my old industrial engineering professor, Russ Buchan, approached me with a big grin on his face. "Look at you, Kris. Look how far you have come. It seems not long ago you were a student of mine, and now here you are presenting a paper!"

The following year, I flew to Tucson, Arizona, and Atlanta, Georgia, to present a paper about the case cart system that Mrs. Gilreath and I developed. At that point, I was known at the national level in the Hospital Management Systems Society, and I felt like I was walking on air to be able to wear a blue ribbon and walk around the hotel as a speaker. After attending these conventions, I came to be known as a good speaker because my presentations were results-oriented.

Chapter 19

In late May 1981, my family and I visited India so our parents could meet Rajan for the first time. They were overjoyed to see Rajan and hold him close to their chests. He bonded with my father right away. While there, my father said the words I longed to hear.

"We have gotten our passports," my father informed me. "Now we just need a visa to come to the States."

After four weeks, I returned to America early for work, and once my parents completed all the requirements a few weeks later, they came to the States with Raj and the boys. They agreed to stay six months with us in the States because I persuaded them that they would get a much better taste of America the longer they stayed. Also, I simply missed my parents, and I did not want them to come, only to leave in hardly any time at all.

I hoped my parents would see our big house and two cars and find comfort in knowing we were doing well. I hoped my mother would see how comfortable I was and wouldn't feel that I should move back to India. Also, I hoped they would see my lifestyle in the US and decide to stay with me. I wanted them to enjoy the same comforts I did—a nice bedroom, a clean environment, and good food to eat.

"It is amazing to see how my son has come so far," my father said proudly after I gave my parents a tour of our house. "You have done very well in the United States. We are happy to be here and to see your way of life and to help you in any way we can. This will be an interesting visit."

"We are proud of you, Krishan," my mother said, smiling. "I am so happy to be with you and Raj for such a long time, and we are looking forward to spending time with our beloved grandchildren this summer."

If only they knew how deeply thrilled I was to have them there myself. I could tell them all day long, but words could not express my deep emotions at that moment.

A few days after my parents came to stay, Raj started managing Bressler's ice cream store. We had purchased the store, located in the mall, a few months earlier, and Raj had attended a two-week training program in Chicago to learn how to manage it.

Since Raj was often at the ice cream store, my mother helped her with whatever she needed at home. Right away, she took over unloading the dishwasher. However, my mother was too short to reach the cabinets, so instead of putting the dishes away, she set the dishes on the counter and my father put them away. While Raj and I were at work, my father would answer the phone. "If the phone rings," I'd told him, "go ahead and answer it, but state, 'Mr. Bedi is not home. Call later.'"

My father wrote down my instructions, and the plan worked well. Our friends would simply call later when we were home. However, one day the phone rang, and it was Raj's brother, Satish, on the line. While Satish tried to tell my father who he was, my father kept repeating, "Mr. Bedi not home, call later." Satish, realizing what was going on, waited for my father to finish, and then said in Hindi, "Baiji, I am Satish. Satish Verma from Nabha."

Immediately my father perked up, stating, "Oh Satish mal, why didn't you tell me that was you?"

"Baiji, I was trying to tell you," Satish said, "but you kept saying, 'Mr. Bedi not home, call later.'"

During the day, my mother walked around the neighborhood to strengthen her knees. People, being polite, would wave at her and say, "Hi."

My mother did not know how to respond, and, one evening, she brought up the matter to me.

"While I am walking, this woman with light-colored hair who lives in the blue house keeps saying 'Hi, hi.' There are several others who say the same thing. I'm not sure what illness they have. They keep saying 'Hi, hi.' It is very strange."

I just chuckled because in Hindi, people say "Hi, hi" when they are in pain due to sickness.

"Bibi, there is nothing wrong with them," I said. "What they are saying means *Namaste*. You can also say hi and wave your hand."

"Oh," my mother said, laughing, too, at her mistake.

Another evening, my mother related to me what happened when she picked up the phone.

"I told them, 'Mr. Bedi not home, call later,' but they kept talking. So I say in Punjabi, 'Why you keep talking? I just knew only this much English.' *Then* they stopped talking."

I always enjoyed hearing my mother's stories and seeing life in the States through her eyes. While everything around her was American culture, from the way people spoke to each other to how they behaved, she only knew Indian culture and the Punjabi language, and many times the American way of life left her feeling puzzled.

Meanwhile, at Providence Hospital, I was proud of the results my management team and I continued to achieve. However, the inflation rate was high at the time, and we were not receiving salary increases. Looking for a way to fix this, Mr. Gilreath and Finance Director D. M. Hass hired a consultant to work on an administrative compensation package.

After a few months, the consultant's recommendations were approved. As part of the package, each of the administrative staff was granted $2000 towards an IRA and a company car, with certain limitations, such as a monthly lease payment.

Needless to say, I was excited about choosing which car I wanted to lease. The car was only granted to four of us: D. M. Hass, Bill Poll, Mr. Gilreath, and me. Mr. Poll liked the Camaro. As part of the lease agreement, he paid $1,000 out of pocket. Mr. Hass chose a Toyota Corolla with no money out of pocket. I liked the sporty Camaro and chose a white one, also paying $1,000 of my own money. The hospital paid $200 a month for each car. When I drove the car around town, revving the engine and gliding effortlessly through the streets, I felt on top of the world. The car had eight cylinders, so when I drove to Lawrenceburg to see my friend Harbans Gill, it was exhilarating to test its speed on the country roads. Harbans and his wife were amazed to see me pull into their driveway.

"Bedi Saheb, what's going on?" they asked.

I felt as though I were up in the clouds—owning an ice cream store, a company car, receiving a $2,000 financial package, my kids going to a private school, my parents staying with me, and earlier that year, I had invested in two apartment buildings. At the time, I bought gold and silver coins, giving Raj a gold Krugerrand coin to wear as a pendant. Harbans Gill's wife also wanted one, and one day, he said to me, "Bedi Saheb, what's going on? Have you won the lottery? You are making it difficult for us. Now my wife wants one."

There wasn't much else I could ask for, and it seemed life just kept getting better and better.

❀ ❀ ❀

One late night, at around 2:30 a.m., Raj and I were awakened by a phone call. It was the security guard from the mall where our store was located.

"Mr. Bedi, there is some melting ice cream through the small opening of your main freezer, and it is running into the open drain," he said.

Raj and I were stunned to hear this, and we didn't know what to do at such a late hour.

"I just noticed it during my rounds and wanted to give you a call," the security guard said.

"Thank you for calling," I said, "We'll be right there."

Once we got there, we opened the freezer door, and to our surprise, there was an inch and a half of melted ice cream on the freezer floor. It was leaking from the heavy cardboard containers and flowing down the drain. Even though the situation seemed hopeless, we tried to salvage some of the ice cream containers, putting them in our showroom freezer and stacking them as much as we could. The rest continued flowing right in front of our eyes, and, as the saying goes, we were watching our money go down the drain.

The freezer's compressor had simply conked out, so there was nothing to do but let the ice cream flow. Disappointed and tired, we returned home and slept until it was time to get up and start the routine for the next day—getting the kids ready and going to work. While I attended to my responsibilities at Providence Hospital, Raj found someone to fix the freezer compressor. It took three to four days to repair. Needing to order a new supply of ice cream was an additional setback. We had not foreseen such a disaster.

Even if we hadn't suffered a setback, our business still might have struggled. The mall was fifteen years old at the time, and there was not as much traffic as before. Later, I learned this mall was in decline because a newer mall built elsewhere in Cincinnati was attracting more business. In the meantime, the economy was down, and people were not spending as much money on non-essentials like ice cream. All these factors contributed to a bleak outlook for our store. Not long after this incident, we sold the store to another couple. We could not afford to put any more money into a store which made no profit.

It was a sad day in our household when my parents chose to return to India after their eleven-month visit. I tried to persuade them to stay with us indefinitely, but my mother missed her daughters and other grandchildren and her friends from the village. My father missed having control over his properties, and he'd had news that my brother was not managing the cloth shop well.

As they boarded the plane, I almost cried, thinking how I was living comfortably while they must go back and live with my brother in terrible circumstances. He did not give them any respect, and along with the hot weather, no air conditioning, and no heater during the winter. I could not bear to think of it. But it was their wish, and they missed seeing their daughters as well as being in their own culture.

My sister Krishna told me later that when my parents reached New Delhi, she and her husband, Krishan, received them at the airport. Not only was my mother walking easily, but she was also wearing dark glasses and a nice sari. Even though the weather was warm, she wore her topcoat to show it off. She had also lost a little weight and looked entirely different and happy. As my sister told me, she could not even recognize her own mother.

Chapter 20

In October 1982, when Rajan was five years old, I had no idea my life would change, but it did, at first gradually, and then all at once. At the time, I had recently discovered, through a round of testing at the Cleveland Clinic Foundation, that Rajan's growth hormone levels were abnormally low, and he would need to be put on a waiting list for a trial of growth hormone therapy. With Rajan in my thoughts, I received a phone call from Satish. He had seen an ad from a large industrial group known as the Goels.

"The Goels are looking for an administrator for a new hospital to be built in New Delhi," Satish said. "The requirements are an Indian national in a Western country experienced in hospital administration and willing to move to India to be head of this state-of-the-art, five-hundred-bed facility to be built in the suburbs of New Delhi."

I laughed. "Satish, we are well-established here," I said. "We have no thoughts of moving back to India. My kids are at a prestigious private school, and I have a good, secure job here."

"I know, I know," Satish said. "Why don't you just apply and see what happens. Who knows? You may be qualified."

Later, I discussed this job opportunity with Raj. She laughed also. "We are all set here. We don't need to move."

Those were my thoughts exactly, and we just laughed at how ridiculous it would be to move when we were comfortable as we were. However, that evening as I lay in bed, the thought crept into my mind—*What if I did get the job offer? Wouldn't it be great if I applied, just out of curiosity, and they wanted me to be the administrator?* The words "newly built," and "state-of-the-art" floated in my head. By the next morning, as I got ready for work, I had decided to apply just to see if anything happened. Not that I wanted to move—I really didn't. But now that the idea settled into my mind, I wanted to see if I would be offered the job. It would boost my ego.

On a whim, I decided to mail a letter to New Delhi inquiring about the position. To my surprise, I received a phone call three weeks later from the Hospital Corporation of America (HCA), a profit-making organization which owned and operated many healthcare facilities in the US. They were known for buying failing, nonprofit health care facilities and turning them into profitable entities.

During the phone conversation, the HCA representative told me the Goels liked my qualifications and wanted HCA to interview me. When could I come to Nashville?

Taken aback and pleasantly surprised, I set a date. Later, I shared the news with Raj, and while she seemed happy that they had chosen to interview me, she wondered why I was going through this if we were not going to move to India.

"Hey, I haven't gotten the job yet," I said, "so moving doesn't come into the picture. Let's see what happens."

In a way, the phone call from HCA made me feel good, indicating that I was qualified for the position after all. The next month was a whirl of activity. After my interview in Nashville, HCA wanted me to fly to New York City to meet Z.M. Goel, the head of the hospital project. With Mr. Gilreath's permission, I took two days off to go there. Z.M. Goel talked to me briefly about my experiences at Providence Hospital. I explained everything to him fluidly, also speaking about finances and how we were able to increase revenue in several departments. After the interview, he shook my hand vigorously, saying they would be in touch.

After I returned to Cincinnati, Arun Mangal called me to set up a time for Z.M. Goel and himself to come to Providence Hospital to spend the whole day with me. When I spoke to Mr. Gilreath about it, he was excited that people from India were interested in me and wanted to see Providence Hospital. He asked the food service department to serve a fabulous lunch for the Goel team. I informed Mr. Mangal that my boss would like to set up a luncheon while they were visiting, and as the next few days passed, excitement spread like wildfire through the hospital as everyone learned that people from India were coming to see the facility and were interested in hiring Kris Bedi as the administrator of a new hospital in New Delhi.

The day of their visit, Mr. Mangal talked to me one-on-one in my office. Then, the entire day, as I went from department to department, he followed me, observing, wanting to know exactly what I was doing in order to make sure I really was the assistant administrator of this facility and that everything I had told them about my professional background was true. Z.M. Goel arrived later that morning. Mr. Gilreath and I treated him and Mr. Mangal to a nice lunch, and I gave them a tour of Providence Hospital, especially going through the SPD department. All the supervisors and managers greeted Mr. Gilreath and me with big hugs, and they showed positive attitudes while performing their activities. All the departments were clean and well-organized, and the Goel team observed the quiet and the automation on the patient floors as well as the interactions between patients and nurses. The Goel team was impressed, and at the end of the day, they wanted to meet Raj as well.

I called Raj ahead of time to let her know we would be coming at around 4:00 p.m. When we arrived, she set before us an elaborate tea and snacks with formal china. Z.M. Goel spoke with her for several moments before presenting her with a beautiful, expensive sari brought from India.

After drinking tea and eating snacks, Z.M. Goel and Mr. Mangal stood to leave. "Once we get back to India, we will let you know our decision," Z.M. Goel said. After they left, Raj and I breathed a huge sigh of relief.

❀ ❀ ❀

In January 1983, Raj and I stepped off the plane after traveling in executive class to the New Delhi airport. The Goel brothers had personally invited Raj and me to India to further discuss my role in the hospital project. Looking back, it was a daring decision to leave three young children behind while we traveled so far away. Mr. Gilreath gave us confidence that he would take care of the kids in any emergency situation. While we were gone, he visited the children every day after work and also checked on the sitter to see if she needed any help.

Mr. Mangal met us in the terminal, and the three of us stepped forward into the uncertainty of New Delhi with its endless maze of streets. I kept telling myself we weren't going to move there, and Raj seconded this thought. We had many comforts in the States, and to move to this big city in the northern center of India would be a great risk.

The Goels owned a helicopter, and the next day, Mr. Mangal invited me to join him for a helicopter ride. "Take a look over there!" Mr. Mangal yelled over the thundering roar of the helicopter engine. We had flown eighty miles to Goelnagar to see the city named after the Goel family. "This is a great bird's eye view of Goel Mills. See, right down there!" Mr. Mangal exclaimed. "Late Mr. Ashoka Goel established the Goel group in 1933 here in Goelnagar, along with his brother, Gobind Lal Goel."

Ashoka was the father of five of the Goels. He had passed away, and the hospital would be built in his name. Ashoka, an entrepreneur, had started the Goel Industries which his sons kept going. Gobind Lal Goel was the father of two of the brothers, and he was also the chairman of the group.

I could tell the Goels were proud of their family history. As I sat in the helicopter's front passenger seat, I felt amazed and excited to be with these businessmen high up in the air.

"We take our businesses seriously," another Goel brother said. "Whether it is a mill or a rubber factory, we uphold the highest level of quality and service. It will be the same with our new hospital. Perhaps even more so."

I nodded thoughtfully. I was on board with that statement. My sole mission at Providence Hospital was to improve the quality of service and operations in each of my departments. It helped that the Goels and I held the same vision in that regard. In fact, what I was beginning to like about the Goels was their visionary attitude for every project they started. It was clear that this helicopter ride was meant to impress me, but I was most impressed with the way they did business.

During the next two weeks, I met new people everywhere I went. In the meantime, the seven cousin-brothers interviewed me individually at their own convenience. In India, a cousin-brother refers to a male cousin from the same generation as you. Gobind Lal Goel interviewed me as well. I never knew exactly when I would be interviewed, only that when they called, I needed to be ready. Gobind Lal cautioned me, saying "Right now you are 'Mr. Bedi' and you are walking by my side. If you do not manage the hospital efficiently, then you will walk behind me and no more 'Mr. Bedi.'"

All this time, Satish reveled in the fact that his brother-in-law was being interviewed for such a prestigious position and would be well-connected to the Delhi high-level politicians, such as chief ministers, if I landed the job offer. Also, an intense discussion ensued among my relatives in New Delhi about my flying in a helicopter. They were in awe that I was being given so much respect, and, indeed, I felt gratified. The Goels wanted to impress me as well as persuade me to move to India permanently. I could not help mulling over the fact that in this position I would be the director, the one in charge of the facility.

When Raj and I visited my parents, they were surprised to see us, since they had come back from the States a few months earlier. I told them only briefly about my visit, not elaborating on details, because we had no intention of moving back to India at the time. Deep down, my parents felt happy, thinking it would be great if this job matured for me.

At one point, I visited the construction site of the new hospital and met with the project director and several architects, including one named Abhay Chawla. One evening, Chawla invited Raj and me to his residence for an entertaining cocktail and dinner party. First the hostess, and then a guest, asked Raj if she wanted a cocktail. Both women were surprised when Raj declined the offer of alcoholic beverages, saying that she did not drink. Many women at the party were drinking hard liquor, and they were amazed that Raj had lived in the US for so many years and did not drink. We also saw one woman smoking at the party. Normally, in our experience, Indian women did not smoke or drink. However, the impression of American women was that they all smoked and drank. Smoking and drinking in India was a status symbol, signifying they had adapted to Westernized culture and were doing well.

Quite a few important people were invited to this party to meet me and to impress me so I would accept the position if it were offered. It seemed the longer I stayed in India, the more discussions I held with my relatives; and the more these people tried to impress me, the more difficult my decision was becoming.

Raj and I had planned to spend two weeks in India, but after that time passed, the Goels wanted me to see more people. So Raj returned home while I stayed in India. On the last day of my visit, Mr. Mangal offered me the job, indicating the salary would be 5,000 rupees per month—$500 in US currency compared to my current salary of $4000. I would also be provided with a furnished house, servants, a chauffeur driven car, and a *chokidar* or gatekeeper, to watch over our house. In the advertisement, the salary range had been 5,000 to 8,000 rupees. I mentioned this, but Mr. Mangal was firm. They could not increase the salary at that point. However, he could work it out so that my wife was added to the payroll without needing to do any work.

With all those perks, it seemed an attractive offer. I told Mr. Mangal that I would discuss it with my wife and let him know my decision.

❋ ❋ ❋

Once I returned to the US, everyone's eyes were on me as they wondered, *What is Mr. Bedi going to do?* I told Mr. Gilreath about the entire visit and how this was the hardest decision of my life. "I don't know what I'm going to do, Mr. Gilreath," I said at the end of our conversation. "In my heart, I feel my place is here, beside you. I love my job here, and if I decide to move, it will be a very difficult decision."

Mr. Gilreath acknowledged my statement, and I could tell he felt the same way. Looking at me directly, he said, "Kris, this decision is totally up to you. I want you to do whatever you feel is best for you and your family. Do not think about me."

Now that I was back in the States, I started receiving phone calls from Mr. Arun Mangal, as well as D.P. Bakhsi, an accountant and the liaison for Z.M. Goel. "What is your decision?" they wanted to know.

After thinking about it and discussing the matter with Raj, four things came to my mind. First, it would be great to take my education and experience in the healthcare field and use it to provide and improve patient care to the poor, setting an example of excellent quality of patient care. Second, I would be contributing to my birth country by making an impact on the healthcare profession. Third, I would be near my parents to provide comfort and take care of them with their health care if needed. Finally, I would be the top man, number one, the person in charge of the design, to staff, to develop policies and procedures, and to open this hospital from scratch.

At the same time, my cousin Ved Bedi had said, "Krishan, you should think twice before moving back to India. It's not going to be easy. Things are not the same here. Like they say, the grass looks greener on the other side."

Since Ved had lived in the US, earned his master's degree, and worked there for a couple of years before moving back to India to settle with his parents, he could tell me that the adjustment was not easy.

On the other hand, Satish responded differently. "Bedi Saheb, it would be great if you moved. Once the hospital is built, this will be a great position. Every important person in New Delhi will be approaching you, wanting to have good relations with you because it is difficult to be admitted to a good hospital or get a medical consultation when you need it."

At that time, there were no private hospitals in New Delhi, and there was a great need for good facilities throughout India.

Another issue on my mind was Rajan and his health. I spoke to Dr. Redmond about it, and he seemed to think it might be good for Rajan to move to India. One, he should be drinking goat milk, and two, a more vegetarian diet might be better for him because of his less than normally functioning kidneys. I also questioned whether or not growth hormone would be available in India, since Rajan was going to start that treatment soon. He was much smaller than other kids his age, and we hoped this treatment would help him to catch up. Dr. Redmond inquired about the growth hormone medication and found that it was available in England and could be shipped to us.

So Raj and I discussed all these factors, especially those concerning Rajan's health, but in the end, Raj was not in favor of moving back. "Why are we moving?" she would ask.

My answer was, "To help the poor and to provide good healthcare."

In the back of my mind, I thought Raj also might be happy since she would be close to her parents and siblings. However, she seemed reluctant. Since Subhash was twelve years old and well settled at the school, I shared my thoughts of moving to India with him.

"Why?" he asked, a sad look on his face. I did not have a good answer, simply stating it was a new job.

At the end of April, I decided to accept the position. I would join them by mid-November after finishing my projects at Providence Hospital and resigning, as well as selling my house, the apartment buildings, the rental house, and our two cars. For several weeks, the environment at the hospital was subdued with everyone processing the news that Mr. Bedi would be leaving them. Most of them hoped Mr. Gilreath would convince me to stay. Even though I had decided to leave, I worked as hard as ever and assured Mr. Gilreath I would continue doing my best for Providence.

Mr. Gilreath nodded. "I have no doubt, Kris. I have full confidence in you. After all these years I have known you, you have done so much for Providence."

In a way, our relationship remained the same, and over the following months, we continued working together as normal. However, deep down in his heart, Mr. Gilreath did not want me to leave.

Chapter 21

I arrived in New Delhi on November 13, 1983. Raj and the boys had moved to India in July so the kids could start school at the beginning of the school year. Rajan was in first grade, Christopher was in fourth grade, and Subhash was just starting middle school. They attended Delhi Public School, a school with a good reputation. The Goels helped get them accepted on such short notice.

The car driven by our chauffeur brought Raj and the kids to the airport to meet me. Raj hugged me tightly, and the kids jumped up and down, wrapping me with hugs and shouting out loud. I hugged each of them, but to Rajan, I gave the biggest hug of all, lifting him off the ground and holding him in my arms.

Being so far from my family the past four months had been a trial. During that time, I struggled to sell my properties, finding it necessary to sell them for much less than their worth before my departure to India. Losing these investments and watching my money go down the drain was almost more than I could handle. On top of it, my cousin Raj Dev Bedi called after he returned from a visit to India with the news that my entire family had contracted malaria. "Why are you in the US and not in India taking care of your family?" my cousin chided. My wife, not wanting me to worry, had not said a word about it.

I broke down and cried that day. Shutting myself in my bedroom, I fell to my knees and cried out to God in anguish. At one time, my net worth had been $125,000, and now, although I still had $30,000 in a 401K plan, I had barely $3000 in cash. My properties were not selling for the prices I had hoped for, and now I feared for my family, knowing it was my fault they were in India, instead of in America where malaria was not a threat.

I would wake up every morning, drag myself to the pictures of my Guruji and Lord Krishna set up on a table, and fall to my knees, crying out to God. Tears of desperation flowed down my cheeks, and for the next fifteen minutes, I wept. *Please God, please help me,* I said over and over in my heart. After saying the Gayatri Mantra, I wiped the tears from my face and resolved to put my best foot forward. No one else could help me, and so no one else would see my tears.

Now my family was well, and I was finally in India. As the chauffeur drove us to our house, I tried my best to look forward and put on a cheerful face for my family. Raj warned me about the house D.P. Bakhsi pressured her to choose. "It's not in the best neighborhood," she told me, "but it's the best I could do out of the options they gave me."

The chauffeur pulled onto a narrow street in the Masjid Moth area. All the houses were crowded together, and our house looked small and plain with peeling paint and scraggly bushes in front. The chauffeur helped me unload my suitcase and bags from the trunk, and we all entered the house. There was not much furniture inside, just a couch, a table and chairs, and some bedding to tide us over until our custom-built furniture arrived.

Oh God, what is this? I thought, looking around at the dingy walls and dirty concrete floor. Even though the windows were open to let in the breeze, the air felt stifling hot. I gestured for the chauffeur to set my suitcase and bags in the bedroom, and then I turned around and smiled at Raj. She watched me nervously.

"This is fine," I said. "When I've been working at the hospital a while, I will have more influence with the Goels. Mr. Bakhsi will not be an obstacle. Then we will find the right house for us." I hid my true feelings, not wanting Raj to sense my disappointment. She had worked hard to find a house.

Upon our arrival, a servant prepared tea, and Raj rang the bell to be served. She showed me the bell ringing system connected from the bedrooms to the kitchen. Whenever we needed a glass of water or cup of tea, we could ring the bell and the servant would appear, asking, "What do you need, sir?"

The next morning, I met with Mr. Mangal at the Goels' office to discuss the hospital. Afterward, D.P. Bakhsi escorted me to the construction site. The construction team had built a few temporary offices on the site, and one of them was reserved for me. The office contained only a table and chair, nothing more. I was crestfallen at the sight of the tiny, dank office. I could not imagine meeting with staff members and important hospital figures in this confined space. I had hoped my office would resemble Mr. Bakhsi's spacious office with its large desk, shelves, and comfortable chairs. I hid my distaste, knowing Mr. Bakhsi enjoyed seeing me working in such conditions. He was jealous of the importance given to me, and he failed to hide his dislike.

Mr. Bakhsi introduced me to the staff—one architect to coordinate construction, a retired colonel in charge of the construction, an accountant, a draftsman, four peons, two secretaries, and a medical doctor just returned from the Middle East. I liked the colonel right away. He had an open, honest nature I could trust. While the staff filled me in on the project's finances, construction, and architecture, the colonel took me aside, fixing me with a serious expression.

"There are some elements assigned to this project who might not be honest with you," he cautioned me. "They might try to pull you down in every effort to make you fail."

Mr. Bakhsi came to mind, but were there others too? Puzzled, I simply thanked him and moved on. I was here to do a job, and I planned to do it the way I knew best. Besides, I preferred to have a fresh start with the staff. I would draw my own conclusions.

Later that day, I met with D.P. Bakhsi. Sitting in his site office, I could look out the window and see the construction workers building the frame of the hospital. It looked like hot, dusty work, and the sound of drills and hammers made its way into D.P. Bakhsi's tidy office. Mr. Bakhsi sat behind his desk looking at me intently, not with an expression of dislike, but one of boldness, almost bordering on insolence. I already detected friction between him and the colonel, and this was to be confirmed later, but at that moment, there were several factors to discuss.

"Prior to your arrival, the colonel has been holding weekly meetings with the project staff members," D.P. Bakhsi said. "Now that you are here, you should hold the meetings."

I nodded my head. In a way, it made sense, but at the same time, it was obvious he was attempting to create friction between the colonel and me. Nevertheless, I spoke to the colonel about it, and he said it would be okay. "Bedi Saheb, just to be sure," he said, "I am the project director of construction, and any issues related to construction you should communicate with me."

"Yes, I will make sure to do so, Colonel Saheb," I said. With that, I gave him a firm handshake, a friendly yet professional gesture to say I meant no ill will.

After being in Delhi for a month, I held my first meeting with the organizations associated with the hospital project. To my annoyance, people arrived thirty minutes to an hour late. Right away, I established a few rules, the first rule being that everyone must arrive on time, and we would start the meeting at the scheduled time. Second, we must listen to each other, and only one person could talk at a time. "There will be no meetings going on within the meeting," I said. If we were going to accomplish anything, the meetings needed order and discipline.

During the first few months, I toured several hospitals in Bombay and Madras (now known as Chennai), in order to familiarize myself with healthcare facilities in India. When I returned to New Delhi, I tried to conduct business in my small office at Nehru Place. This was more difficult than I anticipated. First of all, there was no phone. Second, I could not hold meetings with anyone because of the room's size. To make phone calls and talk to people, I used D.P. Bakhsi's office, feeling uncomfortable because he was supposed to be working for me. Since Z.M. Goel was a busy man, most of my communication was with Mr. Arun Mangal. One day, I proposed to Mr. Mangal the idea of moving from my much smaller office into D.P. Bakhsi's office, and he could find another office in the Nehru Place building. I also talked to D.P. Bakhsi about it, and while he didn't outright say no to me, I could tell he did not want to move.

In the end, Z.M. Goel gave me the go-ahead, and I moved into the nicer, more spacious office. D.P. Bakhsi did not appreciate my pushing him out of the office. He was considered a big man in his profession, and since he was dealing in finances, everyone was afraid of him, especially because he pushed his weight around and usually got what he wanted. He felt I had undermined him in front of his staff by taking over his office.

This was simply the way things should be. As executive director, a title I requested in place of "administrator," I couldn't let D.P. Bakhsi control me. It seemed only fair that I should have an office to conduct business in, since I was in charge of the entire hospital, not just one area of it. To D.P. Bakhsi, my position and responsibilities did not matter. From that point on, whatever I tried to accomplish, he found a way to interfere.

The first week of January 1984, my family and I moved into a house located at 333 East of Kailash. We lived on the second floor, and an American man who worked with Goels Sterling Drug lived on the first floor. The second floor had three bedrooms and was clean and well-furnished. The third bedroom was located above us, and there was a staircase to the roof with a table and chairs. We felt lucky to live in a nicer house, and having an American living below increased the status of our new home.

After a couple of months in India, I sensed the financing of the hospital wasn't coming through. The State Bank of India rejected the initial proposal, forcing the Goels to scale back the project to a 350-bed facility. But when the papers were prepared, the project was still not financially viable. The Goels arranged for me to meet with the minister of health, explain the scope of the project, and plead our case. I also met with Pranabh Mukherjee, the minister of finance who was also the right hand man to Prime Minister Indira Gandhi.

As the months passed, I became more discouraged. The funding for the hospital was not coming in, and what had seemed like a sure thing was now full of uncertainty. A few weeks earlier, I'd spoken with Mr. Gilreath to follow up on my financial matters—the bills needing to be paid in the States as well as house payments that needed to be deposited to our accounts there. I casually said, "Maybe I should come back. The project is not going as planned." However, Mr. Gilreath only sympathized with me and did not give any indication that I would get my job back if I returned. I decided to continue working hard to see if the project would still come through.

The entire time, I also dealt with the politics of seven cousin-brothers and the competition and jealousies arising between them. Even though Z.M. Goel was managing director of the project, the other cousin-brothers were also members of the board. G.B. Goel, for instance, wanted to be the managing director, and his father, Gobind Lal, also wanted him to be in charge. There was a lack of professionalism and no organized structure. The Goels did not show as much interest in the project as they should if they wanted it to be a success. In fact, it was extremely difficult for me to meet with Z.M. Goel on a regular basis to give him updates on our progress, financial or otherwise.

The Goels scaled back the project to 200 beds, and we still weren't getting loan approvals. D.P. Bakhsi was the director of finances and had played a major part in getting the loans approved. Now he was a failure. He only did the required amount of work, not putting his heart and soul into it. Sometimes it seemed he was spoiling the project, throwing in a monkey wrench. He wanted the colonel out, resenting him because the colonel threw him out of a meeting, telling Z.M. Goel he did not want Bakhsi coming to the construction site at all. I dealt the best I could with these obstacles and controversies, hoping this project would somehow come out on top.

❀ ❀ ❀

In India, bugs and mosquitoes flourished at our house on East of Kailash. The only spray available to kill insects was DDT, a chemical spray banned in the US. I hesitated to spray DDT, but the bug problem worsened until I had no choice. The night after we sprayed, Rajan's breathing became heavy and labored. We took him to a hospital for treatment, and I felt deep remorse for exposing Rajan to harmful chemicals. The environment in India was twenty years behind the US, and in times like these, I wondered why I had brought my family to India. Environmental dangers lurked all around us, not to mention the traffic, which only added to the stress and chaos.

During the summer months, the temperature reached over one hundred ten degrees, and sometimes the air conditioners would shut down because it was so hot. The children tossed and turned sleeplessly in their hot rooms, so I sprinkled cold water on their sheets each night. My parents and I did the same thing when I lived in Malaudh. The water creates a cooling effect on the body when air blows on it. As I sprinkled water on my sons' beds, I couldn't help thinking to myself, *After twenty years of living in the US in houses with central air, here I am in New Delhi, creating a cooling environment just as my parents and I had done in Malaudh.* It was the only effective way to keep cool at night, and at times, Christopher said he felt like he was sleeping in a bucket of water.

❀ ❀ ❀

As always, Rajan's health challenges lay heavy on my heart. I did not share all my son's medical challenges with my relatives and parents because it would worry them tremendously. His testes had not descended, and there was still concern over his kidneys and his small stature, but Rajan looked healthy and normal. He brought joy into our lives just by his presence.

In April 1984, I decided it was time to go to the Naina Devi temple. Years earlier, I made a pledge to Naina Devi, a goddess of Hindu mythology: "If you keep Rajan well during his surgeries, I will come to the temple and do pushups across the 1.5 mile distance up the hill to your first gate."

There are many phrases, called *jaikaras*, chanted over and over by people who come to Naina Devi with their requests. A common one is "*Jai Mata Di*," meaning, "You fulfill everybody's wish." On the appointed day, I would lie down at the beginning of the path with my arms stretched forward, and I would mark the dirt at the point my fingers reached. While saying my own jaikara in Hindi, "Please accept my plea," I would stand up, move to the mark in the dirt, and lay down again, still chanting my chosen jaikara. This ritual was called a *Dandhot*, and I would repeat it over and over until I reached the temple gate.

When I arrived at the temple with my wife, my sons, and my parents, only Raj knew what I planned to do at the temple site. Neither my parents nor my sons knew anything. It was a matter I kept close to my heart, knowing I must be strong and determined to accomplish the strenuous feat.

We arrived at the parking lot two miles away from the Naina Devi temple. The steep steps leading up to the temple gates were unmistakable. I could see devoted worshipers climbing to the top. On either side of the steps, there were souvenir shops selling religious items. As my family members got out of the car and stretched, I tied a red bandana around my head, a symbol of a devotee of Naina Devi. A few minutes later, we walked together to the winding pathway that led up the hill and through the trees. My sons, who had been noisy and talkative in the car, were now quiet and observant, curious to see what would happen next. Before beginning our walk to the temple, we hired an Indian boy to carry Rajan on his back because Rajan was small and would have trouble walking up such a steep hill in his orthopedic shoes.

The steep path zigzagged, making the ascent much longer. My parents were amazed I was doing the *Dandhot* ritual, and they prayed for me to successfully complete it. As I ascended the hill, my mother and father spoke encouraging words to me while Raj and the kids walked a few steps behind. Thirty minutes later, I reached the steps where I took a short break. There were more than 450 steep steps, and since my mother could not walk up them, we hired two men to carry her in a *palki*, a chair roped to a long, thick wooden rod. With the men on each side of the rod, they began to carry her.

Gathering my strength and taking a deep breath, I climbed the steps in the same manner I climbed the hill. Other people were walking up the steps at the same time, and they looked toward me. Many of them chanted with me to help fulfill my vow. Others spoke encouraging words, saying, "You can do it. Not much farther to go." The sun blazed hot on the concrete and marble steps. Subhash and Christopher walked behind me. Raj walked to my left, and the boy carrying Rajan was on my right. Rajan, seven years old, was too young to know that my prayers were for him, but I prayed all the harder, chanting until my throat felt raw. My lips were parched, and my bandana soaked the sweat from my forehead. I prayed for his health with all my might, and at the very last step, I remained prostrate a moment longer, saying my *jaikara* with as much feeling as I could muster. Tired and my shirt soaked with sweat, I smiled as I came slowly to my feet. I made it to the top, finally accomplishing what only the truest devotees would do as I fixated on the promise of my heart.

The Indian boy set Rajan on the ground, and the two men helped my mother out of the *palki*. Together, my family and I entered the temple, where I stood in front of the statue, praying, "Please accept my pledge and continue to protect and provide good health to Rajan." It had been a good day, one of hope and joy, and despite the troubles Rajan faced, I knew his life would be blessed.

❊ ❊ ❊

In May 1984, New Delhi's temperature rose to a sweltering 120 degrees. During this time, Rajan would come home from school red-faced and sweaty. Without saying a word, he would go straight to the bedroom he shared with his brothers and sit in front of the A/C. When mealtime came, he was uninterested in any food we gave him, and he would go to bed in the evenings having eaten next to nothing. After a few days of this pattern, Raj and I became worried. He was not a big eater to begin with, but now he was losing weight. Looking weak and pale, he walked slowly, dragging his feet.

One day, I called a pediatrician and told him of my son's symptoms. He told me to bring Rajan to his office the following Monday.

"My son is losing weight and has not eaten for the last four days," I said, desperation creeping into my voice. "I would like to bring him to you today."

Upon my insistence, the doctor finally agreed.

"Bring him to my residence, and I will take a look," he said.

Raj and I took Rajan to the doctor's house, and after a brief examination, the doctor said, "He may have lost his appetite due to the heat. Give him something salty. That will make him thirsty. Try giving him potato chips, and little by little, he will start eating and keeping cool."

On our way home, we bought several bags of potato chips, something we normally didn't allow our kids to eat, but we were hoping Rajan would eat as many chips as he wanted. Slowly, Rajan began eating, first the potato chips, and then a peanut butter jelly sandwich, and later, a cheeseburger. After a few days, his eating patterns returned to normal. After then, we made sure Rajan stayed cool and that his bedroom A/C was working at all times.

Rajan's health was one concern continually on my mind. My cousin Ved Bedi's wife, Usha, was a doctor. Every month, we took him to Usha's clinic to get his blood drawn to monitor his creatinine levels, and even though we gave Subhash and Christopher regular milk to drink, Raj would mix Rajan a drink from the Similac PM 60/40, which we had shipped from the US in large quantities before we moved to India. The Similac was designed for children with poor renal function. Also, Rajan had grown little in the past year. I made several calls to Dr. Redmond in Cleveland to check on the growth hormone medicine. To my disappointment, he always had the same reply—it was not yet available.

Despite the challenges we faced, my family and I experienced fun, light-hearted moments, and the holidays in India were always a chance to let loose and celebrate life. *Holi*, in particular, is the most vibrant and joyful of all the festivals. It is a celebration of the arrival of spring, a season of joy and hope. We would go to Satish's house in the afternoon, and we all would dump water of different colors on each other and rub red powder on each other's faces. Out in the streets, the people of New Delhi ran about, throwing red, green, orange, yellow, and purple powders at each other. Afterward, we would share sweets with each other and laugh because we all were covered from head to toe in an array of color.

We also visited Mussoorie, also known as the Queen of Hills, a hill station in the State of Uttarkhand where the air was cooler. We enjoyed visiting local tourist attractions, such as Gun Hill and the temple Nag Devta, dedicated to the snake god, Lord Shiva.

One day in June 1984, Satish called. As soon as I heard his voice at the end of the line, I knew something was wrong.

"Bedi Saheb, have you heard the news?" he asked.

"What news do you mean?" I asked, even though I heard it on the radio that morning.

"Operation Blue Star," he answered. "Today, Indira Gandhi ordered the Indian Army to attack the Golden Temple. Can you believe it? *The* Golden Temple. The Sikhs are not going to be happy about this."

Everyone was talking about it, and everyone was on edge. The self-styled leader of a Sikh separatist movement called the Khalistanis, Bhindranwale, and his followers were taking shelter in the Golden Temple along with their ammunition. He was considered a freedom fighter by some Sikhs, but others saw him as merely a terrorist. Ordering an attack on Bhindranwale would rile up the Sikhs, posing a serious danger.

"I have heard, Satish Ji. I hope the Indian Army can keep the insurgents under control."

"Yes, I am afraid things might get out of hand," Satish said. "You remember what happened last October, don't you? Those Sikh militants stopped a bus and shot six Hindu passengers."

I heard about that attack when I first moved back to India a month after it happened, shocking me to know these tragedies still happened. The Sikh separatists were stockpiling weapons in the temple in an attempt to take over the state of Punjab and form it into their own country. The revered holy place had sustained much damage, and the Sikhs and others who worshipped there were furious that the Indian Army attacked the insurgents who were using it as their hideout. I told Satish I would be on watch for anything out of the ordinary.

Upon speaking with my parents, I learned there was a great fear spreading through the state of Punjab. Bhindranwale had gathered a following of hundreds of thousands of khalistanis who also wanted to create their own country, killing Hindus in the process. Now the people of my beloved home of Punjab trembled at the sound of his name.

On October 31, 1984, a year after I'd returned to India, I was in Bombay to make arrangements with a transportation company to transport boxes of camera film to New Delhi. Satish had asked me if I wanted to be a part of his side business of importing film. While taking care of the transportation, I learned that at 9:20 a.m., Indira Gandhi had been shot at her residence in New Delhi.

She was in critical condition and had been taken to a hospital.

Two of her Sikh body guards shot her as revenge for the Operation Blue Star assault on the Golden Temple in Amritsar a few months earlier. Indira Gandhi was declared dead that afternoon and the news of her assassination spread throughout the country like a tidal wave. Tension lurked behind the eyes of everyone I met, and it seemed the air was touched by an electric current of fear. The great prime minister of India had fallen.

At three o'clock, I called Satish to inform him that the consignment was on the truck, en route to New Delhi.

"Very good, Bedi Saheb. But please be careful. Right after Indira's death was declared, riots broke out all over New Delhi."

With the country in chaos, I boarded the plane from Bombay to New Delhi, arriving at 9:00 p.m. Instead of my chauffeur waiting for me as I expected, Satish's driver waved me down. "Bedi Saheb, get in the car quickly," he said. "We will be going to Punjabi Bagh instead of East of Kailash, because people are already damaging moving vehicles, and riots have started on that side."

Satish had communicated with Raj, and she informed him that people were throwing bricks at cars, and it did not seem safe for my chauffeur to go to the airport. As Satish's driver brought me to Punjabi Bagh, where Satish and his family lived, I couldn't believe I was heading for the safe part of the city while Raj was alone with our three sons. I could not get them out of my mind, and I prayed continuously for their protection.

When we reached Satish's house, he met us at the door, relief written on his face. "Good, you are safe," he said. "Bedi Saheb, I just spoke to Raj on the phone, and she wants you to know she and the kids are okay. They have gone to the neighbor's house."

Satish and I went to the living room, and as he talked about the assassination and the riots, I felt strange being so far from my family while so much violence and chaos was around them. There was no telling what might happen in the days to come.

That night, I could barely sleep. I spoke with Raj at around 11:00 p.m., just before she and the kids moved back to our house to go to sleep. They would have the chokidar stay awake and watch the house the whole night, but I still couldn't sleep much. I did not like being away from my family on a night such as this.

The next day, I wanted to get back to my family, so Satish's driver took the back streets until we reached my house. The riots were spreading all over New Delhi, and it wasn't safe to go into the streets anywhere. I was overwhelmed with relief and happiness to be home, and as I walked in the door, my kids ran to greet me. Raj, especially, was relieved to not be alone with the kids while the riots were happening right outside our doorstep. We stayed inside the house, and every now and then, we would go to the balcony to see what was going on. People were breaking into shops and carrying out items such as TVs, radios, air conditioners, and clothes. Any cars that risked venturing out were pelted with rocks and bricks.

On the second night of the riots, our doorbell rang. With great hesitancy, I opened the door and saw a Sardarji standing outside. He was the owner of the taxi stand in front of our house, and although he was a Sikh, I was always friendly with him and his partners, speaking Punjabi with them and greeting them pleasantly. Even though I am not a Sikh, I have always had good relations with them, and so whenever I needed a taxi, I would always get one from their stand.

On this evening, the Sardarji trembled with fear. He was taking a great risk to be outside our house at this moment.

"Saheb, can you help us?" he asked quickly.

"Sure, tell me what I can do," I responded. I could hear the sounds of a fight breaking out just a block away.

"I have a nephew who is only eighteen, and he has nowhere to hide. Is it possible for you to give him shelter?"

Raj was standing next to me, and we both looked at each other, thinking the same thing: *Giving shelter to this Sikh boy might put our family in danger.* At the same time, my heart could not say no. Turning back to the Sardarji, I said, "Tell this boy, don't say a word and just stay inside the garage."

"I will do so. Thank you, Bedi Saheb. Thank you. We will not forget your kindness." The Sardarji placed his palms together and bowed his head to me before rushing to tell his nephew the good news. The boy hurried to the garage and closed the door.

I shut the door, and Raj looked at me, a worried expression on her face. "I just couldn't say no," I told her. "What if he is killed tonight or tomorrow? I would not be able to live with myself, thinking that I said no and later learned this boy became a victim of the riots."

Raj nodded in understanding. "I didn't want to say no either," she said.

On the second day, the Delhi government started a curfew to control the rioting. Hindus all over New Delhi were killing Sikhs, and the violence only seemed to be increasing. I witnessed with my own eyes a Sardarji being pulled from his scooter by a group of men who beat him, kicking and hitting him over and over. It was the cruelest thing I had ever seen. I did not like watching what was happening merely a few yards from our house, but there was nothing I could do. My heart aching with sadness, I went back inside and shut the balcony doors.

I advised the kids to remain in their bedrooms because I did not want them to see the violence. Raj leaned against the wall, her arms crossed as I came inside. Her face mirrored mine. We were not happy about these circumstances, and we wished for it to be over as soon as possible. In the meantime, we could only sit and wait it out, feeling helpless and praying that the riots would not affect the safety of our family. We also made sure our servant gave food to the boy, and we also instructed the servant to not spread the word that there was a Sikh boy in our garage.

After three days of rioting in New Delhi, the government finally put an end to the chaos and got everything under control. The Sardarji and his partners from the taxi stand came to us, each with both hands pressed together, palms touching, in front of them and thanked us over and over. The Sikh boy joined them, and our lives slowly returned to normal. However, it took several months for their taxi business to return to normal. Many Hindus expressed hatred toward the Sikhs by refusing to use their taxis.

Chapter 22

A few months after settling in New Delhi, I convinced my parents to visit with us. They agreed and came to stay for about two months, but they were anxious to go back to Malaudh. I didn't understand why they were so eager to leave and would argue with them.

"We have come back to India," I said, "and the reason we are here is partially so you can stay with us and live a comfortable life rather than live in Malaudh with my brother, who shows you no respect, and his children, who give you a hard time. It hurts me to know how they treat you, and yet you always want to go back."

Many times during that visit I raised my voice, in a way, taking all my frustrations out on them. The hospital project was not going as planned, and now I was unsuccessful in keeping my parents with me. After returning to their home, they came to stay with us a second time for several months, but the story was the same. They still wanted to return to Malaudh.

In November 1984, my youngest sister, Sita, informed me that my father was not doing well. He was having heart problems and was in Ludhiana with her. Disheartened by the news, I told Sita I would come right away, feeling that I should be with my father while he was sick.

My driver and I left first thing in the morning. It normally took six hours to drive the two hundred miles from Delhi to Ludhiana because of the many different types of traffic on the road—bullock carts, tractors, bicycles, water buffalo, cows, and goats all traveled on the same single lane road. Plus we faced congestion in all the small towns and cities we passed through on the way. No one followed any traffic rules.

We started driving at 5:00 a.m. We had barely left the city when my driver got stuck behind a small herd of water buffalo meandering in front of us. *Why don't I drive?* I thought. *I will be able to drive faster and better than my driver, and we will reach Ludhiana in five hours rather than six.*

"Why don't I drive, Keshyp?" I said. "We will get there faster."

My driver just shrugged his shoulders. "If you say so, Bedi Saheb," he said, stopping the car and getting out.

A thick fog blanketed the early morning air, so one could see no more than thirty yards ahead. Once in the driver's seat, I maneuvered around the water buffalo and began driving fifty-five miles per hour. After covering seventy miles in an hour and a half, a tractor trolley sitting in the middle of the road suddenly appeared out of the fog. I thought to go around the trolley, but another car was coming in my direction. Holding the steering wheel tightly, I slammed on the brakes, but I had been driving fast and did not see the trolley soon enough. The car skidded and crashed into the back of the trolley. My driver flew forward, hitting his head on the dashboard. I hit my chin on the steering wheel and felt a sharp pain from the ring of the wheel cutting my chin.

Thinking the car might catch on fire, I stumbled out, hurried to the passenger side, and pulled my driver out by the shoulders.

"Keshyp, are you okay?" I asked.

He rubbed his forehead for a moment and looked at me. "Yes, I think so."

The front of the car was smashed up, the hood had popped open, and the radiator was spewing water on the road. The car behind us honked, and as traffic backed up, several people yelled at us from their windows. I opened the passenger door on the driver's side and took out my shoulder bag, which held my .22 caliber revolver. While it made me feel more secure, owning a handgun was also a status symbol in India.

Keshyp and I stood on the side of the road. I could feel blood dripping from my chin, and I pressed the front of my shirt against the wound to stop the blood flow. No one stopped to help us or to see if we were injured. I stuck my thumb out, trying to hitchhike as it was done in the States. No one hitchhiked in India, but I thought I'd give it a try. The cars and buses simply passed, seeing we obviously got in an accident with the trolley. While disheartening, it came as no surprise. People simply sped around our car and the trolley, and the traffic pandemonium continued on as before.

I was shaken up, my adrenaline still rushing as I realized we might both be dead if I hadn't hit the brakes hard enough. I kicked myself for making the decision to move to India. Nothing seemed to be working out, and here I was bleeding on the side of the road. *In the US,* I thought, *the ambulance, police, and first responders would quickly arrive at the scene to help us.* I told myself that as soon as I recovered from this accident, we would return to the States. Another thought crossed my mind: *Here I am trying to be with my parents in their old age, yet where would my own family be if I died just now?* These thoughts circled in my mind until a car slowed to a stop several feet from us.

"We need a ride to Naraina," I told the person sitting in the back, who appeared to be the owner of the car. He nodded and gestured for us to get in. Naraina was where Satish and his family lived. It was about sixty-five miles on the way to New Delhi. We arrived at around 8:30 a.m., and with my hand still covering my chin, I told the servant, "Go tell Saheb I'm here and I'm hurt."

The servant returned several moments later. "They are sleeping," he informed me.

"Wake them up," I said, feeling exasperated.

A moment later, Satish came out. "Bedi Saheb, what happened?" he exclaimed, a worried expression on his face. He frowned at the sight of my bloody chin.

After I explained, Satish called Raj right away to tell her what happened and to let her know I was okay. Raj was concerned, and so Satish's driver drove Keshyp and me home. As soon as we arrived, Raj ran downstairs to see how I was. "Kris, your chin!" she exclaimed, worry in her eyes. Hearing the commotion, the boys ran into the room, and their mouths dropped open when they saw my blood-stained shirt and the deep gash on my chin. Raj hurried to the phone and called Usha, telling her to come immediately.

"This may require stitches," Usha remarked when she examined my chin. "Let's find a small private nursing home to admit you. They are usually like mini hospitals with only fifteen to twenty beds. You will receive good care compared to a public hospital."

After checking into a private nursing home, we were told I could have either a general surgeon do the stitching or, if I preferred, I could get a plastic surgeon who would do a neater job. Since it was my face we were talking about, I decided to go with the plastic surgeon. I waited several hours for him to arrive, and after he performed the surgery, he came out to talk to Raj, Usha, and Satish.

"Krishan will have a small lump right under his lip," he told them. "This is because I had to stretch his skin in that area."

"It doesn't matter what he looks like now," Raj remarked. "I am already married to him."

I stayed at the nursing home for three days, and during that time, I would joke with the manager, asking if I could have a beer. He told me he would check with my doctor, but of course the doctor always said no. The manager promised he would present me with a six pack when it was time for me to go, and he did. My family looked amazed when I came out of the nursing home carrying a six pack of beer. It became a joke that when that facility discharged you, they threw in a little something extra. They also joked about my chin roll, saying, "Don't worry, you're looking okay, so Raj isn't going to leave you."

One early Sunday morning in May 1985, I heard popping noises in the living room. Subhash and Christopher also heard them, and we all ran into the living room to see what was going on. The television was clicking on and off and so was the VCR. At the same time, Raj noticed the A/C had stopped running. Perplexed at what was going on, I scratched my head and tried inspecting the plug-ins. Just then, we heard popping noises coming from outside. Looking out the window, I saw people running toward our house, shouting "Fire! Fire!"

We all hurried outside and saw the electric meter inside the garage had caught on fire and was making popping sounds. Raj, the kids, and I rushed to the street as people gathered around us, wanting to be helpful but unsure of what to do. Several people brought buckets of water, but I said, "No, do not use water on an electrical fire!" Others began picking up dirt and throwing it on the meter board, but the fire kept burning. Having just moved to India, we were not aware of any fire department and never thought we would need to know. Even if there was a fire department, it might have taken half an hour for them to get to our house. Either way, no one on our street was calling the fire department, which indicated to me that perhaps there wasn't one in that area.

Shouts filled the air as the crowd continued throwing dirt at the fire. Finally, after a few minutes, the fire went out. The meter board was burnt badly, but since there was no other combustible material around the meter board, the fire did not spread. Luckily, the fire did not spread inside the house through the wires either. After the chaos died down, we called the electrician and he came to check the burned meter and to repair it. After the repair, we entered the house cautiously and found that the TV, computer, several A/Cs, the microwave, and VCR all were electrically burned beyond repair. It was heartbreaking to see such loss, but nothing could have been done.

In all honesty, I wanted to cry. The troubles with the hospital filled my head, and now this. I didn't know how much more I could take, but I knew one thing for sure—I must keep a cheerful attitude for the sake of Raj and the children. If I broke down in front of them, what was there to keep us all together? Instead, I took a deep breath and smiled down at my three sons. Rajan was nearly in tears, and Subhash and Christopher stared sadly at the burned appliances and electronics.

Life was tough in India. School was difficult at times. The boys did not know the language, culture, or living amenities, and because they grew up in the US, they were different from the other Indian students. Coming to India for a visit was one thing, but living in India was a culture shock. Christopher came home from school one day and told us the teacher slapped him on the cheek. Also, the kids sometimes bullied the boys, especially Rajan, because of his short stature. These were situations unknown to them from their experience of school in the US. Then, there was the constant heat and now this electrical fire. We were thankful we were safe and the fire had not caused any structural damage, but it put one more damper on our experience in India. Staying calm and wearing a cheerful face was the only way I knew to instill a sense of equilibrium in our lives.

In the meantime, I received word that Z.M. Goel had completely washed his hands of the hospital project. G.B. Goel took over, and during meetings, he would insult the colonel, calling him a dummy and other names. I couldn't believe what I was hearing, and I disliked the way G.B. Goel was overseeing the project and conducting meetings in his office. The colonel also became fed up with his behavior. He had held a high-level construction managerial position in Sri Lanka, and now here he was on a dead-end project being called names. One day, he finally turned in his thirty-day notice.

❀ ❀ ❀

The summer of 1985, I experienced a new challenge. During a much needed vacation to the US with my family, I experienced a herniated disc in my lower back. At the time, I was having so much fun visiting old friends across the country that I didn't realize the physical stress our travels put on my body. At first, I didn't know why pain was radiating down my leg. On our way back to India, our flight landed in London, and my friend Mr. Luthra introduced me to several individuals who claimed they could heal my "slipped disc." Blinded by the pain, I naively went along with their methods, hoping it would be so simple. One older man used a tall stick to balance himself as he walked across my back. Another man brushed my back with a bundle of peacock feathers while chanting mantras. Yet another friend of Mr. Luthra's told me to tie a string to my big toe while sitting cross-legged in a chair. Desperate to be rid of the pain before leaving London, I complied with each suggestion, but to no avail. The pain was relentless and ruthless as a hot poker sticking me again and again. On the flight back to India, I lay down in the back of the plane, the only position that gave any relief. To my great irritation, a stewardess scolded me for lying down when the plane ran into some turbulence. I refused to sit up and put on my seatbelt, even when she threatened to tell the captain.

Back at our home in India, I spent the next few months undergoing traction therapy with the guidance of my sister-in-law, Usha, and a trusted doctor. The traction, using bricks tied to a rope which was tied to my waist over a pulley, would lengthen my spine and allow the disc to slip back into place. Since the hospital project was at a standstill until the Goels provided more funds, it did not matter if I lay in bed all day. Standing even for a few minutes to brush my teeth, shower, or go to the bathroom was too painful. Raj tended to my needs, and our servant placed the bricks throughout the day, alternately increasing and decreasing the weight as instructed by the doctor. At one time, our servant tied ten bricks tied to the rope. In this way, my body slowly returned to normal over a four-month period.

After three months of bed rest, getting up only to use the bathroom and do physiotherapy exercises my doctor prescribed me, we began reducing the number of bricks little by little according to the doctor's recommendations.

During this time, the Goels continued to pay me, and they also paid for my medical expenses. Once I began feeling better, I was able to socialize, enjoying a drink and a good meal with relatives and friends. It took me almost four months to rehabilitate myself and get on my feet again.

✿ ✿ ✿

Before leaving for India, I had put the contract for the sale of the Boudnot apartment complex property in the care of Mr. Jones, a lawyer referred to me by Mr. Gilreath. One evening, I called him to see if he had collected the money owed to me according to the contract the buyers had signed, agreeing to pay the full amount at the end of five years. Now, five and a half years later, and I looked forward to good news. My share was seventy percent and totaled $85,000. R.P. Singh, my limited partner, would receive the other thirty percent.

To my surprise, when I inquired in late 1988, Mr. Jones informed me that the men had not made any payments because they knew I was out of the country. I was in shock. How could they go against the contract like that? Just because I was thousands of miles away didn't mean I wouldn't do anything about it. Remembering that one of the men was a doctor who would not want his reputation ruined, I instructed Mr. Jones to prepare legal action against the men.

Mr. Jones informed me I needed to pay him $3,000 up front before he would do anything. Not having this money on hand, I called R.P. Singh and persuaded him to help out with this amount. After all, if we didn't do anything, we both would be out of a large sum of money.

A few months later, Mr. Jones informed me by letter that he had recovered the money. I wrote back, instructing him to give thirty percent to R.P. Singh and to put the remainder in a trust account. In the back of my mind, I thought, *If I return to America, this chunk of money will create a good cushion to fall back on as my family and I transition to life in the States.* I could not put my relief into words. It seemed to be the one thing going right when the past few years had only brought me financial frustration.

At the same time, I asked Mr. Jones to settle a matter with the IRS that had plagued me the past few years. In 1984, I received letters stating I owed the IRS more than $8,000. An investment shown in my tax returns had been disqualified for a deduction, and I now owed them that amount plus interest. Later, in 1985, I learned that the accountant who had calculated the figures in my tax return was wanted by the FBI for fraud. He and his wife had fled to Florida after the IRS audited him for fraudulent filing of tax returns. At the time, I did not have $8000 to pay the IRS, so I did nothing, hoping the matter would go away after a few years.

Now that I had the money from the Boudnot properties, I told Mr. Jones to settle the matter with the IRS. After some time, Mr. Jones informed me that he had paid the amount which had gone up to $12,000. Relieved that this issue was taken care of, I insisted that Mr. Jones obtain a letter from the IRS stating the matter was resolved. I felt it was necessary to have something in writing to prove I was in good standing with the IRS. A short time later, Mr. Jones mailed me a copy of the letter written and signed by the IRS. I tucked it away into my files, thankful this issue would no longer haunt me.

Chapter 23

Near the end of 1985, Satish persuaded me to become a partner in his television manufacturing business. At first, feeling reluctant, I finally agreed to run the factory he planned to open in Indore, state of Madhya Pradesh. There is a word in the Punjabi language, *rozgari*, meaning one should not pass up any opportunity that could provide income for his family. *Maybe God has created this opportunity through Satish, so I can have a prestigious income-producing business in India*, I thought to myself. Since the proposed 500-bed hospital had been reduced to 125 beds, and the Goels still could not get a loan, I did not have anything to do at the hospital.

Although I knew nothing about the television manufacturing business, Satish assured me I would learn easily due to my management experience and education. Satish's marketing associate, Girish Bhatt, accompanied me to Indore where we found a rental space to open the factory. While my family stayed in New Delhi to finish out the school year, I checked into the Shree Maya hotel in Indore and threw myself headfirst into opening the factory and running a successful enterprise. I had spent two weeks in Satish's factory in Noida, near New Delhi, learning everything I needed to know, and with a newfound confidence, I told myself this would be a successful venture.

I named the company, Suny Electronics, and after six months, we were manufacturing and selling close to three thousand televisions a month. However, Mr. Bhatt and I began running into problems with a certain distributor who was complaining about the dealers he sold the televisions to. There were cash flow problems, and Mr. Bhatt, displeased with this distributor, gave him two weeks notice. We switched to a new distributor.

The old one became angry at us for canceling with him on such short notice, and the news spread all across Madhya Pradesh.

In the meantime, Raj called to tell me Christopher had fallen off his bike and broken his tooth. The neighbor took Raj and Christopher to see a dentist who had returned from England. The dentist said, "If you can find the broken tooth, I may be able to put it back in place. If you do find it, place it in cold water and keep it in the water until you can bring Christopher in to see me."

After returning home, Subhash, Rajan, our driver, and a servant went to the site of the bicycle accident and looked for the tooth in the dirt. After sifting through the dirt for several minutes, one of them found it. Raj cleaned the tooth and kept it in water just as the dentist said. The next day, she and Christopher returned to the dentist. He placed the tooth where it broke off and, according to Christopher, used a regular hammer to pound the tooth back into place. Although in great pain, Christopher did not scream or protest. The dentist told Raj this tooth would be good for fifteen years, and then Christopher would need to get an implant.

Christopher told us later that as he sat in the dentist's chair, he thought, *Here I am in a dentist's office, where this dentist is using a hammer to put back my tooth that was in the dirt for several hours!* This was a very different picture from the dentist's office in the US where we had taken Subhash for his dental check-ups.

When I heard stories like this from my wife and sons, I wished with all my heart for different circumstances. How could I have known that the Goel hospital would never be built? I left New Delhi without any prior notification to Arun Mangal or Z.M. Goel. No one objected, since there was no progress on the project, and Z.M. Goel had stepped out. Now G.B. Goel was pursuing the project just for the sake of it. They continued paying me until February 1986, and in late 1986, I discussed the matter with Mr. Mangal, claiming that my contract was for three years, and they needed to continue paying me. As of that moment, it had only been two years and three months. Feeling bad since he had been the one to interview me and show me the good side of the Goels' organization, Mr. Mangal said he would see what he could do. He discussed the matter with D.P. Bakhsi, who did not wish to give me any money, but in the end, Z.M. Goel approved paying me for the remainder of my contract period. It did not take much persuasion, since he also felt guilty for bringing me into their mess. The way I left the Goel organization was unusual and unprofessional, but under the circumstances, it was the best way for me to depart at the time.

After three years of running the television factory, I didn't know how much more I could take. *I am in a prison,* I said to myself one day. *The distributors are telling me what to do instead of the other way around.* The five distributors in the state had me by the tail, and the dealers who sold the televisions were dancing around me, knowing I was helpless to do anything. Although I felt trapped, I still tried to talk sense into the dealers. For months, Mr. Bhatt and I traveled from city to city to learn their problems and answer their concerns. We hoped they would pay, but no one offered to repay the money they owed. Suny Electronics, running on five months of credit, could not survive much longer without payment. The amount owed to us was thirty lakh rupees, the equivalent of $150,000.

As a last resort, I refused to send the distributors more televisions unless they paid first. In one case, a distributor finally agreed and gave us a bank draft number and draft amount over the phone, saying the draft was in the mail. Then, as soon as Suny Electronics sent the shipment, he canceled the draft, depositing the money back into his account.

Even when Satish invited the distributors to meet with him at a hotel and discuss their complaints and concerns, there was no change in their behavior. Not even the owner's presence could push them to do the right thing. Furthermore, Mr. Bhatt took a passive stance with his responsibilities, only acting if I told him to. He did not like asking me for approval of the marketing promotions as I requested. Later on, I learned he had been selling a different brand of cheaper televisions under the table to our distributors. Infuriated, I informed Satish. When Satish confronted Mr. Bhatt about the matter, the man broke into tears, saying he was having trouble communicating with me and could barely keep up with the marketing pressures to maintain sales.

Satish decided to bring Mr. Bhatt back to New Delhi, since he had previously been a loyal employee for many years, and he promised to assign his best marketing man to my factory. In the meantime, the distributors took advantage of my lack of marketing experience. They formed a group to share with each other their complaints about the Indore factory, and they refused to pay any old amounts until we sent them new material.

Each night, I returned home to have dinner with my family, and even though I was mentally exhausted, I kept my chin up for the sake of Raj and the kids. At night, I cried myself to sleep because even though I was the owner of a television factory, I felt like a prisoner locked in a small, dark room.

In April 1989, Satish informed me of his decision to move my factory to Pithampur due to the end of the seven percent sales tax exemption in Indore. In Pithampur, we would have advantage over the competition because the city was in a Special Economic Zone, meaning it was also sales tax exempt. Moving to a new building would reduce our operating costs by $5,000 a month. While still running the Indore factory, I traveled fifty kilometers back and forth to Pithampur to make preparations. I put in sixteen-hour days, and by the time I reached home, poured a drink, and sat down to eat, I had never felt so exhausted.

I was sad about so many things at the time. The Indore factory I put so much work into was coming to a close, and even the name, "Suny Electronics," was scrapped for a new one. I was sad because out of the eighty employees at the Indore factory, I could keep only twelve. Telling so many people they no longer had work took a toll on my heart.

I felt like I did not belong in this environment. I did not fit in with the people in the television manufacturing industry who thought nothing of ignoring their debts while telling you they would pay. What they said never matched what they thought or what they actually did. I based my entire profession in the States on honesty and straightforwardness, telling my colleagues and the employees working for me exactly what I thought. There was no hidden meaning, no dealings under the table. Here, you couldn't trust anyone.

And it is strange how even the smallest, least significant things can make you sad. As I left the Indore factory for the last time, my tears overflowed at the sight of the flowers and the mango trees I had so carefully chosen for the landscaping around the factory. They were a touch of love and beauty I hoped to give to a cold and unfeeling place.

In June 1990, I received the accounting report for the fiscal year 1989. I shut the door to my office and sat at my desk, staring at the impossible figure. Suny Electronics had made a net profit of only fifty thousand rupees, the equivalent of $2,500. My share totaled a whopping $625. I could have cried, knowing my yearly share equaled one-eighth of my monthly salary in America. I had worked for next to nothing day in and day out, year after year, with no assets to show for it—no house, car, or household furniture to call my own.

The sales for that year totaled more than one *crore*, or ten million rupees, which at the time was the equivalent of $600,000. How could our profit be so small? Yet looking back over the budget, it became clear: the cost of television materials and factory expenses was much higher than expected.

I went home that day, looked at Raj, and finally spoke my mind.

"I want to go back to America."

Raj looked at me, a stern expression in her eyes, and without a moment's hesitation, she said, "Let's go."

She did not ask why, nor did I discuss any reasons with her. We both were thinking the same thing. Before, I thought Raj would not want to leave her parents, sisters, and brother. Now that I saw Raj was on my side, I felt an enormous sense of relief. A huge weight was lifted off my chest, and for the first time, I realized how much it had been suffocating me. I had wanted to return to America for a long time, but I continually suppressed the idea, thinking we had gone to so much trouble coming to India in the first place, and it would be a mistake to uproot our family, leaving our parents and relatives behind once again.

I also did not want to let Satish down. He and his other partner had put great confidence in me, so while I felt relieved about my decision, I also felt guilty for leaving the business. It was not in my nature to give up, but I knew leaving was the right thing to do. I could not go on much longer in a business culture where people considered you foolish for speaking openly and honestly. I was thought of as naïve, a dummy who didn't know what was going on, whereas in America, I was respected as intelligent in making decisions and achieving results.

On my next trip to New Delhi, I told Satish my decision.

"I will stay two more months with the new company to make a smooth transition," I said, "but I do not fit in this culture. It is time for us to go."

Rather than blaming a particular person or pointing out the problems with the business, I took it upon myself to say the culture simply was not a good fit. Satish listened quietly, absorbing the news.

"Bedi Saheb, it is your decision," he said. "I understand it has not given the profit we were expecting. We can call a meeting tomorrow at my residence to inform the other partners as well."

The next day, I sat around the dining room table with Satish and the other partners. When Satish told them my decision, one of the partners said, "Bedi Saheb, we are not going to let you go back to the States. Tell us what we need to do to help you run the Pithampur factory."

Another partner asked, "Why do you want to go back? Share with us so if there are problems with the factory, we will try to rectify them."

Again, I stated, "I am not a good fit for this culture. I have failed you. Satish placed his confidence in me when I did not have any experience in the television manufacturing industry. I have failed all of you."

Before I knew it, tears poured from my eyes. I excused myself to go to the bathroom, and once I calmed down, I returned to the dining room. Everyone gave me a hug, saying they respected my decision. At the same time, no one came out in the open to say it wasn't me who failed them. No one took responsibility to say that things did not run smoothly and there were problems from the start.

During my last days with the company, my partners tried to persuade me to stay, and one of them threw a party for me. Being in high spirits, everyone began singing parts of songs, and at one point, someone said, "Bedi Saheb, you also sing a song."

One song came to my mind. As I sang in Hindi, I put all my emotion into every word.

Sab kuchh sikha hamane, na sikhi hoshiyaari
Sach hai duniyawaalon, ki ham hain anaadi
(I have learned everything, not learned cunningness.
This is the truth to the world that I am clumsy.)

I continued the song, substituting my own experiences in each line. Everyone became quiet as they listened. They had not known until then the depths of my struggle.

❋ ❋ ❋

The following months were a whirlwind of activity. There was much to do to prepare for our departure for the States, but after I made the decision to leave the television manufacturing business, Satish talked me into joining him and two other partners in his leather jacket export business. With no job prospects in America, I would need a way to support my family.

"It will be the best of both worlds," Satish said. "You can live in the States, selling leather jackets there, and you can travel to India on business."

Satish assured me the business could potentially earn multi-crores. Since a crore was equal to about ten million rupees, we would be millionaires. I decided to invest in the business. At my request, Mr. Jones wired me the $18,000 I needed to become a partner in the company. After spending a few months learning about the trade of leather garments, in January 1991, I spent time in Germany showing wholesale buyers our leather jacket samples. One of Satish's partners had a son named Vinay Jain, whom he sent to Germany, also, and together we tried to expand the business. The son's wife, Seema, joined us later on, and she became involved in every aspect of the business. She tried to control everything, and as time went on, I feared that she might be deflecting business away from us.

One day, in March 1991, I was at the train station in Frankfurt with Vinay and Seema when their briefcase holding all their travel documents was stolen. Seema was supposed to be watching it while Vinay and I went to buy tickets, but she, being a friendly woman, caught the eye of two young men who approached her. While one distracted her, the other ran off with the briefcase. Luckily, I carried mine with me, or I also would have been stuck in Frankfort.

My main role was to help the couple establish business in Germany, and now that my time with them was over, I was glad to leave. The couple had been quarrelsome and not pleasant to work with.

I took a flight to Boston, Massachusetts, and after spending several enjoyable days with the Cheemas, I traveled to New

York with Yusef, the Cheemas' eldest son, to attend the biggest annual exhibition on marketing leather garments. While there, I attended a fashion show of the latest jacket styles and designs. As I sat in the audience watching young girls modeling the jackets, pants, and skirts, I shook my head, thinking to myself, *I have a master's in industrial engineering and have healthcare administration experience, and now, here I am watching a fashion show. I know nothing about fashion.* I couldn't help feeling a little ridiculous, but at the same time, I could only laugh about it. Yusef sat next to me, wide-eyed and enjoying the fashion show as beautiful young girls paraded in front of him, flashing smiles as they showed off the leather jackets, purses, and pants.

The exhibition was overwhelming due to my lack of experience, yet I kept moving forward. After Yusef left, I stayed for three more days, approaching many wholesalers and showing them my leather jacket samples. From New York, my travels took me to Washington, DC, back to Boston, and again to New York to see more exhibits and connect with more wholesale buyers. I was not having much luck. Since no one knew about our company or our product, it was difficult to get an initial order. Two months passed, and in May, I boarded the plane back to India, my brain bursting with knowledge I hoped would be useful in marketing the business. I couldn't wait to get back to my family, pack our things, and board a flight back to America by June or early July before the school starts.

"Life won't be as easy as before we came to India," I told Raj when I returned to India. Once we're in the States, you may need to get a job to help with expenses. I'm not sure what is going to happen with my career. Are you sure you don't want to stay in India with the kids until I can get reestablished in the healthcare field?"

"I can work," Raj said quickly. "I don't want to stay behind."

Christopher and Rajan didn't want to stay behind either. Subhash, in his third year of Engineering College at Manipal Institute of Technology, needed to finish his degree and was the only one remaining in India.

Excited that the time was ripe for us to go to America, I contacted Satish to inform him we would be leaving soon.

"Oh, but you can't move to America yet," Satish said. "Things went terribly wrong in Germany while you were gone. The leather company is nearly dead."

"What happened?" I demanded.

Satish explained that while Vinay and Seema were in Germany, they spent the company's money lavishly. Because they lost their visa documents, they were forced to leave Germany abruptly and return to India, and since they could not continue the business in Germany, they siphoned 40,000 DM ($25,000) into Vinay's father's bank account in Hong Kong.

"Bedi Sahib, only you can resuscitate the business," my brother-in-law pleaded. "If you do not, we will simply bury the company because it is on its last breaths. We need you to spend six more weeks in Germany to revive contacts with wholesale buyers. Bedi Sahib, if you can receive one large order, you will be able to bring the company back to life."

I sighed. America would have to wait.

"Yes, I will do my best," I replied.

"I know you will, Bedi Sahib. I know you will."

I spent one month in Germany, and at the end of my trip, I received an order for one thousand jackets. Satish met me there just in time to seal the deal.

"Bedi Sahib, you have brought the company back to life!"

Satish praised me endlessly, and while I was grateful to have helped Satish with his company, I felt more than ready to return to America.

My wife and sons were staying in Nabha with Raj's parents, and one sweltering mid-afternoon, the car driven by Satish's chauffeur pulled up in front of their house. Raj had done all the packing on her own, and to this day, I think back to the stress she faced making sure our affairs were in order, all our belongings packed into boxes and shipped from Indore, and every loose end tied up while I was away in Germany. All the decision-making about what to keep and what to sell rested on her shoulders, and she made sure we kept the basic necessities while selling other items such as the two televisions, the refrigerator, washer and dryer, and any other large items too expensive to ship. However, we did keep the large sectional sofa we bought in America, as well as the wooden bed frame custom made in India. All this she arranged, and not once did I hear her complain. My kids did not complain about moving to the States either. They readily accepted my decision, willing to move on to the next adventure.

The day I boarded the plane with my wife and two of my sons was the day that all the rivers of emotions flowing through me met at one point. I was leaving the place that caused me great stress, fear, and anxiety. It was the place I once thought of as my home country, but now I did not think of it as "home." Looking forward, I could see a path filled with more challenges, but for the moment, those were clouded over by intense feelings of joy, peace, and excitement to be finally returning to the US. While I was overwhelmed with gratitude to be with my wife and sons again, at the same time, I was sad because I would be leaving one son behind. Before boarding the plane, I hugged Subhash tightly, knowing we would soon be thousands of miles apart.

And then I knew I must leave my beloved parents behind, although I had promised my mother I would return to stay for good. This broken promise weighed me down, and as I bowed to touch my parents' feet, the tears welling in my heart overflowed from my eyes. My father wished me safe travels and many blessings for the road ahead. My mother, downhearted to see me leave, hugged me one last time, her tears wet against my face, mixing with my own.

My heart was torn. While I wished to stay near my parents, a larger, stronger part of me longed for America and the terrain on which I had initially sown the seeds of success, growing up from nothing and reaping the reward of a fruitful career. Now

I must start all over again. How long would it take to reach the top again?

On the plane, I sat in the window seat, looking out at all of India sinking far below me as the plane rose higher and higher until we were above the clouds, and I could no longer see the people or villages or countryside. It would be a long flight, and I would have much time to think and to plan the next steps I would take once back in America. I hoped I could pick up where I left off with my career in healthcare administration. Even though I might start at the bottom of the ladder once again, I was thankful for my family being with me every step of the way.

Someone once said, "Men make their own history, but not in circumstances of their own choosing." We try our best to live our lives, go a certain way, do what we think we should do, but when all is said and done, a mysterious force takes things out of our control. Maybe a majority of events play out the way we would like, but as I look back over my life, I see jobs that came and went, classes I failed, dreams that did not happen the way I planned, a career with more ups and downs than all the roller coasters at a theme park, and a beloved son with medical issues and endless questions of whether I could have done something differently. I have learned to not worry about uncertainties, but instead, to do my best and leave no stone unturned.

It was a long flight, and with thoughts of the future heavy on my mind, I dozed off. Next thing I knew, I woke up to hear the captain announcing, "Fasten your seat belts. We have started descending and will land in twenty minutes."

Our plane landed in Boston on a beautiful afternoon on August 10, 1991, and as I stumbled off the plane, I dropped to my knees and kissed the ground, thanking God that we were finally in the US for good. This was my true home.

Acknowledgements

With a heart full of gratitude, I am first thankful for my good-looking wife, Raj, for bearing with me through the tough times and helping me remember many details for this memoir. I am indebted to her unconditional love in supporting this long, painful, and rewarding endeavor. I would also like to thank my parents who made my very first dream of moving to the States possible. They never stopped praying for me, especially my mother. Many thanks to the Cheemas for befriending me as a struggling student in America and for all the years we kept in touch. To Dariush Hanrahi from whom I learned to eat American food and enjoy simple things in life. To my friend Sewa Singh, a guy with a huge heart, who always helped me throw a good party. I am indebted to Professor Buchan for making it possible to achieve my engineering degree and for becoming a friend. I am grateful to Mr. Earl Gilreath for providing me with the opportunity to grow professionally and also becoming a lifelong friend. I am very thankful to Ved Bedi and Dr. Usha Bedi for providing us with unconditional moral and medical support when we moved to India. I wish to thank Satish Verma for teaching me business sense and for providing business opportunities for me. Thanks are also due to my relatives for entertaining us while we were in India. Much gratitude goes to Raj Dev Bedi and Swaraj Bedi for all the times they lent a helping hand, and for being friends I could always count on after my family and I returned to the States.

I am truly blessed to have very understanding, undemanding sons. Their wives have exceptional spirits as well, and through them, Raj and I feel as though we have truly inherited three daughters. I wish to acknowledge Manu Sharma Bedi, who not only inspired me to write this memoir, but gave me tremendous feedback for the writing and publication of this memoir. Subhash Bedi's encouraging words that this would be a bestselling memoir kept me going through this journey. I would also like to thank Emily Winne for helping me articulate my stories in a clear and concise manner. She made several revisions from a 200,000-word memoir to bring it to less than 100,000 words and still retain the deep meaning of my story.

Thanks to my publisher, Brooke Warner, editor, Kelly Malone, and Lauren Wise, project manager, for their endless coaching and editing the manuscript to this final stage.

Lastly, many profound thanks are due to SparkPress, for accepting and refining my memoir, and making it possible to share my stories with thousands.

Also, thanks to my publicist, Crystal Patriarche and Tabitha Bailey for the tremendous publicity campaign throughout the country and placing me on the book publishing map.

St. Jude Children's
Research Hospital

ST. JUDE
MEMPHIS TO
PEORIA
RUN

The St. Jude Runs, co-founded by Mike McCoy and Gene Pratt in 1982, is a relay -style event benefiting St. Jude Children's Research Hospital. Runners begin their journey from St. Jude in Memphis, Tennessee, or one of 36 satellite communities, **all concluding in Peoria, Illinois, home of the St. Jude Midwest Affiliate.**

Since inception, 35 years ago, the St. Jude Runs has **raised $45.5 million**. The Memphis Run has over 200 participants, one of them being a long-time dedicated runner Kris Bedi. Kris has been a St. Jude Runner for 10 years and has raised over $80,000 for St. Jude kids.

Please join us in our mission of finding cures and saving children by visiting and donating at stjuderuns.org.

The Punjabi Express carrying the victory torch of St. Jude Memphis to Peoria Theme Run in 2016

About the Author

K rishan Bedi came to the US by boat with only $300 in his pocket in December 1961. A twenty-year-old from the tiny village of Punjab, India, he had big dreams and ideas of what he wanted to do with his life. He eventually earned a master's degree in industrial engineering at the University of Tennessee. After nine years in the US, he returned to India to have an arranged marriage; together, he and his wife returned to the States, where Bedi developed a career as a healthcare executive. He's since served as member of several healthcare professional organizations, and is currently a member of the board of Indo-American Society of Peoria. Bedi is a contributing author to *The Magic of Memoir*, edited by Linda Joy Myers and Brooke Warner.

In his spare time, Bedi enjoys reading, cooking, spending time with friends and family, and participating each year in St. Jude's 465-mile Memphis to Peoria relay-run, which has raised over $80,000 for the St Jude Children's Research Hospital in Memphis, Tennessee. He now lives with his wife in Peoria. They have three successful sons and five grandchildren.

Author photo © JCP Portrait Studio

SELECTED TITLES FROM SPARKPRESS

SparkPress is an independent boutique publisher delivering high-quality, entertaining, and engaging content that enhances readers' lives, with a special focus on female-driven work. Visit us at www.gosparkpress.com

The House that Made Me: Writers Reflect on the Places and People That Defined Them, edited by Grant Jarrett. $17, 978-1-940716-31-2. In this candid, evocative collection of essays, a diverse group of acclaimed authors reflect on the diverse homes, neighborhoods, and experiences that helped shape them—using Google Earth software to revisit the location in the process.

Quiet the Rage: How Learning to Manage Conflict Will Change Your Life (and the World), Richard Burke, $22.95, 978-1-943006-41-0. Where there are people, there is conflict—but conflict divides people. Here, expert Certified Professional Coach R.W. Burke helps readers understand how conflict works, how they themselves may actually be the source of the conflict they're experiencing in their lives, and, most important, how to stop being that source.

A Story That Matters: A Gratifying Approach to Writing About Your Life, Gina Carroll, $16.95, 9-781-943006-12-0. With each chapter focusing on stories from the seminal periods of a lifetime—motherhood, childhood, relationships, work, and spirit—*A Story That Matters* provides the tools and motivation to craft and complete the stories of your life.

The Natives are Restless, Constance Hale. $40, 978-1-943006-06-9. Journalist Constance Hale presents the largely untold story of the dance tradition of hula, using the twin keyholes of Kumu Patrick Makuakane (a Hawaii-born, San Francisco-based hula master), and his 350-person arts organization. In the background, she weaves the poignant story of an ancient people and the resilience of their culture.

About SparkPress

SparkPress is an independent, hybrid imprint focused on merging the best of the traditional publishing model with new and innovative strategies. We deliver high-quality, entertaining, and engaging content that enhances readers' lives. We are proud to bring to market a list of *New York Times* best-selling, award-winning, and debut authors who represent a wide array of genres, as well as our established, industry-wide reputation for creative, results-driven success in working with authors. SparkPress, a BookSparks imprint, is a division of SparkPoint Studio LLC.

Learn more at GoSparkPress.com